The White Devil Discover'd

American University Studies

Series IV
English Language and Literature

Vol. 5

PETER LANG
New York · Berne · Frankfort on the Main · Nancy

Frederick O. Waage

The White Devil Discover'd

Backgrounds and Foregrounds to Webster's Tragedy

PETER LANG
New York · Berne · Frankfort on the Main · Nancy

Library of Congress Catalog Card Number:
83-48766
ISBN 0-8204-0055-6
ISSN 0724-1453

© Peter Lang Publishing Inc., New York 1984

All rights reserved.
Reprint or reproduction, even partially, in all forms such as
microfilm, xerography, microfiche, microcard, offset prohibited.

Printed by Lang Druck Inc., Liebefeld/Berne (Switzerland)

To

Ginger

Acknowledgements

To Robert Fagles, whose drama seminar first introduced me to Webster; to David Bevington who encouraged my work on Jacobean drama; to Carolyn Peeples for preparing the manuscript.

Contents

		Page
Preface	. . . .	vi

Chapter

I.	The Movements of *The White Devil*	1
II.	First Movement: "Wee are ingag'd to mischiefe and must on"	11
III.	The Arraignment of Sir Walter	39
IV.	Second Movement: "Through darkenesse Diamonds spred their ritchest light"	47
V.	Whoredom	73
VI.	Third Movement: ". . . Strange fowle, from this foule nest . . ."	83
VII.	The Black Book	111
VIII.	Fourth Movement: "The bed of snakes is broke."	119
IX.	Thomas Adams's White Devil	139
X.	Fifth Movement: "Cease to dye by dying."	147
XI.	*The White Devil* and *Biathanatos*	161

Notes

I.	. . . .	169
II.	. . . .	169
III.	. . . .	175
IV.	. . . .	175
V.	. . . .	178
VI.	. . . .	179
VII.	. . . .	181
VIII.	. . . .	182
IX.	. . . .	183
X.	. . . .	183
XI.	. . . .	184

Preface

My title is deliberate: despite their diversity, studies of Webster have often been those of the "middle ground": thematic but not close readings; contextual, but not sharp juxtapositions of external works or events.

The present study of Webster's first, and less often examined, great tragedy does not pretend to be revolutionary or portentious. It seeks to do two things: first, to present the first sequential "close reading" of the entire play available (the foreground); second, to provide a few meditations on the relationship between this play and certain specific works and events of its time (the background).

My reading of the play may be disconcerting, because it does not seek to be doctrinaire or complexly allusive. In fact, despite what I feel I have perceived in the play, I remain of of two or more minds about a number of important issues in it. I have also chosen to use as my text of reference in the study that of F. L. Lucas in his Complete Works of John Webster, where the majority of modern studies use the more recent one of J. R. Brown (I do make reference throughout to significant points made by Brown in his edition). There are several reasons for this choice. Lucas's text is still a standard complete works edition, and the only such, placing The White Devil in close proximity to his other writing, in a consistent scholarly format. More importantly, I feel, it is an old-spelling edition, and, as in the case of visual puns, much original meaning is lost when it is obscured by attempts to make contemporary meaning clearer. The new edition of three Selected Plays of John Webster (The White Devil, The Duchess of Malfi, The Devil's Law Case), edited by Jonathan Dollimore and Alan Sinfeld (Cambridge: Cambridge Univ. Press, 1983) may come to be a standard reference in criticism, but still lacks Lucas's completeness.

I have considered The White Devil in terms of "movements" (see Chapter I below); intervening between my discussions of those movements are shorter background chapters relevant, as nearly as possible, to contiguous sections of the play itself. These chapters are meant to be suggestive, and to stimulate further inquiry. They are in no way to be conceived as pretending to demonstrate actual influences involving Webster's play and other words considered. They might best be considered "exercises in juxtaposition," which relate ideas and modes of expression to each other, and, at the most, collectively assert the involvement of Webster in the literary and philosophical life of his immediate time.

Any student of the drama of this time must come to terms with Richard Levin's <u>New Readings</u> vs. <u>Old Plays</u>: <u>Recent Trends in the Reinterpretation of English Renaissance Drama</u> (Chicago: University of Chicago Press, 1979); no doubt this text is prone to many of the errors in thematic, ironic, and historical readings that Levin describes. I would attempt to evade his accurate darts partly by categorizing my approach as a "tentative reading," seeking to open up possibilities, and courting strictures and alternatives. Also, I would accept his "fundamental principle," that "the Renaissance dramatist wanted to be understood" (p. 202). I have avoided categorizing themes to which everything that happens in the play must relate; I have sought to avoid objectivizing my subjective apprehensions so as to have Webster's characters always meaning the opposite of what they say; and I have neglected to encrust my text with layers of footnoted references to Renaissance works, or to top it off with layers of history-of-ideas generalities.

The result may not, and I hope not, appear as a nightpiece; I am sure it is not my best.

Chapter I

The Movements of The White Devil

    Along with morbidity and decadence, and the general question of "moral tone," discussions of Webster's plays have been be-devilled by questions of form and formlessness, by the assumption that his construction deviates from an aesthetic ideal, and that his deviation cannot, whether excused or deplored, be evaded. The ethics and aesthetics of Webster's plays are closely intertwined. Apologists for his presumed "moral" deviations can find support in the intentionality of his aesthetic chaos: the lack of a dominant tragic protagonist, the lack of a strong dramatic presence of virtue to counterbalance vice, the lack of clear sequential and culminating action, the lack of a moral stance in the choric satiric commentator, Flamineo, and so forth. Similarly, the presumption of a necessary moral stance on the part of the author can be deductively applied to both the ethics and aesthetics of Webster's plays such that his failures in form are evidenced to support the statement of his failures in theme (ethical) and vice-versa.

    Webster's own famous prefatory comments on the initial production of The White Devil have been used to substantiate these contradictory evaluations. In his "To the Reader," Webster himself plays the white devil, praising and blaming himself, and presenting himself as the adherent of contradictory aesthetic theories. He easily confesses that "this is no true Drammaticke Poem," of the classical model implied in his references to Horace and Euripides, and yet views with approval the most classicizing humanistic contemporary playwrights, Chapman with his "full and haightned stile," and Jonson with his "labor'd and understanding workes." Yet, within this contradictory disclaimer of the mode he in his next breath professes to emulate, is another paradoxical presentation of an ideal of ethically and aesthetically formal drama. He outlines "the most sentenious Tragedy that ever was written, observing all the critticall lawes, as heighth of stile; and gravety of person; inrich ed with the sentenious Chorus, and as if were life'n Death, in the passionate and waighty Nuntius . . ." It is this sentenious and critically lawful play that Webster says his play is not--not because of any confessed failings, or proclaimed opposition to its ethics or aesthetics, but because "the breath that comes from the uncapable multitude is able to poison it . . ."

    Those who criticize Webster's ethics and aesthetics, at least as they are manifested in The White Devil, appear to define the paradoxically presented classical tragedy as his ideal, and to see in his criticism of the uncapable multitude the same (even justified) sour grapes Jonson often hung on his stubbornly Aristotelian structures, all the while their popularity decreased. But if we read it closely, Webster's statement does not exist declaratively; rather it is conditional. It is not that he has actually written such a tragedy, and it has been unappreciated; but that if one _were_ to write so pure a work, productive of "divine rapture," even such a one _could_ be poisoned by the multitude. In fact Webster has "willingly, and not ignorantly" chosen _not_ to write such a play; he has "faulted" _willingly_, not in that he has been _unable_ to write a Jonsonian or Chapmanian sententious tragedy. The "faulted," like the whole overstated characterization of the ideal classicizing tragedy, is ironic. Webster has chosen not to write a "pure" tragedy because he knows that it will be misinterpreted by the multitude. Webster does _not_ say that he has created "the most sentencious Tragedy that ever was written," but that even such a play would be ill-received.

On the other hand, the entire import of his "To the Reader" _is_ a condemnation of the audience at the specific theater, the Red Bull, for failing to understand and appreciate what he was trying to do. His clearest definition of his audience's propensities is by analogy with those "ignorant asses" who go to book stores to ask for "new" rather than "good" books. In this matter Elizabeth Brennan is surely correct to present Webster as using "old-fashioned" revenge tragedy conventions, and disappointing his audience by not even providing them with the fulfillingly restorative catharsis such conventions demanded;[1] of course he and his characters are aware of the "old fashioned" nature of the conventions they "look backward, to a more inclusive and exalted vision; they know what they have lost."[2] But Webster does not simplistically equate good with "old" in opposing it to "new"; and if he does not identify The White Devil with the ideal "sentencious Tragedy," the preface cannot be said to equate "good" with "ethical," or with drama that is unambiguously didactic.[3] It might as well be said that contemporary readers who could be disappointed at not finding clear structure and clear moral vision in this play are as much a misunderstanding auditory as was Webster's original one.

If Webster's own commentary on The White Devil provides only a calculatedly ambiguous view of his own thematic and aesthetic purposes in the play, and if it is inadequate to discuss his success and failure in these realms _via_ a simple dichotomy between order and chaos or morality and amorality, how can one approach the question of defining the _general_ shape and purpose of his play?

If we are to consider "form," and shape, it might be on the basis of one of Webster's own comments, and a certain mediative direction in recent criticism of his plays. In a fairly uncommon "postscript," Webster provides, instead of an epilogic apologia by an actor in his play, a personal commendation of the actors in the first performance, particularly "Maister Perkins," and a non-ironic definition of the virtue of their representation; he praises them for ". . . the true imitation of life, without striving to make nature a monster." If we are to take "true imitation of life" at its face value--and particularly contrast it to the "monstrous" behavior and language of characteris in the play who distort life by false acting, as the Cardinal does at Vittoria's arraignment, or Francisco at Padua--it cannot but connote "realism" as opposed to stylization. The full-fledged sententious Tragedy, with its high rhetoric, grave personages, Chorus and Nuntius, is surely a monster, in terms of how people actually behave and speak. Webster may well idealize the stylized dramaturgy of Jonson and Chapman, as of a higher order than the "happy" work of Shakespeare, Dekker, and Heywood, yet these latter writers certainly more "truly" imitate life, with fewer interventions from philosophical and aesthetic ideology-- or from "critical laws." The White Devil, and Webster's other tragedies, are pervaded with a sense of human complexity, duplicity, and irresolution. One can never tell whether the black man is really white, the monk really a murderer, the suicide really a homicide. If for Webster "life" is so elusive and difficult to didacticize, then a drama which was a "true imitation of life" would also have to avoid adhering to the formulaic principles of a classicizing, or any other, aesthetic.

I would suggest, then, that Webster's plays, and The White Devil as prime exemplar, are best approached as wholes in terms of a "modern" sense of "realism"--they imitate the irresolution of "real life," and their characters and structure have a relatively "open" form. It is this openness of form which makes the corrupt and inverted rituals which periodize the play's structure, such as the arraignment and the barriers, such "monstrous" violations of nature; nature which is for Webster, as for Montaigne, "divers et ondoyant." I would suggest characterizing the form of Webster's drama, anachronistically, as "organic."

Of course, such a view as the above is not itself new; it was precisely Webster's "open form" and seeming contemporaneity that made him appeal to such contrasting early 20th-century champions as Rupert Brooke and Jacques Copeau. But to see Webster as closer, in form, at least, to Heywood, say, than to Jonson, would not have been considered in a literary-historical context, viable, until recently. And it still is not, to a great extent. A signal expression of a different view was Ekeblad's "Webster's Constructional Rhythm," which proposed that "such scenes in Webster's tragedies as are dramatically very tense tend to have a certain 'rhythm': a way in which the dramatic situation and the language--inextricably united--move together and are gradually intensified."[4] But the sense of "rhythm" as a play of movement between diffusion and intensification was not applied to the whole play or plays, only to specific scenes. Dallby, in his book on The White Devil, names "tempo" as an important element, but chooses not to discuss it since he finds no way of measuring it objectively.[5] Another recent study considers a "romantic" view of Webster's art as defined by a "design of activity in space, of movement in and out of closure,"[5] which is akin to a sense of "organic form" but not carried consistently through any of his plays. What Coburn Freer defines as the difficult "coming to terms with works that are disjunctive in their characterization, language, or action" applies particularly to Webster. "Both the dramatist's perception of his task and the forms he creates from it may not be linear or ordered in any systematic fashion, much as we may succeed in abstracting discursively organized patterns out of the swirling motion of a play."[6] In The White Devil "swirling motion" would seem to be the defining principle of form, and the imposition of "systematic" patterns on it be "monstrous." But the patterns of concentration and diffusion in Ekeblad's idea of "constructional rhythm" may come closer than other "systems," to articulating the play's ethical and aesthetic shape as a whole, without being untrue to its life.

In the interest of finding the rhythm of The White Devil, I have chosen to pay strong attention to the fact that the edition of the play that Webster himself deliberately chose to publish lacks act and scene divisions. While the anciency of an act/scene premise in Renaissance drama is an ancient debate itself, it is hard to avoid the simple fact that Webster took the "liberty" to have his own play published without such divisions at a time when an expressly five-act structure was becoming increasingly "standard," and with it, of course, the neoAristotelian critical premises of unity of time, place, and action. In The White Devil Webster is formally allying himself with the "happy" Red-Bull-scale popular playwrights in defining the movement of his play by the rhythm of exits and entrances of characters. If we are to give credit to any formal principle in any drama divided only by sequential scenes, we have to involve an "organic" pattern modeled not on critical laws, but on qualities of the living drama itself. I would consider The White Devil to progress via a sequence of "movements" which play moments of concentration of action, attention, emotion, off against moments of relief, stasis, reflection. The "movements" of The White Devil have an "organic" quality in that they are defined by the sort of changes that define human action in "real life"--changes of mood, location, behavior brought about by circumstances, not by fiat. As an artist Webster uses his authorial fiat to imitate the pressure of circumstances more than to impress an abstract pattern on his characters' lives. Although he does not progress accord with a particular aesthetic principle, he still involves complex patterns of equivalence, symmetry, and repetition in the working out of his form. For example, he constantly employs foreshadowing and recurrence to play ironically against movement as fatalistic as the growing, blooming, and blasting of a flower.

The White Devil's movements, as I have proposed them--and other sequences than those proposed may certainly be defensible--in their broadest outlines work through concentration and diffusion of action. When action is diffused, a goal has been reached in the assumptions of the actors; a place is presumed immovable and secure; a view of life has been affirmed and seemingly shared by the participants; motion and violence are at a minimum. With concentration, a split develops between individuals' views of how things are and how things ought to be; physical or psychological spaces seem insecure and threatened; action to change circumstances is deemed necessary, decided on, and effectuated. The state of peace is the state of diffusion; the state of war is the state of concentration. The culminating, cathartic action, which relieves the necessity for war, and heals the split between how things are and how they ought to be, is death. If the social analogy of the movements of concentration and diffusion in The White Devil is war and peace, and its psychological analogy madness and sanity, its physical analogy is the progress of lust, from desire to fulfillment, to satiation or sadness.

The play's first movement is from a point of initial diffusion to one of concentration and high tension, just prior to the precipitating action; it does correspond to the first act as apocryphally established. In it, three fundamental factions or individuals are presented in an initial condition of diffusion, or low intensity, and heightening circumstances are introduced that move them towards concentration and culminating action.

In the first scene, the reprobate Count Lodovico, "decay'd," and his friends, Antonelli and Gasparo, are presented in a transitory, undefined place, philosophizing on Lodovico's banishment, proclaimed by him in the play's first word. There is a deceptive diffusion of energy here, because banishment would seem to be a resolution of tension between the banished one and the milieu from which he is excluded. But it is precisely the freedom and autonomy provided by the banishment which creates the conditions that allow Lodovico to become the tool of others in building towards murder. Lodovico's literal isolation, the freedom of his stage space, his civil status, his amoral philosophy, all create a sort of "harmony of condition" in him that is akin to the initial conditions of the two subsequent scenes: the Duke of Brachiano in amorous intimacy with Vittoria Corombona in her husband's enclosed garden, and Francisco de Medicis with his family and allies, including Cardinal Monticelso, in the bosom of his own establishment, a room of state in his palace. Lodovico, though, is in his own mind abused and a victim of injustice at the very outset; the other two groups seek to restore an abused stability as their scenes progress, but the only stability or peace acceptable to Lodovico would be the destruction of that of the others. And although he seems to be the free agent he has characterized himself as, he is "bound" (I.i.59) to those who are "Dependants of the Duke of Florence," and therefore is attached to whatever movement toward culminating action the Duke becomes engaged in. Thus the initial, paradoxical condition of Lodovico: in a condition of free movement, he is actually bound to a search for stasis whose nature will be the disruption of others' order.

The second scene is also paradoxically diffuse: the Duke of Brachiano, "lost" in love for Vittoria--his "secretary" Flamineo's sister, and wife to Camillo, nephew of the Cardinal Monticelso--dallies with her within her husband's own walls. As Flamineo gulls Camillo into accepting the fulfillment of their adulterous desires, and as Vittoria's mother condemns this treachery with increasing violence, this peaceful space becomes the terrain of conflict. More than this, the fulfillment of love becomes itself an act of violence against all three "families" originally involved in peaceful interrelations, and combined by the marriages of Brachiano and Vittoria into a harmonious oneness. The interlude between the lovers creates irresolvable tension between Brachiano and his wife, Isabella, sister of the Duke of Florence, between Vittoria and Camillo, and between all three members of Vittoria's family. All sorts of precipitating actions are suggested: Cornelia renounces her son, Brachiano calls for Doctor Julio, the arrival of Brachiano's wife Isabella in Rome is announced. These specific actions are complemented by the rhetoric of anticipation: Brachiano foresees "ensuing harme," and Flamineo announces "Wee are ingag'd to mischief."

The next scene occurs in the condition of ceremonial stasis--the noble family of the Medici peacefully gathered together--but this stasis contains equally ceremonial expressions of forces gathering to break the stasis into action. Its central event is the prolonged rupture between Brachiano and Isabella. This divorce occurs _en famille_ as though parodic of other events connoting stability such as feasts or marriages. The names "honourable brother," "Sister," circulate much, contraried in action by their opposites. The scene also presents Brachiano's noble and martial son Giovanni, whose non-involvement in the brewing intrigue complements that of the "free agent" Lodovico, whose orbit through the play has commenced earlier. It is noteworthy that these two do not come into proximity until their confrontation in the last scene; as the least involved initially, their fates become enmeshed totally at the end. With the hostile, separated groups on stage at the end of the scene--Marcello, Camillo, Francisco on one side, Brachiano, Flamineo, the poisonous Doctor on the other, victims and killers, _in potentia_, on each side--tension has reached its highest point, and a precipitating action is fated to occur.

The second movement of the play I see as a long exhalation, beginning with death, which realigns forces and relationships, and ending with the outcome of the trial which is the _de facto_ rectification of the disorder caused by the deaths. This movement also has its integrity because it contains in miniature a universal and, supposedly, harmonious human drama: crime and punishment. In a moral universe, this would be the only play. Its classical symmetry is ironic here, because the identities of guilt and innocence are not clear before the crime, or during and after the punishment; and the punishment is itself a crime, requiring a new punishment.

The concise dumb show (II.ii) wherein the obstructive spouses to Brachiano's and Vittoria's union are done away with deliberately contrasts to the laborious and extended show trial (actually an "arraignment") wherein the crime's perpetrators are mere observers, and Vittoria receives a punishment, sequestration in a corrupt "House of Convertities," which is both unjust and too lenient. The arraignment itself is mockingly balanced between prologue and epilogue scenes in which the main mover in the murders of Isabella and Camillo, Flamineo, is seen interacting with the two characters he will be involved with in future deaths. These involvements are themselves initiatory actions to the future killings, and therefore are preludes to a new crisis set in the middle of what presents itself as the "diffusing" aftermath of a previous crisis. In III.i Flamineo quarrels with his brother Marcello, a quarrel leading to Marcello's murder which initiates the fourth movement (as Camillo's murder initiated the second). In III.iii he gets friendly with, then quarrels with, Lodovico, whose murder of him in V.vi will conclude the play.

The four scenes following the crime and punishment sequence (IV.i, IV.ii, IV.iii, V.i) seem to me to constitute a slowly rising action, a movement from diffusion to concentration paralleling of the swifter movement of the first (as the second movement's concentration-diffusion sequence follows the fourth's). The diffusion here involves movement in space as well as in quality of character and action. IV.i presents the Medici interest (in a replay of II.i), as Francisco, aided by Monticelso, contemplates revenge against Brachiano, and initiates action--a deceptive love-letter addressed to Vittoria in the House of Convertites. The purpose of the letter is to induce Brachiano to steal Vittoria away with him to his seat at Padua. In this he succeeds, but he is aided by the intimate war-and-peace exchange between Brachiano and Vittoria at the House of Convertities in IV.ii (an intensified replay of I.ii), whose result is an even tighter and more erotic-suggestive union than that in their earlier love-scene. Both hatred and love conjoin to create the movement toward the wedding procession of V.i, the very image of stasis and diffusion, escape from death. IV.iii plays a key role in this mode of order and stasis too. The ceremony of the Papal election (spiritual marriage as Brachiano's is earthly) is likewise formal and likewise corrupt, since it is the scene in which Lodovico is bribed to go to Padua as Brachiano's assassin. It plays a role in relationship to the two preceding scense such as I.i plays to the two that follow it.

In the marriage scene and its aftermath (V.i), we can find both a gathering action towards crisis, and a recapitulation, in a new locale, of the forces which in the first movement led to murder in Rome. The romance of Flamineo and Zanche recapitulates the parodies that of Brachiano and Vittoria in its early stages; Marcello attacks their relationship as Cornelia did the other couple in I.ii. The conspirators in the Medici pay embrance, like an unholy family, and it is announced that the combatants are donning their armor for the ceremonial barriers, which celebrate love, as the vaulting-horse gymnasts in II.ii celebrated war.

There are two subverted "honest" conflicts that constitute the initiatory deaths of the play's fourth movement. As in the second, they occur with devastating swiftness, as though impelled by a pressure of life beyond willed control. Flamineo stabs his brother Marcello without warning, pre-empting a formal duel arranged between them, in the short interval between the girding for the barriers combat, and the combat itself. This murder is followed by a rushed and absolute judgement of Flamineo by Brachiano, here the accuser, with Francisco (disguised) the spectator, in a multiple inversion of the arraignment of III.ii. Immediately after the judgement, ritual stage-fights lead to the poisoning of Brachiano *via* his helmet, and a drawn-out, agonized death-scene, in which Brachiano's energies literally diffuse themselves slowly. Within this death scene we find Brachiano in mad judgement of his society and his associates, and another violent strangling of him by Lodovico when he does not die soon enough. This movement balances two faces of death: it appears painful in its abruptness, and painful in its duration. The main action of the final scene in the movement (V.iv) is pervaded by the deep presence of death: Cornelia singing as she winds Marcello's corpse, Brachiano's ghost appearing to Flamineo. Two faces of death are encompassed in this movement in another sense, therefore: death as the act of dying, death as a presence in the lives of the survivors. When paired with the short appearance of the first paired deaths of the play, in II.ii, these deaths seem to convey a weight of ethical suggestion. Those who initiate death eventually become drowned in it, if they do not die themselves. Except for the concentrating action gesture of Giovanni, his father's successor, exiling Flamineo from the court at Padua (anticipating the final movement), one might feel the collective movement of the whole play is toward a hopeless form of diffusion, a social embodiment of the idea of "entropy."

Of course, the energies of Lodovico, and Francisco's aim of revenge, have not yet been fulfilled, so a final movement ensues which becomes a third diffusion-concentration sequence, accelerated desperately. The movement towards concentration in V.v is very swift and abbreviated, as though there is no further energy left in the collective participants to luxuriate in intrigue. The situations of death in the earlier movement are ridiculed by the pretended urge to suicide Flamineo presents to Vittoria and Zanche, and their actual attempts to murder him in betraying his own suicide pact, which fail because there is no charge in the guns he has given them (guns very different from the sword he has given Marcello). This scene presents death as so powerful that it has spared only itself to prey upon. Suicide, and murder within a sibling relationship, seem to be manifestations of solipsism and sterility, as though the whole organic process of stasis and motion, diffusion and concentration, breathing itself, has slowed to a stop. This ultimate stasis is represented by the closed room in which the failed suicide and murder take place. Those who break into it, in turn, are the vicious and virtuous "outsiders" to the sequential intrigue--Lodovico, who has the trio killed, and Giovanni, who captures Lodovico. It is left to speculation as to whether Giovanni's presence can introduce new life, and movement, or whether he merely delivers to <u>coup-de-grace</u> to all motion.

Chapter II

First Movement: "Wee are ingag'd to mischiefe and must on."

I.i

As well as being dramatically vital, Lodovico's initial exclamation "Banisht!" (I.i.i)[1] sets a thematic premise of the entire play. "Some form of Lodovico's 'Banisht!' was from earliest medieval times the sign of Satan's arrival in hell."[2] But, in human terms, the first banishment, of Adam and even from the land and condition of innocence, irrevocable, is the prototype evoked here, by the absoluteness of the word. But Lodovico's banishment, as punishment, is itself a corruption of fallen justice: he returns from it easily, midway through the play's action; those who banished him are his equals in corruption; his mortal retribution against Vittoria, which culminates the play, is motivated by jealousy, thirst for vengeance, and other sinful attributes of fallen humanity.

The punishments--from banishment to death--undergone by most of the major characters in The White Devil take place in amoral space. These punishments both parody the Christian assumption that suffering and reward are sanctioned and justified, and illustrate the "banished" condition of corrupt and depraved humanity: "in Adam's sin we sinned all."

The play's initial dialogue between Lodovico and Antonelli, serving a conventional plot-expository purpose, is also rich in deeper implications. Lodovico (with philosophical inaccuracy apostrophizing a "Democritan" polytheism), also invokes Fortune as his deity, as "a right whore" (4), and as one who gives only to take away. Norma Kroll's "The Democratean Universe in Webster's The White Devil," argues that "the philosophy of Democritus serves as Webster's unifying principle,"[3] taking off from Lodovico's initial evocation of him. She would have the amoral universe of the play be that of Democritean "atomic" theory, "where events are caused, not by cosmic intention, but by an indifferent chain of random action and reaction."[4] For example, Fortune's "smal percels" (5) are "atoms." Despite her derivation of Webster's Democritean knowledge from Montaigne, and other acknowledged intermediate sources, the weight of allusion to one system strains at the diversity of intellectual strands in Webster's background. "Fortune," for example, applies too diversely, and lives in too many philosophical realms, to be made a creature of Democritean atomism. Murray may be closer to Webster's frame of reference in seeing Lodovico, devotee of Fortune, as the "World" of medieval Christianity, Vittoria as the Flesh, and Monticelso as the Devil.[5] Whatever their associations, the qualities of divinity Lodovico invokes are all anti-Christian, and paint the primary background of the supposedly Christian realm he lives in. Catholic Rome is, of course, to the English, the anti-Christian Whore, as in the flesh Vittoria is the whore of many imaginations in the play.

    Imagining his banishment as the conspiracy of powerful enemies, Lodovico "prays for them" (10). Disingenuously defending his double-faced morality with the metaphor "The violent thunder is adored by those / Are pasht in peeces by it" (11-12), he both takes secular mortals as his divinities on the basis of their material power to banish him, and uses the transcendent attributes of pagan nature-divinity to describe them: the wielder of thunder is Zeus. "It is the Machiavellian princes, the 'great men' of the play, who are seen and who see themselves, with unconscious irony, as wielding, God-like, the power of thunder."[6] Although Lodovico's credo, like that of his colleagues and some of his victims, has the materialistic faithlessness of the archetypical English "Machiavel," it often puts on the mask of fulfilling the higher commands of non-Christian powers in nature.

    Antonelli and Gasparo add irony to Lodovico's self-evaluation by recalling the latter's "sinful" life, to support the argument that his banishment was "justly dom'd": he has been a prodigal, a drunkard, a glutton, and a murderer. All of Lodovico's supposed crimes fit into both a moral and a legal context of sin, and his companions recite them strophically in a parody of an indictment read at an arraignment in an ecclesiastical or secular court of law. Of course they are in direct anticipation of the similarly parodic indictments similarly read before Vittoria, Lodovocio's eventual extra-legal victim, in an actual, confusedly ecclesiastical and secular, court.

    Part of Lodovico's "doom" (in the senses both of <u>sentence</u> and <u>fate</u>, the willed and the inevitable), is that the noble guests at Lodovico's "prodigall feastes" (22) have laughed, like the cynical gods of Democritus, at his misery. Devotees like himself of Fortune, they have prejudged ("fore-doomed," 24) his banishment, which is here cosmically likened to that of a Meteor banished from the earth's atmosphere. Lodovico's prodigal hospitality, a sinful and pernicious excess of charity, is unrewarded by his peers. In fact, like Vittoria later, he has been deterministically judged on amoral grounds prior to his actual crimes. Also, as an uncontrolled meteor, Lodovico has been banished from the realm of freely-willed ethical or unethical action; he is now "on the loose," a complete subject of Fortune. The implication of his collaboration with his associates in his demise is that he is partially a creature of, at least half-created by, the evil nature of his milieu.

    The parodic indictment of Gasparo and Antonelli includes Lodovico's crime of participating in a non-Christian, non-ethical system of reward and punishment, <u>and</u> of being a victim within the terms of that system, which Gasparo and Antonelli, in their jocular manner, profess to believe in. The paradoxical self-incrimination in these exchanges is, in accord with Thomas Dekker's motto <u>seria jocis</u>, serious laughter. Webster does not mean merely to hold Italianate corruption up <u>en masse</u> to an obviously contrary English mirror, but to demonstrate the difficulty--even impossibility--of sustaining a credible system of justice and ethics based on Christian principles in <u>any</u> state. The alternative to achieving such a difficult ideal seems to be its extreme opposite, represented by the world of <u>The White Devil</u>: a total moral and legal anarchy. Lodovico's "This well goes with two buckets, I must tend/ The powring out of eather" (27-28), as McLeod suggests,[8] presents the emblem of "duplicitous balance" present in other scenes of false conflict, such as Brachiano's barriers and Flamineo's suicide pact. The assumption of order in any world system is mocked by the use of the system's assumptions as tools for asserting individual will in a void of order. Lodovico's scorn for these assumptions is expressed in his single dismissive "SO!" to Gasparo's presentation of a model of order. Responding to his indictment, Lodovico has half-seriously indicted in his turn the workings of justice: if he committed so many murders, "Why tooke they not my head then?" (33). Gasparo responds, in the deliberative cadences of a commonplace:

> The law doth sometimes mediate, thinkes it good
> Not ever to steep violent sinnes in blood,
> This gentle pennance may both end your crimes,
> And in the example better these bad times. (34-37)

Gasparo's philosophy of justice creating order here is the ideal of a Christian commonwealth where the tempering of justice with mercy and a Biblical ideal of forgiveness induce voluntary reformation in individual and state. It is overtly anachronistic in this environment.[9] The only system of punishment Lodovico will respond to is the merciless one of death, which he suggests, and which he will welcome at the end of the play. Nonetheless, an English audience in 1612 would certainly respond positively to Gasparo's ideal commonwealth here, precisely because it is ridiculed by those who are corrupt and Italianate--as another Gasparo's more elaborated commonwealth is in <u>The Tempest</u>. Lodovico <u>can</u> be seen as evading, or "rationalizing" guilt he actually <u>feels</u> for living contrarily to such ideals, as can other characters in the play.[10]

Lodovico's eye-for-eye philosophy presents Justice as a coparticipant in the unjust, un-balanced system it is supposed to equilibrize. Gasparo's "gentle pennance" is so ineffective as a regulator in this world that it cannot participate in it at all; the ineffectuality of mercy cannot help but cast doubt on the veracity of its Christian premise--that one may be led to know, and eventually voluntarily to choose, "good" over "evil." The concept of penance which justifies Lodovico's banishment is as devoid of substance here as is the penance supposedly induced in the House of Convertites to which the "whore" Vittoria is banished. In her life, the house of conversion becomes one of assignation, and similarly Lodovico's banishment merely provides him the opportunity to plan more murders.

The elaborate discussion of banishment in this scene allows Webster to have Lodovico allude to the necessary background of the as yet unbanished Brachiano's lust for Vittoria. Lodovico's words do not make clear his own jealous lust for Isabella, whom Vittoria will supplant, as it will emerge later, but his bitterness has thematic point when he names Vittoria as "she that might have got my pardon/For one kisse to the Duke" (43-44). While exclaiming on Brachiano's unpunished prostitution of Vittoria's honor, Lodovico complains at her implicit unwillingness to prostitute herself (presumably for pure charity) to Brachiano, in exchange for Lodovico's "pardon." Buying pardons with a kiss is possible in the kingdom of Judas, not in that of Jesus. Our first oblique view of Vittoria here is creditable in Christian terms, since she has incurred Lodovico's wrath for not living in accord with his philosophy. (We could also note that the Virgin Mary is Judas's antitype as female interceder for pardon from a divine publisher, and thereby ironically related to Vittoria the Magdalen; see Ch. V , here, where she is reported to refuse a corrupt intercession.)

Antonelli stays Lodovico's wrath at this betrayal, by expressing more moral commonplaces, which must be taken ironically in their context: he euphuistically asserts that "affliction/Expresseth virtue" (48-49), a traditional Christian consolation inapplicable to Lodovico, who is too sinful to have any claims on Christian comfort, and for whom virtue is (as we have seen in the case of Vittoria) a negative attribute. In terms of his dramatic situation, Lodovico is correct in naming Gasparo's platitudes "painted comforts" (50), but they are likewise so in view of subsequent afflictions suffered by others. Only for Isabella and Cornelia does affliction have any ethical connotation, either as overtly unjust or as bringing out, revealing, strengthening, the virtue of the one afflicted; both these women possess no mitigation for their affliction, and receive no reward for their virtue.[11]

Contrasting to the "painted comforts" of what we might consider Christian stoicism, is Lodovico's strongly asserted fatalism, which is dynamic, in contrast to the "dead" rhyming stasis of his companions' speeches. "Ile make Italian cut-words in their guts" (50) is his response to these commonplaces. The cut-works are an opposite form of artistry to "painted comforts," ostentatious, not subdued, but artistry nonetheless. The metaphor of art, for Lodovico, communicates amoral action, or ridicules assumed moral action.[12]

Although predicting murder of his enemies, "patient" (52) Lodovico follows up with a comparison of himself and the condemned criminal who "grows familiar" and intimate with the hangman, "And would account them nobly merciful / Would they dispatch

me quickly" (56-57). Lodovico imagines himself almost
simultaneously as both the executioner and the one executed, as
both justified punisher and one justly punished by the ultimate
penalty. The psychologizing interpreter might judge that
Lodovico harbors a secret and overwhelming guilt, and courts
punishment to expiate it.[13] But since he is, with his "nobly
merciful," satirizing Gasparo's Christian view of his banishment
as mercy, it seems more likely that he speaks for an ultimate
condition of anarchy--wherein those emblematic of ultimate moral
oppositions--criminal and hangman--are fused into one being.
This fusion of opposites is heightened by the homiletic couplet
wherein Lodovico defines "the worlds almes" as their opposite--
cupidity--in a commonplace which also inverts the Biblical connotation of the shepherd: "Great men sell sheep thus, to be cut
in peeces, / When first they have shorne them bare and sold their
fleeces" (61-2). Not only is Lodovico's self-characterization as
a sheep the opposite of the truth (if a sheep at all, he is a
wolf 11.8.9 in sheep's clothing), but the shepherd-sheep
relationship is one of commercial exploitation and dismemberment,
and, as the play will demonstrate, not limited to the "Great men"
of the piece.

I.ii

Having shadowed governing themes and circumstances, Webster
proceeds to establish the central intrigue of the play--the
blasted romance between Brachiano and Vittoria. When the audience first witnesses it, it has progressed less far than Lodovico
(exaggerating from resentment?) has initially suggested. This
love-scene is one of several night-pieces in the play; here,
other members of Vittoria's family, the future victims of her
love, hang around the couple as moths around a flame in the darkness. It can be fruitful to see the scene's exchanges in the
context of a traditional Morality debate between personified
qualities--Love and Lust, Body and Soul--manifested particularly
in a struggle of Brachiano and Cornelia for Vittoria's allegiance.[14] Of course the scene is a corrupted débat since the
choice of Vittoria has already been irrevocably made. In the
irrevocability of this choice might be seen the "class
consciousness" of Webster, expressed in his ambivalence toward
commitments that cross the boundary between "noble" and "common"
realms (represented here by Brachiano and Vittoria).[15] We will
be faced with inquiring whether the lovers' "fall" is the
result more of their violation of social, or of ethical and
divine, laws. The social element is crucial in that the seduction of (or by) Vittoria is made simultaneous with the inward
disintegration of the lovers' respective families and social
alliances. In the play's third scene, Brachiano's family and
circle will be shown falling at odds; here, the strife within
Vittoria's family is displayed, at the very moment it attaches
itself successfully to Nobility. Flamineo, as Pandarus, con-
ceitfully leads his sister and Brachiano together and into
adultery, while the Hecubesque mother Cornelia disowns him and
the situation he has created.

Brachiano enters as Vittoria's guest; he is "Quite lost" (3), in the dark literally, and takes on a mode of tentative eagerness at odds with his reputed, and later manifested, bluster and arrogance. The "Quite lost," terse as, and equivalent to, Lodovico's "Banish't," is as it were the governing premise under which his existence will operate. Unlike Lodovico's, it is a self-created decree. Brachiano might be seen as banished henceforth from "wholeness" and self-knowledge, lost to the confidence in his own position and nature that have directed him to this point. But he is surely not meant to become an "absolute victim" of Vittoria and his brother-in-law's avengers; the weight of "lost" is on the side of a spiritual, not a wordly, hopelessness. Since Brachiano is lost when we first meet him here, it is hard to credit his course in the play as following the lines of Aristotelian-based tragedy, "the downfall of a great man through a flaw in his character."[16] If his love for Vittoria is a "flaw," it <u>defines</u> him; it doesn't undermine him.

To Flamineo's unctuous praises, and announcement of his "dealings" for the lovers' assignation, Brachiano exclaims, "We are happie above thought, because 'bove merrit" (16). The condition of being mastered (perhaps obsessed) by a transcendent emotion, sustained by him throughout, contrasts to Flamineo's scurrilous and self-consciously obscene rhetoric here as disturbingly as the two philosophies of crime and punishment, and their verbal presentation, did in the first scene. These polar romantic and anti-romantic views of sexual attraction are embodied in motifs of "consuming," here and throughout the play. Here, Flamineo considers ladies "polliticke--they know our desire as increas'd by the difficultie of injoying; whereas satiety is a blunt, weary, and drowsie passion" (20-22). Eating both nourishes and annihilates that which nourishes. Sexual appetite is abased whenever it is made gastronomic in the play, particularly by Flamineo--as when, in the first scene and in the arraignment scene, it is associated with banquetting.[17] Here, though Flamineo's appetitive and Brachiano's spiritual presentations of love differ as black does from white, their actual aims are both "black," and as in the case of Lodovico's two buckets, a seeming symmetry between good and evil that defines a system of order actually collapses into one condition of pure appetite.

Circumstantially also, despite their different styles, the duke and his secretary are still collaborators in an act which to an anti-Italianate audience would have a simple "black" moral identity. Flamineo, as satirist, describes this very situation of paradox. In his banter he uses one of a number of reminiscences--here, being "unwisely amorous" of a lady disliked by others who have already "enjoyed" her--in a similitude with birds inside and outside a summer bird-cage, each wishing to be in the other's position. Not only does this similitude covertly suggest to the audience that Vittoria has already been enjoyed by others before Brachiano got to her, but it describes a "subjectivity of vision," often analogized to Renaissance ideas of "perspective," pervading the attitudes of many of the play's characters. Psychologically, this subjectivity manifests itself in dissatisfaction, a constant search to deny it which merely emphasizes it more as an inevitable human condition: Lodovico, Flamineo, Vittoria, Monticelso, seem to seek the "impossible" state of being, as it were, both inside and outside of the bird-cage at once. Flamineo's search for this state of abolished subjectivity reaches its most fevered point when, in the final scene, with his mock-suicide, he seeks to be both dead and alive at once. There, as here, he can abolish subjectivity only at the verbal level, not essentially.

The set-piece dialogue which follows Flamineo's bird-cage figure exemplifies non-fulfillment: Flamineo toys with the gullibility of Vittoria's complacent husband Camillo--who by his "aparell" (45) appears to be the "pollititian" Flamineo fancies himself to be, but who is actually an "Asse," unable to obtain even his own wife's sexual favors. As an ass, Camillo in effect takes on the role of the jealous old father of Renaissance romantic drama, who stands in the way of the two star-crossed lovers,[18] and Vittoria seems in the strange guise of his daughter--a role association emphasized by such details as her meek-seeming assertion that she carved before him at the preceding meal (123). Flamineo continues his banter with Camillo in order to "tricke" him into sleeping apart from Vittoria, on the excuse that he can win her back sexually by denying himself to her. Thematically, in their exchange Flamineo and Camillo elaborate the bird-cage paradox. Brothers-in-law, and presumably similar in dress, they articulate totally discordant intelligences and temperaments in strangely harmonious dialogue:[19] Camillo shares Flamineo's bawdy puns on his wife, her "flaw," and his gaming puns (bowling), as well as the awareness that Brachiano is in pursuit of her (the lovers apparently remain on stage during this time). Camillo even shares Flamineo's disbelief in his own advice to secure Vittoria by locking her up like a bird in a cage.

Then, in a radical change of tone and language, Flamineo, saying "I will be bitter," (90), suddenly interjects (from Montaigne) the opposite of this advice: "women are more willinglie & more gloriously chast, when they are least restrayned of their libertie" (92). The assertion that the bird released from the cage will seek to get back in is a dubious axiom governing behavior analogous to Gasparo's assertion that light punishment induces self-restraint. It is similarly false in the play's realm of relationships, and similarly presented with a cogency that demands initial belief. The characters of the play refuse (save perhaps for Camillo) to accept voluntarily the primal limitations inherent in the laws that govern, cage in, the whole world. Many experiencers of The White Devil continue to accept Flamineo's deceptive axiom, and seek a cage of structuring significance, wherein the play's conflict in some way is ultimately between good and evil.

Those who do not succumb to the "morality play syndrome," as Whitman calls it, may, like him, find some other redeeming cage of categories to which to relate Webster's characters; in his case it is the "Apollonian" and the "Dionysian."[21] But Flamineo and others try to subject the limiting circumstances of life to their wills in different ways and in terms of different distinctions they describe and then seek to overreach. I believe Webster can be seen as upholding a traditional Christian metaphysics and moral law without his characters having to be situated within the structure of some moral or amoral system themselves.

Flamineo continues, in the rhetoric of low comedy, his critique of restraint, to the effect that "pollitique inclosures of paltry mutton" breed "rebellion in the flesh" (95-96) equivalent to that caused by purgatives. Here we have an elaboration of Lodovico's pastoral cynicism (I.i.61-62), with the mutton-made sheep as prostitutes (the _sale_ of flesh is a similar connotation), and with an incendiary reference to enclosure as a politic--therefore approved--act. As a would-be politician, Flamineo uses exposure of politic actions as a way of covering up his own. The politician maximizes his own liberty of action by finding indirect ways of inclosing the liberties of others. The perceptions of Flamineo, who uses words to manipulate others' actions, and Lodovico, who acts directly himself in assumed freedom from moral constraint, are similarly distorted from a traditional Christian perspective by their inability to acknowledge that all human action is ultimately "inclosed." Flamineo discounts Camillo's jealousy as analogous to the multiplication of illusory images like those produced by "perspective" glasses, which multiply twenty times the view seen through them (100-106).[22] But this familiar analogy really applies to _him_, as an analogy of his own undefined, amoral vision as figured in the birdcage similitude. Flamineo would give any one of many contrasting images of the same object, goal, or experience, equivalent validity if they served his purpose. The chosen one would become "true" by virtue of his choice of it, colored by the subjectivity of his own state at the time of perception. Thus, Flamineo's judgement of Camillo's jealousy is actually a psychological self-description: ". . . they that have the yellow Jaundeise, thinke all objects they looke on to bee yellow" (108-109).

The dramatic exemplum of Flamineo's theory of his own perception is the act to which his engagement with Camillo has been indirectly leading. "I will make you friends and you shall go to bed together" (118) is the way the gull Camillo perceives Flamineo's purpose, and is the substance of his discourse with Vittoria (who enters, as though summoned, while he confides his plan). But we share with Flamineo, through _his_ perspective glass, knowledge that the same discourse is an inducement to Vittoria to betray Camillo and go to bed with his deadly opposite.

Flamineo's dual speeches (122-155), to Vittoria covertly, and in the hearing of both Vittoria and Camillo, are distinguished in the text by parentheses, connoting asides. The contrast between the derogatory character of Camillo which we hear, and the admiring character which he alone hears and responds to with naive credulity ("He will make her know what is in mee," 140), parallels the contrast between Brachiano's idealizations and Flamineo's derogations of Vittoria, which began the scene. Similarly, Flamineo promises to deliver great joys to the aspiring lover. Camillo sees these promises through his rose-colored perspective glass, considering Flamineo a "virtuous brother" (145), absolutely contrary to the audience's perspective of him, as he is, and will become: a violator of all brotherhood and eventually a fratricide. Camillo is, as it were, "smothered in roses" (149-50) of rhetoric, a dramatically ironic foreshadowing of his ultimate punishment for his innocence.

Flamineo's tone changes again: ". . . so perfect shall be thy happinesse, that as men at Sea thinke land and trees and shippes go that way they go, so both heaven and earth shall seeme to go your voyage" (150-153). This prominent borrowing from Montaigne, as rhetorically incongruous in Flamineo's mouth as his earlier recourse to lyrical commonplace (90-91), is also tactically incongruous, as a different "way" of seeing. It of course describes the condition of subjective perception, which Flamineo is exploiting to destroy Camillo's happiness. But the condition of illusory fulfillment it describes, a harmony of the individual with the movement of the earth and the heavens, is not less a happiness to the experiencer of it because some other perceiver happens to see it as an illusion. In fact, even though it encourages Camillo's illusion of felicity in order eventually to insure his unhappiness, the commonplace describes a condition of fulfillment from which Flamineo is forever exiled, as Lodovico is exiled from salvation because he cannot accept the moral limitations which give meaning to mercy or penance.

This powerful phrase is underscored by Flamineo's next words, addressed to Vittoria: "Shalt meet him [Brachiano], 'tis fixt with nayles of dyamonds to inevitable necessitie" (152-153). Of course "inevitable necessitie" is what Flamineo most fervently denies; this necessity is that Camillo's happiness be an illusion. A necessity hammered by nails must allude to the Crucifixion, and in this context to the inevitable course of Christian history, with the limits it has placed on human freedom, flowing from it. This is the author's, not the character's, conscious allusion, and thereby in a way Webster's own trick on Flamineo, who does not believe in a secular or a religious necessity, and who will necessarily die in the end, "nailed" on a sword. Coming from Flamineo, this promise of necessary union is as baseless as the promise of happiness which it contradicts. Flamineo's nails are not too solid either, being like Vittoria's of diamonds, a very multi-faceted substance, both valuable and superficial, hard and frangible.[23] Vittoria's continued association with jewels, glass, and other hard and brittle substances, is really initiated in this reference--although, slightly earlier, she is a foil, "covered" (a sexual quibble) by Camillo's "counterfeit dyamond" (138-139). The qualities of these substances, indirectly mirroring her personal qualities, are those of the non-Christian values that govern in the supposed heart of Christendom; her nature, like that of her realm, is vulnerable despite its seeming hardness.

Continuing his two-faced dialogue, Flamineo urges Camillo to show a "supremacie of Judgement" (160) by spurning Vittoria in order to draw her to him like adamant. This suggestion appeals to Camillo as a "philosophicall reason" (165), but thereby, of course, an illusory one in a world where actions are not justified philosophically. His ill-judgement leads Camillo, in a vivid working-out of Flamineo's birdcage philosophy, to offer voluntarily to be locked (we might say inclosed) in his room, "because you shall not think ile gull you" (177). This offer of voluntary submission is subtly paradoxical, and functions as a gathering metaphor, "figure of action," for the ideas broached in the scene. To a politic mind, voluntary confinement to a limited system of belief, such as Christian necessity, is self-destructive, and it is precisely such voluntarism that Lodovico's companions ridiculed in the first scene. Camillo is certainly being literally and prophetically self-destructive in so offering himself like a martyr to sacrificial self-entombment.

From Flamineo's point of view, Camillo is renouncing his imaginary ability to gull his "brother" in an act which most sublimely demonstrates his own gullibility. But, contrary to all this, Camillo is as perfect gull perfect innocent, unbanished in his own mind from the imaginary, he might say "philosophicall," garden of oneness with the Christian universe and its laws. I suggest the English audience is being asked to feel some approbation for his voluntary martyrdom, as it might for any other even partial imitator of Christ. And Webster does make Camillo's offer figurative as well as literal. Flamineo says, ". . .ile be your jaylor once,/ But have you nere a false dore?" (179-80), and Camillo replies, "A pox on't, as I am a Christian . . ." (181). The politician's rooms always have false doors; the Christian's, presumably, never.

The retribution for this gulling into confinement is visited on Flamineo only in the last scene, where he is locked into Vittoria's chambers as he seeks to extort his "reward" from her, and where there are no false doors but the "false keies" of the court allow Lodovico to enter and wreak ultimate vengeance upon him. While Camillo is gulled into giving up his key to Flamineo, Flamineo is ultimately gulled by keys beyond his control to hand over. Every politician is ultimately the gull of a more politic politician; Francisco, through his creature Lodovico, gulls Flamineo, as Flamineo has gulled Camillo. Flamineo is ultimately encaged. It is interesting that a mysogynistic judgement of Vittoria and all women accompanies both these encagements. In V.6, women are accused of murderous intent, and here, of lechery, as dogs let loose in the night (188-90). In both cases encagement is also associated with acts of faith, defined as a futile activity. A Christian might consider that, as all life is entrapment in flesh, only faith--expressed through prayer--can offer the keys to an ultimate liberation.

At Camillo's departure, Brachiano enters, his wish that "time would stand still" (191) possessing courtly-amorous associations that seem hypocritical in contrast to the preceding deception. The stage directions ritualize this scene: "Zanche brings out a Carpet. Spreads it and layes on it two faire Cushions."[24] It would seem as an impudent allusion to this carpet, with its erotic and luxurious connotations, that Brachiano brings his rich gown to sit on at Vittoria's arraignment.[25] Here the artifice of scene-setting, and the blackness of Zanche as stagehand, create a context of falseness and manipulation in this love-scene. Brachiano himself, with more grace of diction than awareness of his own meaning, philosophizes, "all delight doth it selfe soon'st devour" (193), and prays Vittoria ". . . if you forgo me / I am lost eternallie," calling her (as we suspect he would never allude to Christ) "a sweet Phisition" (197-99). Vittoria compares "ladies cruelties" to doctors' funerals: both take away their credit (200-02). Brachiano's language clearly establishes that he has transferred to Vittoria the worship that should go only to God and Christ, suggesting strongly Vittoria's diabolical nature, as substituting herself for the divine and taking on its guise. The "lost" and the medical allusions ironically foreshadow Brachiano's death-scene, where Vittoria, who has lost him, also cries that she is lost, and where doctors of the body are called in, are impotent, and are figuratively abused.

The choric observers of this scene are present also in a manner anticipating the observation of Cornelia's bereavement and Brachiano's dying. Here the observers express themselves antiphonally. Zanche and Flamineo, almost as a couple whose harmony caricatures that of the lovers (and who will become lovers later on), harmonize over this "happie union" (205). Cornelia, probably positioned symmetrically with them on the opposite side of the stage, prophesies in this same happy union "our house / Sinking to ruine" (207-8). The observers here are complementary opposites: Flamineo possesses wit and lacks wisdom; Cornelia possesses wisdom, but no wit to rule her offspring. The audience observing the limited and vulnerable awareness of each of the three factions on stage, can be drawn to feel a force beyond their ken, which none can see whole and forestall, leading them to disaster. Cornelia's "house" implies by force of allusion such a force--whether of fatality or divine will--with its suggestion of generational and dynastic disaster, as in the fall of the house of Atreus, to which later allusions are also made.

Brachiano and Vittoria also quibble on the word "jewel," whose connotations will continually expand in the play. Their exchange of jewels, which substantizes a pledge of love traditionally, here becomes fleshly and lubricious, as in Flamineo's bawdy aside, ". . . His Jewell for her Jewell, well put in Duke" (215), and Brachiano's continual urging of Vittoria to wear her jewel "lower." The implicit staging of the "lower" exchange is that of suggestive gestures or touching, connotating the relationship of a whore and her client. It is precisely the relationship played on by Vittoria's accusers later, and in total opposition to the atmosphere of romance the setting and Brachiano's words create. Vittoria's valuation of her "jewel" is brilliantly candid: "Tis the ornament / Of a weake fortune" (211-12); that is, her sexuality, specifically her probably nonexistent maidenhead, is of value only for what its sale can bring in increasing her fortune. For someone of little fortune, it is the only ornament that can be worn. Such a lamb can be sold only as mutton. By extension, a woman of weak fortune will remain that way unless she considers her sexuality--her potential to possess or lose her fortune--as solely ornamental, not as something basic to her nature. Brachiano, presumably, either does not understand, or understands too well, the subtle self-definition here: "ile have it" (the jewel), he says (213).

There is a contrast between the elegance of the setting Zanche lays, and all these exchanges that take place in it. This is not the flowery bank where lovers experience "exstasie" and time stands still, but the <u>agora</u> where a bargain is struck between an aristocratic prostitute (i.e., courtesan) and her client. The trouble, in perspective of this scene, with Cardinal Monticelso's charge that Vittoria is a whore, is not that it is false--the audience has witnessed its truth more substantially than he probably has--but that it is of the same nature as the crime, a <u>prostitution</u> of Astraea (Justice). The hypocrisy of Vittoria's arraignment can be paired with the hypocrisy of this assignation. Both are "white" social rituals used to "black" ends.

Vittoria interrupts her byplay with Brachiano by telling him a "dream," whose interpretation has been much debated. The extreme, contrasting interpretations this dream has engendered might please Webster. Norma Kroll, the Democratean, sees the "cross-sticks" on the grave in the dream, for example, as "the completed symbol of Democratean reality. Each of the overlapping images marks off four cone-shaped or 'Piramidall' forms--Montaigne's emblem of the Democratean gods."[26] For West, the Demonologist, the cross-sticks are archetypal charms of witchcraft.[27] The whirlwind in the dream is "the most dynamic of all possible images for Democratean activity."[28] but it is also a traditional natural tool of witches, and represents "the ancient witchcraft that Vittoria is trying to substitute for [true religion]."[29]

In Vittoria's dream, she has spied Isabella and Camillo preparing to dig up a Yew ("Eu") tree rooting in a church graveyard; the two say that they will replace the Yew with a "withered blacke-thorne," and bury the dreamer alive in the bargain. Vittoria says that for all her terror in the dream, "I could not pray" (239), to which Flamineo interjects "No the divell was in your dreame" (240). "The hidden dread that Vittoria perhaps really feels, here becomes for the audience also a dread of Vittoria."[30] However, a whirlwind rises and blows a "massy arme" from the yew, which strikes the two diggers dead.

This is a politic, two-faced dream, connoting either a successful murder or a murder's successful revenge.[31] It is meant not to be a perfect allegory of past or future action, but to be suggestive. Even within the play it has two different interpretations, both of which hold some truth. Flamineo, approving Vittoria as an "Excelletn Divell" (245), sees it according to his own perspective glass as a covert lesson to Brachiano on how "To make away his Dutchesse and her husband" (248). Brachiano, publicly, interprets it "sweetly," with the suggestion that he could interpret it bitterly if he wished. In his perspective it shows that he is Vittoria's protector; she is sheltered in his arms against the jealousy of Camillo and the envy of Isabella. Of course his commitment to protection is a commitment to murder.[32] Brachiano extends his magniloquent sweetness beyond the above interpretation though, as if inspired: "I'le seate you above law and above scandall" (253)--absolutely false both as a prophecy and a vow.

Vittoria's Eu is obviously "You." The graveyard setting of the dream seems more traditionally derived; Flamineo uses borrowed imagery of life rooting in death often (as in IV.ii.67), as a way of asserting the fundamental corruption of various high ideals. Surely here Webster speaks through his character to have us perceive the garden of love of Vittoria and Brachiano as actually a graveyard--and, filled with "earth & scattered bones" (237), as the "black charnel" that Flamineo ultimately judges his life to have been. As death was the penalty for the Fall, profane loves cultivated in imitation of the seduction which doomed the parents of humanity can have as their Eden only the terrain of death, from which there is no redemption. In such a context of reference, Vittoria's dream (beyond her own intention) may seem to present Isabella and Camillo as potential purifiers, uprooters of the tree (Brachiano) that lives on, and shelters, physical and spiritual death. To murder those who would remove death from Eden would be, thus, surely an act of the devil.

The unburying of the dead in this dream is connected with the fate of unburied Marcello, another uncorrupted figure, in the fourth act, as Cornelia's elegy of him elaborates it. Marcello must be buried deeply (by non-human creatures) or the wolf will dig him up again. This wolf is the Church, whose excommunication denies burial to him. The opposite extreme of the unburying of the dead is the burial of the living, which threatens Isabella in her dream. Justice is not served when this burial does not occur. Isabella, Camillo, and Marcello, unlike her, all have a degree of innocence; they do not create deracination and death, but suffer it. They are the truly "harmelesse" (231) ones. They seem to function in the dream of Vittoria and the song of Cornelia in the manner of an oxymoron: the first two are uprooters struck down by a destructive force of nature; the third is uprooted, but buried by redemptive forces of nature. Vittoria does not understand all she has dreamed, or pretended to dream, because those she sees as profaners of the sacred ground are, to the audience's enlightened moral eye, actually possible restorers of sacred ground from profanation. Cornelia does not understand all that she sings, because the Church-yard and its keepers are profane, allied to the devil, and her son has been saved from being buried in unholy earth.

Brachiano's romantic interpretation of this tortuous dream apparently conjures forth Cornelia from her position as observer (Flamineo: "What fury rais'd thee up?", 260). His vision of felicity is to Cornelia the expression of a "light heart" (259), a phrase applying to Vittoria as well. This single phrase deflates a grandiose but inwardly hollow project. What Brachiano offers to Vittoria is an Edenic condition as insubstantial and unattainable as cloudcuckooland, particularly to fallen humanity. He will "give to your thoughts the invention of delight/ And the fruition" (25-24). All her imaginations will become reality without effort: Fantasy Island with a vengeance, and a hyperbolic presumption to powers that are God's alone. He will subject his government, the source of his ducal identity, to the higher priority of keeping Vittoria "great." This is a self-contradiction, for luxurious neglect of government must jeopardize Brachiano's power to sustain greatness.

With her image of Flamineo as mildew on a flower, Cornelia sustains the scene's Edenic references. Mildew is a whiteness of corruption. Flamineo, like a serpent (a white "Winters snake," 346) has introduced the corruption of innocence--if there was any--into this garden with his language and intent, and it has flowered in Vittoria's graveyard dream and Brachiano's fantasy of a bower of bliss. But to the trio involved, it is Cornelia who appears as the serpent in Eden and destroyer of bliss, when she takes on the voice of doom's ancient prophetess, in the manner of <u>Richard III</u>'s Queen Margaret. Interestingly, according to original stage direction, Zanche the Moor exits immediately at Cornelia's entrance, almost as though she is a diabolical familiar temporarily charmed into exile by the arrival of virtue. Cornelia specifically identifies the lovers with witchcraft:

> O that this faire garden,
> Had (with) all poysoned hearbes of <u>Thessaly</u>,
> At first bene planted, made a nursery
> For witch-craft; rather (then) a buriall plot,
> For both your Honours. (264-8)

This garden seems likely to mean literally the space where Brachiano and Vittoria are consorting, centered on their carpets and cushions, not "Camillo's house" in general, as glossed by Lucas.[33] It could be, figuratively, any space of natural innocence on earth. The important point is that Cornelia defines the lovers' tryst as equivalent to the destruction of a garden by non-Christian spiritual powers or by death itself. In a sense, Cornelia's diatribe is her own interpretation of Vittoria's dream: the yew tree is equivalent to witchcraft's poisoned herbs (Eve's tree is often "poisonous" too, as in Donne's sonnet).[34] The Church-yard expresses moral and spiritual death. "Honours" can be a moral attribute and also an honorific; in the latter sense, Cornelia here lays upon them a curse of literal death, which shall be fulfilled. Cornelia's continued lamentation also resonates Biblically; her maternal grief sounds like that of God or Christ at the "curse of human children" in their disobedience, and justifiably so, if we can share the view that Flamineo is dedicated "to the disintegration of his own family," and to the goodness that any Christian family represents.[35]

As well as being a prophetess of doom, Cornelia is the bearer of ill tidings--in this case that Brachiano's wife Isabella has come to Rome. This news brings out the lovers' sense of guilt and confusion, expressed in their broken sentences, and leads Cornelia to lower her tone and catechize Brachiano regarding his uxoriousness: Princes should, rather, be dials whose motions guide the times. This commonplace (<u>Dial of Princes</u>) is archaic, anachronistic, and "behind the times." It looks back to a social ideal as unrealistic as Brachiano's sexual paradise. Cornelia's commonwealth morality appears questionable and ambiguous, as the ideal of another "good" character, Isabella's fidelity, will in the next scene. These ideals are, however true, not viable in this place and time. Still, Vittoria betrays an at least assumed vestige of respect for her mother. Defensively she argues (what to the audience is objectively false) that her choice was between capitulation to Brachiano and death: "If any thing but bloud could have alayed / His long suite to me . . ."[36] This false argument parodies language associated with the Crucifixion, blood shed to allay the consequences of sin. If Brachiano were construed as a diabolical tempter, the imitator of Christ <u>would</u> be obliged to suffer martyrdom rather than submit to temptation. The allusion is sustained by Cornelia associating Vittoria with Christ's betrayer: "Bee thy act Judas-like, betray in kissing--" (291).[37] Brachiano is the one Cornelia's curse designates as sacrificial victim, not her own daughter, to whom Cornelia assigns only the fate "to be pittied" after Brachiano's death.

Vittoria's "O me accurst!" (294) is ambiguous as a response. Ideally a remorseful outburst, it could appear satiric, in view of Cornelia's "mad" (290) behavior. Vittoria might also, given her initial defensiveness, be here perceiving herself as self-cursed, by her own act, as Cain and Judas were. She may be seen, thus, as an ambivalent figure, and not a single-minded exploiter. However, here in her first scene, the traditional laudatory view of Vittoria as a "new woman" should be conditioned. Is she really a "creature of suffragette eloquence who suffers the agonies of sexual and social ambition in a way that Shakespeare's heroines never knew?"38 This is an old dilemma. Struggling with a newly-found will to identity, Vittoria can become as much of an ahistorical stereotype as when she is cast as villainess and wicked witch (let alone white devil). Webster leads Vittoria off the stage before she can conform to contemporary or seventeenth-century female behavior, and the conventionalization of her identity in any sense seems to violate his dramatic purpose. A sentimental stereotype can be created for her even from the assertion of her spontaneity. Is Vittoria really sincere here, and "instinctively react[ing] to the natural law which dictates strong emotional bonds between any members of a family . . ."?39

Vittoria's immediate exit dramatizes a seeming shame the opposite of Brachiano's assumed immunity from shame. In fact, he characterizes Cornelia's moral indignation as "uncharitable" (298), contrary to the basic tenet of Christian faith, which he most absolutely violates, before going off to bed. Simply naming his bed at this time proclaims his contempt for Cornelia's curse (and again ironically foreshadows both his bed-scene at the House of Convertities, and his death-bed scene, where he enters on a bed). Taking a definitely satiric stance here, Brachiano curses Cornelia in her turn: "Be thou the cause of all ensuing harme" (300). Both Brachiano and Cornelia seem almost to acknowledge the inevitability of harm ensuing from each other's actions. It is not a question of forestalling harm, only of distributing responsibility for it. Brachiano's curse is justified only on the assumption that passion takes precedence, as a source of behavior, over ethical principles such as honor, or social responsibilities, such as those to state and family. Brachiano, in this scene, takes a final position like Lodovico's in the preceding one: he outlaws himself from indebtedness to any superior order, and indirectly from indebtedness to the sanctioner of such an order. Like Lodovico, he is a self-exile from the Garden: he has broken a covenant and violated a sacrificial ritual, both of which seal subjection and insure redemption.

The dialogue between Flamineo and Cornelia which concludes the scene develops Flamineo as a similar exile--in this case from the bonds that unite a family. Flamineo, Cain to Marcello's Abel, appears inherently antagonistic to most shared human values. To some observers, his inflexibility in this regard is due to his literary heritage: much of him is stylized Vice and Malcontent. It seems more meaningful to explore the ambiguities which his unique role does provide. As elder son in a fatherless family, he appears to reject the bonds of tenderness and love that unify, yet he seeks to advance his family collectively as parasites of the Duke, to whom a contemporary witness might feel he relates as a petulant teenager does to a biological father. His actions are completely self-contradictory: what he does to prosper his family inherently divides and destroys it; he can gain preferment for all only by prostituting his sister and blasting the honor of all. As Cornelia protests, ". . . because we are poore, /Shall we be vitious?" (307-8). Flamineo is trapped in the paradox of his mother's question and the ambiguity of "vitious." By implication, the society that surrounds him is accessory to his vicious acts. If poverty is seen as a materially vicious condition, the only way to escape it is through non-materially vicious acts. Flamineo initially plays on the consciousness that poverty and morality, advancement and immorality, are inherently twinned, and he does not believe that the meek shall inherit the earth. He protests at the dishonor his mother has done to Brachiano in sending him home without a servant: in terms of advancement, such punctilio constitutes the only realm in which "honor" can have any substance. Only if Cornelia has hoarded wealth unknown to him, Flamineo implies (with "whoorded," 305, Webster employs an evidently typographic pun), can such a devotion to honor not insure continued poverty. Flamineo's definition of poverty is spatial: it is "bearing his beard" at the low level of his Lord's stirrup (306-7). This is a hyperbolic emblem of social inferiority, of "servitude." The discussions of servitude further on in the play (cf. V.i.106-11) relate back to what this emblem suggests. Flamineo always defines his entire condition by this "levell;" no equivalence of intellect, strength, or any other qualities can compensate his social inferiority.

In responding to his mother's profound question, "because we are poore, / Shall we be vitious," Flamineo provides an autobiographical sketch, unusual in the mouth of a Jacobean malcontent, but one extremely stylized, so that Flamineo's life becomes the pattern of the impoverished scholar whose intellect, unrewarded, turns to evil purposes. Initially, Flamineo responds to Cornelia with rhetorical self-misrepresentation. Unless he uses his sister's honor to rise, since there are no other means, he will end up in "the gallies, or the gallowes" (309), conditions of ultimate servitude which also confront his comrade in another play, Bosola. Flamineo does not mention that tnese two fates are in a lawful state (not Lodovico's) punishments resulting from willed action, not inherent consequences of poverty; unless, of course, his assumption be that poverty is inevitably allied to crime, an idea certainly of wide currency in Jacobean England. The prospective irony is that his rise will, via "courtly reward and punishment" (I.i.3), inevitably be allied with crime.

Flamineo's tale is that his father, to prove himself a Gentleman, liquidated all his property, yet fortunately died before the money was spent. By this we are to understand, "Gentleman" being ironic, that Flamineo's father was seduced by the life of the Court to sell his rural holdings and migrate to its flame, using his now liquid assets to finance a courtly style of life. Such a migration constituted the archetypal "fall" for countless Stuart country gentlemen, in drama and in reality. As elder son, Flamineo is given an education at the University of Padua by his mother. There, impoverished, he spends "at least seven years" in a condition of <u>servitude</u> to senior students, to pay for his keep; (One cause of his jealousy of his brother Marcello might be that though younger, and, thereby consigned to a military rather than a scholarly or priestly career, Marcello is yet more secure and independent than Flamineo). According to his autobiography, after "Conspiring with a beard" to graduate (presumably through influence, not merit), Flamineo followed his father's example and attached himself to the ducal court. There he became "More courteous, more letcherous by farre," but no richer (319).

Flamineo thus "confesses" experience which provides motivation for his amoral actions, and awareness that the courtly pathway to preferment is destructive. He associates moral behavior with infancy, effeminacy, and scholarly claustration. He asserts an illusion of success that his autobiographical narrative has just denied:

> . . . shall I,
> Having a path so open and so free
> To my preferment, still retaine your milke
> In my pale forehead? (320-23)

He contrasts his mother's milk to the "lusty wine" of an unconstrained life. The milk, with its associations, foreshadows the climactic moment of fratricide: Marcello, who still, in Flamineo's metaphor, has the maternal milk of human kindness in him, and is also the non-effeminate soldier, will die in his mother's arms. Cornelia's despairing "O that I ne're had borne thee!" (326) also connects with this ultimate scene of hostility between mother and son. Cornelia's cry affirms Flamineo's already existing renunciation of any family bond, even collaborates with it in banishing him from the bosom of the family.

The tale of the broken crucifix will define a heritage "accurst" from the start, but we could say that Cornelia, by rejecting her son so absolutely, in a visceral way, and primarily because of the immorality of his behavior, is as Brachiano would have it, as partially responsible for his ensuing actions. Her realization of this responsibility might be considered a motivation for her futile efforts to cover up his responsibility for Marcello's murder. Certainly her exclamation spurs him on to collaborate with his own disownment, and to wish that his mother had been a Roman courtesan, because the children of whores have "Plurality of fathers--they are sure / They shall not want" (332-3). This is an ironic commentary on Cornelia's division of poverty and vice; the defense of whoredom is an assertion that it prevents poverty. If whoredom is vicious, though, the children of a whore are assured of not being poor precisely because they have a vicious heritage. Vittoria is to become a Roman courtesan in order to raise her family from poverty. Beyond this, one unexpressed implication is the assurance of fathers, of which

Flamineo has none, and which the final marriage of Vittoria and Brachiano, based on whoredom, will provide him with by proxy in the form of his new brother-in-law.

Flamineo also suggests ironically that Cardinal Monticelso may well "justifie the act" of Vittoria's whoredom, by considering it an act of charity--to future children. Here he seems to suggest that the Cardinal himself may have many children --not a new idea; but it is perverse to justify lechery as an act of faith. Flamineo buttresses his paradoxical encomium of whoredom with one of his many satirically Montaignesque glosses from history:

> Lycurgus wondred much, men would provide
> Good stalions for their Mares, and yet would suffer
> Their faire wives to be barren--   (336-38)

As usual, Flamineo bestializes sexuality. Brachiano (rather than the gelding Camillo) is the good stallion whom Vittoria needs. The analogy by its very nature denies any meaningfulness in marriage as a union transcending sexuality, and justifies him in prostituting his sister as an act of charity on his part; he is interested in posterity, in providing his sister with a better breed of mate.

At Cornelia's exit, Flamineo continues a homiletic monologue similar in tone to his citation from "Lycurgus:" providing amoral philosophy in a moral mode. As an act of policy, he identifies his will with an irresistible force of nature: "Wee are ingag'd to mischiefe and must on" (341). The marital metaphor is implicit in "ingag'd." But this kind of marriage is indissoluble. The fatalism of this statement is ambiguous, because by implication Flamineo's will is married to mischief, which is capricious; he denies the power of transcendent forces over the politician, so he can hardly be the creature of them. He creates a triple metaphor from nature--crooked river, winding path, folded snake--to embody the "winding and indirect" ways of Policy, his divinity. The Machiavellian's mock-confession is a commonplace, but Flamineo expresses his with such harmonious elegance that he creates the illusion of order, even of foreordination, as a principle of "political" action. The path to the mountaintop "Imitates/ The suttle fouldings of a Winters snake;"[40] So, Flamineo defines his future actions as an "imitation of nature," with the additional connotations of sin (snake) and death (Winter). In this speech Flamineo takes on the role of a satiric "presenter" of the entire play: the viewer is asked to follow his path through the play as through a moral landscape led by an amoral guide (so Lodovico after killing Flamineo in V.vi, asks the audience to look back on the chain of events as his work of art).

In fact, as J. W. Lever says, "the total effect of this scene is not to focus attention on illicit romance, on Camillo's marital rights, on the cynicism of the go-betweens, or on

Cornelia's virtue, but to place all these in the wider context of a society where declassed intellectuals [i.e., Flamineo] find the only alternative to galleys, or gallows, in serving without scruple the desires of their rulers."[41]

II.i

After having witnessed Vittoria's family in disarray, we are introduced by Webster to the Medicis, a second family group fraught with discord. It complements Vittoria's family, and differs in being of established, hereditary nobility, not nouvelle richesse. Brachiano's wife Isabella, and son Giovanni, who are devoted to religious and martial ideals respectively, and respectively ridiculed and indulged for this devotion, correspond to the moral and martial Marcello of the Accoromboni (though he does not appear in person in their first family scene). Since Brachiano's wife and son accept the laws and limitations of faith and welfare, they are of course vulnerable to the politicians, who accept none. Yet their paired humility and boldness stand out as jewels against the dark foil of the environment in which they are powerless. Initially in this scene, for example, Webster has Francisco de Medicis, Isabella's sister, recommending hypothetically the burning of Camillo's "Dove"-house only to destroy such "Pole-cats" as Brachiano. Then, immediately, Francisco addresses Giovanni, Brachiano's son, as "my sweet cousin," and, reminded by him, orders the horse and armor he promised him. The horse and armor express an ideal of aggression through action that rebukes the covertness and hypocrisy of arson. That Francisco can endorse these contraries in one breath signifies his potential for lawlessness, in the mold of Lodovico, and his identity as one of many white devils.[42]

Isabella's plea to her brother not to let his "roughness" alienate Brachiano more, at their imminent interview, signals that the family is aware of the potential for destructiveness underlying his seeming righteous indignation and family loyalty. But Isabella's own language is disturbing. In declaring "all my wrongs / Are freely pardoned" (12-13), she may be expressing humbly pure piety, perhaps having undergone a recent general confession which has left her, in her view, so "white" that no chastisement will be possible from her husband. But, considering Lodovico's professed attraction to her, her "wrongs" could as well refer to specific acts of adultery preceding Brachiano's own, covered up by her shows of piety.[43] Similarly ambiguous is her simile of a "preservative Circle" of unicorn's-horn (aphrodisiac) powder which she likens to her circling arms, having a power to "charm" Brachiano into obedience and chastity. Isabella's preservative circle is not that of alpha and omega, sacred, but is pagan and sensual, if not diabolic, as Dr. Faustus's is. It is allied with both sexual excitement and cuckoldry, so that any powers it might have to "force" Brachiano would seem to be similar in nature to the very acts and allegiances of his which have betrayed Isabella.

Cardinal Monticelso's formal address of reprobation complements ironically Isabella's "pagan" conjuration. Neither his words nor her charms can force the submission of Brachiano's will. As a sermon *ex cathedra*, Monticelso's hyperbole is ironic because its passionate language belies his urging that Brachiano "forgo all passion" it may arouse, as well as Brachiano's vow to be "As silent as i'th Church" (26). It also indulges verbally in all the acts it pretends to reprove, and, as in the scene of Vittoria's arraignment, it creates and describes the very licentious behavior it condemns, for whose existence we have no other witnesses. It is also the most stylized in a whole sequence of sermons, homilies, moral advisements spanning the play, from Gasparo's advice to Lodovico to Flamineo's satiric stoic sermon to Vittoria in the final scene. These sermons are consistently contradicted by the obliviousness of their audience or the hypocrisy of their speakers, and through them, Webster's audience may be drawn toward a skepticism of all moral discourse.

Brachiano's initial responses to the speech, and subsequent questions, are bold, yet tersely matter-of-fact, contrasting in the way his exalted yet plain style often did to Flamineo's logorrheia in the previous scene. But Monticelso turns, like Gasparo, to the "soft" line of merciful admonition: Brachiano will "repent" when he has awoken from his "lascivious dream." Brachiano, like Lodovico, denies that his (still qualified as unproven) possession of Vittoria as his "Strumpet" (60) is subject to any moral judgement, and merely asserts that he would fight off any of the martial means Francisco might use to "supplant" her (65). The word "supplant" continues the imagery of trees and uprooting in Vittoria's dream. Hence, Brachiano and Francisco carry on a metaphorically overelaborate war of words, which tends to diminish them when it contrasts to the real wars Giovanni (later in the scene) anticipates waging. Since their war of words is a corrupt and self-destructive one, over love corrupted into lust (as we might say the Trojan one was), the entry of Giovanni becomes a moral symbol. He is ironically described by Monticelso as "a Champion / Shall end the difference between you both" (99-100), though he is as futile in this role as Brachiano is as Vittoria's "champion" (III.ii.187) in the arraignment scene. Yet in the ultimate working-out of the drama, he may be seen as the ender of differences, and in this perspective, he may be a "casket" (106) for their crowns, in the sense of a coffin, as well as of a preservative.

Monticelso continues using Giovanni as the exemplum of the traditional view that

> It is a more direct and even way
> To traine to vertue those of Princely bloud,
> By examples than by precepts: if by examples,
> Whom should he rather strive to imitate
> Then his owne father? Be his patterne then . . .
> (106-9)[44]

Not only does the hypocritical Monticelso practice the opposite of what he preaches, and train by precept rather than by example, but Brachiano and the other paternal role-players in this world provide patterns of vice rather than virtue for their imitators. Flamineo, for example, goes to school with the great, and practices, as he learns, the arts of the politician (granted, he is not of princely blood).

Brachiano, as though abashed and seeking to exemplify the precept that the Cardinal has just uttered, initiates a discussion of war with his son. In this discussion the son instructs the fathers, and provides the pattern of virtue which they do not follow. Encouraged, he imagines a crusade led by a wise yet innocent "child of good discretion" (115),[45] and vows to lead in war against the French foe (not fellow Italians, who are the elders' enemies), as "the formost man" (126). It has been noted that his condition, "if I live" (124), is an ominous foreshadowing, but it might also indicate that as well as innocence, he possesses the awareness of limits (in this case of life) that his elders do not. Like Prince Henry, his probable model,[46] and Henry V, Prince Henry's model, Giovanni would institute chivalric values of a pre-political age, as, it seems, his mother would restore its encompassing piety.[47]

Webster gives Giovanni a political awareness meant to serve but not control his traditional ethic of true nobility. In an Erasmian dialogue with his uncle, he proclaims the charitable policy of releasing prisoners of war without ransom. Francisco asks how he will then reward his soldiers who took the prisoners, and Giovanni replies, "I'le marry them to all the wealthy widows / That fals that yeare" (35.-36). Rather than becoming consumed by domestic intrigue, Giovanni will use the domestic corruptions of others to "nobly mercifull" ends. Giovanni's policy here might be seen as an answer to Gasparo's satire of mercy in the first scene, implying as it does that a principle of mercy need not be hopelessly impotent in the presence of, or outmanned by, a politics of cynicism.

Francisco stands apart after this discussion, as though Giovanni has been acting out an illustration of his <u>sentence</u>: "See a good habite makes a child a man, / Whereas a bad one makes a man a beast . . ." (140-141). The truth of this sentence requires one to see Francisco himself as at least partially bestial, as well as other characters defined by the animal imagery in the play, most of which connotes dehumanization and moral degradation.[48]

Francisco and Monticelso leave the stage at Brachiano's line "You have charm'd me" (149), which coincides with Isabella's entrance likewise, unintentionally, it seems, referring to her false confidence in love-charms. His interview with her ends in what is rightly seen as a sacrament of divorce parodying the sacrament of marriage. Throughout, their exchanges mingle the language of love and of religious faith, paradoxically exploiting their similarities and differences. Isabella, devout Catholic, uses Puritan theological language as basis for her attempts to seduce Brachiano into expressing physical passion for her. Her whole assault on him forms an overtly white, or cold, counterpart to Vittoria's dark and hot encounter with Brachiano in the preceding scene.

   Already committed to disowning his wife, Brachiano insists on interpreting theologically the words she presents with amorous intent, as she does in her expressions of "devotion" and of "casting up" her reckonings (157). Where she cries "You are as welcome to these longing armes, / As I to you a Virgine" (165-66), Brachiano ignores both the suggestions of lust and of purity in this memory, evoking instead Isabella's physical decay, rottenness, and impending death. Dissembling, he condemns her expressions of love and faith as dissemblance (174), and generalizes from Isabella's negative attributes to a negative "character" of her brother, ridiculing him as a miles gloriosus. Thus, he in effect lays down the gauntlet to her whole family. He concludes in the voice of the Devil ("Now all the hellish furies take his soule," 193), cursing his marriage, the wedding priest, his child, and, implicitly, himself.[49] He improvises "the latest ceremony of my love" (197), vowing on his wedding ring a divorce of bodies from Isabella; presumably souls are not involved in a marriage. The fruit of this ceremony will be reaped in V.iii, when Francisco's creatures, as priests, divorce Brachiano from life and hope of salvation with a ceremonial parody of the commendatio animae.[50]

   This divorce is directly parodic of the phases of marriage; in the inversion of the ritual, he curses the matchmaker (Francisco), the priest, and then turns the ceremony of the ring upside down. Although this inversion can represent the Italianate world in general, where "normal values of the Christian world are inverted,"[51] it is hard to know the degree of calculation the playwright wants his audience to discern in it. Despite Brachiano's politic self-righteousness, his wife's offenses to him, like those of Vittoria described by Monticelso, come across as self-contradictory: she is both too chaste and too dissolute, too loyal and too much "wandering." Brachiano's complaint seems almost to be against the entire system of Christian faith that Isabella represents to him. He seeks to make his will transcend and be invulnerable to the "forces" she invokes. When Isabella weakly protests "The Saints in heaven / Will knit their browes . . ." (202-203), he responds "Let not thy love/Make thee an unbeleever" (203-04), tortuously suggesting that for Isabella to imagine the Saints discomposed implies that she is no longer confident in their authority. He also anticipates imagined moral pressure, and repudiates, as Lodovico did in I.i, the possibility of penance. He does so more subtly, though, praying, in effect, that his present sin, if so it be, never be "Satisfied" by any future repentance on his part.

At Brachiano's final dismissal of her ("go, go, complaine to the great Duke," 217), Isabella remains as mortifyingly obstinate for mercy as he is obstinately merciless. She vows to play the role of intercessor by making herself the "author" of his "cursed" vow. This might be seen as the ultimate Christian act of gaining power by martyrdom, taking upon herself the cross both of rejecting him and of doing so from the base motivation of jealously, at which the Saints will surely frown.[52] Also piously accepting predestination, she describes herself as an actress performing her future part with a Christlike "pitteous and rent heart" (226). This individual power struggle between Brachiano and Isabella is also more generally between two ways of negotiating the breakdown of the family, the basic Christian social unit--from without or from within Christian assumptions. For Brachiano strength is strength, for Isabella, weakness is strength. It is brutally ironic to find that even Isabella's near-politic exploitation of the power possibilities in the role of martyrdom will be no match for the Gordian stroke of murder, which abrogates the rules of all social games.

The entry of Francisco (with Flamineo, Monticelso, Marcello) signals the beginning of Isabella's "acting" career as jealous termagant, a play-within-the-play in which Brachiano, despite his repudiation of her, collaborates. Isabella's gulling of her brother has a bitter quality, precisely in that it is ultimately so successful. The politic murder of Isabella, necessary to her husband's remarriage but not to his adultery, which is the cause of her jealousy, is what dooms him to Francisco's revenge. Isabella, by being able to deter her brother's wrath through dissimulation, exercises a power which, working through a chain of circumstances, will eventually make that wrath fatal to Brachiano.

In this encounter, Francisco presents himself as a mediator, seeking peace, and presenting to Isabella the mirrors of other women who suffer wrongs with "patience" and seek "justice." The audience can be conscious that Isabella, in seeming to reject these examples of submission, is actually being submissive to her husband's interests, and collaborating in his duplicity. The words of hatred she comes out with are, given our initial insight into her character, more painful to her the more she uses them to lash Vittoria and Brachiano (unless we accept the possibility that her piety _is_ hypocritical). She anticipates here the attitude that Vittoria, without her calculation, spontaneously assumes when being subjected to defamation in the arraignment scene. When Isabella exclaims "O that I were a man, or that I had power / To execute my apprehended wishes" (246-247), her very affirmation of this distinction is so "brave" that it almost makes it invalid, for her. In her new role of satirist, Isabella does create a verbal picture of the torture and mutilation of Vittoria (248-52) worthy of Lodovico's limning, and she follows this with an aggressive parody of Brachiano's own inverted marriage ritual: "Hence-forth I'le never lye with you, by this, / This wedding-ring" (256-7).[53] Isabella phrases her parodic vow to divorce in parallel to Brachiano's own. In this action she salvages her will from subjection to his, by establishing herself as initiator of divorce before an audience of witnesses, while Brachiano's divorce was proclaimed in intimacy, and cannot be substantiated. It is an act of political mastery from which even Flamineo could learn.

Isabella also apprehends and returns Brachiano's ironic warning against her becoming an "unbeliever:"

> Let not my former dotage,
> Make thee an unbelever, this my vow
> Shall never on my soule be satisfied
> With my repentance, manet alta mente repostum (263-66)

In this case Isabella urges belief in the re-juvenation (from "dotage") of her own will, not the Saints', and imitates Brachiano's own masculine mannerisms of resolutions by uttering a motto expressing absolute resolve ("It rests buried deep in my heart"). It is hard to find specific justification in Webster's text for a judgement that Brachiano's incredulity at this attack ("Nere lie with me?") and expressed innocence ("You see 'tis not my seeking") are those of the dissimulating actor, or also have tones of honest surprise as well. He could well be both playing his part and be disconcerted at the success of Isabella's performance. Isabella has made it hard for him to initiate a public divorce on the pretence of her infidelity, since she has refused to be intimidated by his unilateral divorce, and has made a public issue of his own infidelity. By rejecting Francisco's conventional command to a "mad, jealous woman" to cloister herself in her chamber ["I'le presently to Padua, / I will not stay a minute" (271-72)], Isabella has also put Brachiano in the position of exile from his own seat of power, if she were to claim and stand in her rightful position of Duchess of his domains while he remained in "corrupt" Rome. In fact, not following her, Brachiano would be in a way imitating Cornelia's husband, who presumably initiated the breakup of his family by becoming a court-mosquito.

By placing Brachiano in jeopardy of his public and private repute, Isabella does force him to be resolute in the extreme solution of murder, the ultimate divorcement. On the other hand, in terms of her own character, Isabella's "imitation" of masculine action has imperceptibly become a "real" action and she too is now "ingag'd to mischief." Since she does not have the habit of action, she does not have the resources or will to follow up this coup in a way that will preserve the power she has gained. In fact, her rhymed aside at her exit returns the audience with a jolt to the initial impression of her fundamental submissiveness: "Unkindnesse do thy office, poore heart breake, / These are the killing greifes which dare not speake" (278-79). Isabella would be a self-killer, by way of her own grief, but Webster gives her words anticipatory grim humor: he killing will occur in unspeaking dumb show, and directly on her exit enters the doctor who will do this office as the agent of unkindness.[54]

Immediately, Webster creates an ironic tableau whose purpose is to emphasize the inability of individuals to control their own destiny. While Francisco, Marcello, and Camillo (just entered) confer aside on Camillo's public commission to fight pirates at sea, Flamineo and Brachiano confer audibly on the private commission to the doctor to poison Isabella, and to murder the man of the hour, Camillo. The latter murder is to occur during festivities preceding the taking up of the commission, which is the subject of the parallel discussion going on on stage in the present. In these two symmetical groupings of conferees we might see the cohabitation of initiatives to preserve social order and to insure social chaos, both peaceably occurring together; this doubleness is a fitting "figure of action" for the Italian world. But we will learn shortly in this scene (lines 370 ff.), that the state business of Camillo's commission has the actual private purpose of absenting him so that Brachiano's lust for Vittoria may be fulfilled, and his "name" thereby ruined by the ensuing scandal.[55] Similarly, as Camillo is being sent to battle pirates, for others' personal gain, Francisco is working the pardon of the chief pirate he is being sent to battle, Lodovico (see lines 374 ff.), for the purpose of serving (in more senses than one of the word) Isabella in Padua. Thus the whole state-act of pursuing pirates, its military manifestation as well, are simultaneously parodied by corruption akin to Brachiano's plotting: pursuer and pursued are both tools of the Medicis' wills to private revenge.

The two groups of plotters are overheard in turn by the audience so that their self-revelations have an ironic symmetry. Flamineo, introducing the poisonous doctor, *his* "tool," to Brachiano, compares the whisperings of Marcello and Francisco to a deadly poison: "the Cantarides which are scarce seen to sticke upon the flesh when they work to the heart, shall not do it with more silence or invisible cunning" (285-7).[56] This poison, which reaches the heart so subtly as almost to have no identity as a substance, seems to be Flamineo's metaphor for the quality of politic action he idealizes and tries to practice. Similarly, the thumbnail autobiography of the villainous doctor (291-95) appears metaphoric for general patterns of lives in this Italy. The doctor says he evaded punishment for lechery--which Brachiano and Vittoria may or may not do--by confessing his guilt, and paying a fine whose executor was an extortionist, "an arranter knave than my selfe" (294-95). Flamineo paradoxically praises the Doctor as a "cursed antipathy to nature" (303), and in one of his rare displays of "affection," such as his exchange with Lodovico in III.iii, exclaims "let me embrace thee, toad," etc. Here Flamineo appears as the parodist of his own immorality. But although he is "merry," he is also communing with one of his own kind, and there is an air of self-pity in this jesting. These toads will never become Princes. Flamineo can be intimate only with those who are as self-consciously banished from virtue as themselves.

The imagery of this embrace is in Flamineo's character perfectly consistent with the symmetrical harmony wherein he describes for the audience's anticipation a second murder: "He [Camillo] dies this night by such a polliticke straine, / Men shall suppose him by's owne engine slaine" (313-314). The essence of "politic" action is the presumed noninvolvement of the chief actor. This description of a perfectly politic murder disguised as self-murder analogizes the condition of the satirist as self-satirist, constantly cutting away at even the evil ground on which he stands. The murder of Camillo, as hypothesized here, will of course find an even better manifestation in the play's final scene, where Flamineo satirizes his own politic act of disguising his sister's murder as a suicide pact, by providing unloaded pistols for the purpose.

The Medicis' plot against Brachiano is introduced more deviously. It begins with raillery by the former two against Camillo for being a cuckold. The pretended or actual "Embleme" thrown in his window--a hornless stag with the motto "<u>Inopem me copia fecit</u>"--seems to be introduced by the plotters to make Camillo's condition so obvious, and of such wide currency, that he will be strongly driven to accept the commission to escape shame.[57] It is an ironic emblem, in being predictive, not descriptive. It describes what he will be once he has left Rome, and thus it has the same self-destructive power as Flamineo's plot, which will keep Camillo fatally from leaving. The emblem also introduces a motif of art misused becoming the ally of crime, which will be elaborated in the poisoned portrait of Brachiano, Francisco's love-sonnet to Vittoria, and the fatal masque of Lodovico.

Complementing the emblem is a purposely circumloquacious moral fable, told by Francisco in Flamineo's manner, concerning the complaint of mortals against Phoebus's plans to marry, their objection being that his sons (suns) would create intolerable heat on earth. The incidental topical allegory of Camillo's situation, and the machinations to achieve Frances Herbert's divorce and remarriage to Robert Carr, Earl of Somerset, may be present here,[58] but I feel this allegory does not demand extension beyond its immediate circumstances. Francisco's purpose (and it plays against and with Flamineo's trick on Camillo in I.11 and his comments on paternity and whoredom later in that scene) is to dissuade the gull from having any sex with Vittoria, even before his departure: "Her issue, should not providence prevent it, / Would make both nature, time, and man repent it" (350-51). There is no literal connection between the dissuasion of Phoebus's procreation in the fable, and of Camillo's in reality, not because Webster is sloppily patching together material from his commonplace book; rather, Camillo's credulity is being emphasized by his assumption that there is a "philosophical reason" in the fable. Camillo accepts Monticelso's assurance that he will keep Vittoria from straying in his absence, in the same trusting manner that he accepts Flamineo's curatorship of his bedroom key. Even Camillo's feeling that he has "turn'd soldier" simply by receiving a commission adds to the audience's troubled consciousness of his innocence. He may be ridiculed for his simplicity, but can also be admired for his inability to be politic.

Camillo is willing to be a soldier, even without knowing what it means to be a soldier. Only Marcello (a very uninvolved collaborator in this deception) and Giovanni are willing soldiers who are not fools, in this realm. The martial identity is strongly emphasized as a source of virtue and a defense against corruption. Those who evade, or hypocritically imitate, military virtue, with its frank order and distinction between opposing forces, are the sources of decay in any commonwealth. Thus when Camillo cracks a feeble joke, that it would be best for him, as a soldier, before leaving his wife, to "sell all shee hath, / And then take leave of her" (365-6), his companion's laughter may be imagined as uneasy. This is a joke to Camillo because it is the sort of thing he could not do. But it is the sort of politic action which is the equivalent of martial virtue to his tormenters, and a moral equivalent for what they are doing to him at this precise moment: "selling" the Vittoria ("victory") that he has, as soon as he has taken leave of her.

At Camillo's exit, with Marcello, the politic "brothers in crime" are left, in the absence of the martial brothers, to discuss and reveal to the audience their plot. They will bring Brachiano to some "deathless shame" by opening the way for his love affair, and will repeal the banishment of Lodovico. In grim humor, Webster has his Cardinal protest (there is a similar protestation in IV.i) "It may be objected I am dishonorable, / To play thus with my kinsman" (386.7). He allows Monticelso to feel the necessity of naming and defining for his own purposes moral virtues. But Monticelso's "answer" to this charge has the self-contradictory quality of Flamineo's best statements: "For my revenge I'de stake a brother's life, / That being wrong'd durst not avenge himselfe" (388-89). Monticelso would let his "brother" be killed to save him the dishonor of not being bold enough to defend his own honor. Monticelso has, to the audience's moral eye, and even when he is most charitably viewed, cancelled out one dishonor with another. In the light of succeeding action, even the justification from revenge seems disingenuous, particularly since private revenge, not sanctioned by law, was the object of universal moral condemnation at this time.[59] "Come to observe this strumpet," urges Francisco (390). The two are, in effect, as much pandars for Brachiano as his own pandar Flamineo is, and it is hard to avoid the feeling that they seek to participate in (rather than condemn) Vittoria's profligacy, as the Duchess of Malfi's brothers do in hers. Their problematic participation in adultery will be brought to fruition in her glorious arraignment.

Chapter III

The Arraignment of Sir Walter

Act III Scene ii of The White Devil has a separate title unto itself in the Quarto, "The Araignment of Vittoria." This emphasis directs the reader's attention to the event's self-enclosure as a spectacle, a "play within a play," but I believe it is meant to direct attention as well to another quality of the event as the corruption of a ritual of justice. An arraignment is a specific kind of event, both in legal terms and as a genre of allegory. In both cases it is a "preliminary" event: it affirms that there is a case against someone, states that case, but does not seek to decide guilt or innocence of the one charged, unless that one confesses his/her guilt. An arraignment is not the same thing as a trial, though many have called this scene so.[1]

The fundamental corruption of Vittoria's arraignment is that it is turned into a trial by Monticelso, her judge, who presumptuously takes on the role of her accuser (see III.ii. 63-64), and Francisco, the plaintiff, who presumptuously takes on the role of attorney and of judge. Brought to hear her "charges," and to be "accused" (V.ii.20-22), she ends up with a "sentence" (272), and, whatever her actual guilt or innocence, she can justifiably make a metaphor of the charge of prostitution and in her turn arraign Monticelso on a charge of "rape" of justice.

Of course, an arraignment is the place for the venting of the passions of accusation, and heightened rhetoric is the essence of it. When Richard II is arraigned by his conscience, and faces the accusations of the ghosts of those he has slain thronging to the bar and crying "Guilty!" the pressure of their wills is almost unbearable. But Webster places the passion of accusation in the mouths of the supposedly impartial--particularly the one impartial judge, the Cardinal, is in a sense already disqualified from the role he takes, as he is a blood relative of Camillo in whose death Vittoria is implicated, and by this marriage, of the defendant herself.

In the arrogance of the Cardinal, there is more than the transformation of fictional arraignment into a trial, although this further element is only hinted at. The production of The White Devil came in the immediate environs of the publication of John Cowell's famous Interpreter (1612), whose attribution of prerogatives to James I was so extreme that the King himself was forced to disown it publicly. Cowell attributed to the King the "sole power of making and interpreting the laws," and, more sinisterly, ascribed to James "by law everything that the monarch had arrogated to himself by divine right."[2] The Cardinal, with his lawyer who uses the Latin of the civil law courts, rather than the vernacular of the common law courts, is performing an analogous preemptive act to that suggested as possible by Cowell. He is extending the royal presence and prerogative into those realms where, even though their jurisdiction was limited, the popular will, expressed through Parliament, could define law and the violation thereof. Monticelso can represent, not James himself, but the tendency his belief in divine right represents, because it is as executor of the law of God--not the law made by humans--that the King's right manifests itself in the world. The King, says Royalist Sir Henry Finch, is "immediate under God," and his legal rights are defined by his godlike traits of infinitude and perfection.[3]

Webster is actually presenting a situation wherein the judge, putting on the mantle of the law of God, perverts to his own purposes the institution meant to allow humans to judge other humans in terms of human law. The major charge of whoredom against Vittoria is an expression of this conflict of sources of law; it plays a similar role in Measure for Measure, where Angelo (appealing, it is true, to ancient statutes rather than to divine right), seeks to condemn Claudio absolutely as the absolute violator of a law of God, of which he is the interpreter. Vittoria's crime is seen as the violation of one of the basic "principles of good and evil," expressed in the law of Nature, which is determined by the law of God, which is interpreted and administered by the King alone.[4] Again, there is no neat allegorical relation between Monticelso and James I; there are plenty of obvious inconsistencies in their roles, let alone the fact that the Cardinal's court is expressly an ecclesiastical one. But the power of association still remains: Monticelso, like the King, sees few bounds to his prerogative.

It is instructive to compare Vittoria's arraignment with the description of an actual one which occurred shortly before Vittoria's was written. This is The Araignment of John Selman, who was executed neere Charing-Crosse the 7. of January, 1611 (1612). John Selman's experience was full of ritual potential, since he stood accused of picking a pocket in the Chapel at Whitefriars on Christmas day. The State, including Solicitor Francis Bacon, made much of this violation of Christmas spirit, and presumably publicized this case so widely for its exemplary lessons. Selman aided his captors' moral purpose by his dramatic gallows speech--"I have been the only corruptor of many ripe-witted youth, and leader of them to confusion"[5]--by his providing of a "black book" (see Chapter VII below) of fellow malefactors in his "fraternity," and by the same crime.

But as well as the differences between Vittoria Corombona, who did not confess to any crime, and John Selman, who did, and suffered the penalty of the law for it, there are striking differences between the two arraignments themselves. Since Selman confessed immediately, he was not put on trial, no jury was impanelled, and no witnesses were called on his behalf. Immediately on his arrest he was taken to be Examined by Sir Roger Banistre, Clerk of the Greencloth; he was then committed to Marshalsea Prison, and his citizen's clothing was exchanged for a meaner sort. On December 31, the Marshal of Marshalsea having received a warrant, he was brought before the King's Bench. The King's commission having been read, a "grand inquest" of 18 citizens was called, sworn, the "Bill of Inditement" read to them, the victim and a witness brought to testify, and the examination and prior confession of Selman read to them. The inquest members found the indictment to be a "true bill."

It was only at this point that Selman himself was called to the bar, and had the indictment read to him: "What saiest thou John Selman to this felony, art thou guilty or not guilty?"[6] Selman again declared his guilt, and his sentence of death was pronounced by the Solicitor.

If such were the process of arraignment as commonly perceived by the citizen of London, who might in 1612 have bought and read The Araignment of John Selman or any other such crime-pamphlet,[7] the arraignment of Vittoria, even rendered exotic by Webster's dramatic licence, would have seemed the absolute contrary of good English law, and the English Ambassador's "... the Cardinals too bitter" (III.ii.111) the grossest of understatements. Of course Vittoria benefits from the deliberations of neither a grand jury nor a petty jury; Vittoria is summoned to the bar at the very beginning of the proceedings (III.ii.9) and forced to answer charges directly, without any finding that they represent a "true bill," and without any clear and precise articulation of what they are, an articulation, from which John Selman, despite all the self-righteous bombast of Bacon, does benefit. In a way, her "All this assembly/Shall heare what you can charge mee with" (III.ii.21-22), is a plea for "English" justice against "Italian," which would turn an arraignment into a trial. Of course, not only is she not allowed the participation of her peers, the presentation of her own evidence, or any really clear opportunity to defend herself, but her "sentence" is suddenly declared upon her in the midst of unresolved proceedings, without the actual crime for which she is to suffer being named to her.

I realize that it may seem to be naively literalistic to assume that Webster's imaginative spectacle can be meaningfully evaluated in terms of contemporary legal practice. I would, however, argue both that the explicit definition of the scene as an "Araignment" demands generic similarity with the many pamphlets similarly titled printed in the time,[8] and that no context of meaning in "arraignment" could have been available to most of Webster's audience, and to Webster himself, except that represented by the arraignment of John Selman.

There is, however, one example of English justice much more illustrious than that of John Selman, which figures as a type of the Arraignment of Vittoria, and adds weight to the view that Webster is presenting an arraignment perverted into a trial. This is the actual trial of Sir Walter Raleigh, as begun on November 17, 1603.

At least two allusions to Raleigh's trial and fate have been noted in the play (see below, ch. IV, note 25, and ch. VIII, note 15): Monticelso's reference at the arraignment (III.ii.94) to the loss of an estate for a trivial error in a deed referring to Raleigh's loss of his estate, Sherborne, and Brachiano's daily lease on life to Flamineo referring to Raleigh's condition in the Tower of London. But the whole nature of Raleigh's trial, with its abuse of rhetoric and browbeating of the defendant, is harmonious with the conduct of the Cardinal and the Duke towards Vittoria. Raleigh's trial for treason against the state, with its confusingly multiple indictments, was a "spectacle . . . intended not to assess guilt but to proclaim it. All the privy councillors who in theory sat as impartial justices had for the weeks before the trial been employed cross-questioning the accused with a view to building up a case for the prosecution, while Raleigh was allowed no legal assistance nor even prior knowledge of the precise charges to be brought against him, which he first heard on the morning of . . . the day of his trial."[9] Raleigh was tried before a jury, but the jury was stacked, and it heard charges of treasonous plots and conversations for which no clear evidence was presented; the heated language of Coke, the attorney general, substituted polemic for evidence, and assumed guilt before it had been legally determined.

This is of course not an arraignment corrupted into a corrupt trial; it is a corrupt trial. The defendant was led to the bar, heard the indictment read, and pleaded not guilty to all its charges. Once he had done so, Coke engaged in a verbal taunting of Raleigh amazingly similar to that of Vittoria by Monticelso. After an exhaustive characterization of the Treason Coke asked "But to whom do you bear Malice? to the Children?" Raleigh: "To whom speak you this? You tell me news I never heard of." Coke replied "Oh sir, do I? I will prove you the notoriest Traitor that ever came to the bar . . ." But Raleigh spoke in a manner like Vittoria's "Find mee but guilty, sever head from body" (III.ii.141):

> Your words cannot condemn me; my innocency is my defence. Prove one of these things wherewith you have charged me, and I will confess the whole Indictment, and that I am the horriblest Traitor that ever lived, and worthy to be crucified with a thousand thousand torments.[10]

But Coke persisted in characterizing Raleigh as a white devil: "thou art a monster; thou hast an English face, but a Spanish heart."

The diabolic nature of Raleigh was repeated many times by the Attorney: he pursues a "Machiavelian and devilish policy," he engages in "the most horrible practices that ever came out of the bottomless pit of the lowest hell." Coke repeatedly addressed him directly with the most vituperative epithets: "thou Viper," "thou Traitor." His declaration "You are the absolutest Traitor that ever was," received the reply "Your phrases will not prove it," similar to Vittoria's "Who saies so but your selfe?" (III.ii.232).[11]

In this texture of similarities there is only one absolutely direct verbal echo of Raleigh's trial. When Monticelso criticizes Vittoria for not being in mourning, as though it were evidence of her implication in Camillo's death, Vittoria replies

> . . . Had I forknowne his death as you suggest,
> I would have bespoke my mourning.
> MON. O you are conning.
> VIT. You shame your wit and Judgement
> To call it so; What, is my just defence
> By him that is my Judge cal'd impudence?
> (III.ii.125-30)

When Cecil and Coke had built up an elaborate connection between Raleigh and a treasonable book, the defendant exclaimed

> . . . Here is a Book supposed to be treasonable; I never read it, commended it, or delivered it, nor urged it.
> <u>Attorney</u>. Why, this is cunning
> <u>Raleigh</u>. Every thing that doth make for me is cunning, and every thing that maketh against me is probable.[12]

There are, though, two other circumstantial parallels between the two trials. The first is the prosecution's introduction of Arabella Stuart, somewhat similar to Brachiano's intervention (III.ii.159). As Brachiano is Vittoria's supposed companion in fornication and murder, Arabella is Raleigh's supposed companion (one of them) in treason. Arabella silently, and Brachiano vociferously, deny involvement in intrigue. As Monticelso, toward the end of Vittoria's ordeal, presents an incriminating letter (III.ii.200) supposedly revealing the "plot" of the lovers to rendezvous amorously, so Coke, as a crowning blow toward the end of Raleigh's trial, produced a letter from Cobham directly implicating Raleigh as the inciter of his own treason. Reading this letter, Coke could not resist interjecting again "Ah! is not this a Spanish heart in an English body?" Unlike Vittoria in this case, though, Raleigh produced his own letter from Cobham disavowing the former one, and managed at least a counterstroke.

For all its verbal abuse, Raleigh's trial was to an extent a debate on the nature of law and authority. Raleigh seems to have been well aware (although naturally he could not get his prosecutors to admit), that he was on trial for his values and beliefs, not for his actions; he is a "damnable atheist," defender of "the most heathenish and blasphemous Opinions." His two main vices, ambition and "corrupt covetousness," are being condemned. The unprovable circumstantial charges against him are, as in the case of Vittoria, more or less a front for judging him simply for what he is. In such a process the implication is of an overweening claim of the State to decide and control thought and belief, as well as action. "If this may be," he exclaimed once, having confessions of other plotters in which he was not mentioned, used against him, "you will have any man's life in a week."[13] This is the import of Vittoria's "you have ravisht justice, / Forc't her to do your pleasure" (III.ii. 286-87). This ravishment of justice, in the Raleigh trial, is most clearly demonstrated in his argument with the justices over their inability or unwillingness to present any actual witnesses to his treasonous words or acts. As Raleigh says, "there is a law of two sorts of Accusers; one of his own knowledge, another by hear-say."[14] The closest to witness testimony Raleigh's judges hear is "ordinary and Ryalto talke" (III.ii.257), as it were, yet the Lord Chief Justice defends the proposition that the health of the realm would be threatened if one could not be condemned, in a treason trial, by indirect and circumstantial evidence, without witnesses. To this Raleigh inquires "I know not how you conceive the Law."

>Lord Chief Justice. Nay, we do not conceive the Law, but we know the law.
>Raleigh. The wisdom of the Law of God is absolute and perfect. Haec fac et vives, etc. But now by the Wisdom of the State, the Wisdom of the Law is uncertain . . .[15]

Raleigh would seem to be saying that the State is taking unto itself the absolute power that resides in the Law of God--which does have jurisdiction over thought and belief--and as a result, the actual Law has become a tool of the will of the state.

This subversion of the law's autonomy by the State (the State here being in effect the King's own will) is what Cowell's Interpreter of 1612 was considered to be advocating. It is what, changing the circumstances slightly, Vittoria's judges them selves are doing in her trial. The fact that in both the imaginary and the real trials under consideration an impartial audience may feel the defendants were actually guilty as charged only serves to focus on the corruption of the process of justice, as distinct from the results of that process.

I have sought to point out striking similarities between tone and theme in Raleigh's trial of 1603 and Vittoria's of (c.) 1612. I certainly have no evidence such as Boklund has unearthed regarding The White Devil's sources to indicate what printed or oral account of Raleigh's trial might have been accessible to Webster ten years later; it is certainly hard to doubt that such a notorious event, with its victim, reprieved at the last minute, visible taking walks every day in his tower captivity, would have been "ordinary and Rialto" talk in its every detail as much as sensational trials are today. Nor do I dream of contending that Vittoria "is" Sir Walter Raleigh. God forbid! I do suggest that Webster may be alluding to, <u>not</u> allegorizing, in Vittoria's arraignment, a famous trial that was also construed by many as an abuse of the power of the great; alluding in the same way that he often alludes to Montaigne, Sydney, <u>et</u>. <u>al</u>., with telling borrowing and paraphrase. The power of the allusion works in the play in both cases, but the audience is not being asked to interpret the play as only a commentary on the works or events alluded to.

Chapter IV

Second Movement: "Through darkenesse Diamonds spred their ritchest light."

II.ii

The dialogue in this ritualistic scene, where the potential actions held in solution in the first movement are precipitated, mainly serves to provide the context for two dumb-shows--the murders of the two spouses, Isabella and Camillo, in the way of a union between Brachiano and Vittoria.[1] But the conjuror who arranges Brachiano's (and our) vision of these acts, although he is a conventional stage-conjuror of Friar Bacon's lineage, is not a gratuitous character. Isabella's metaphor of conjuration (II.i) has brought up the possibility of a power both non-political and non-Christian, and this conjuror proclaims himself an adept of such power, unlike those who by "Sophisticke tricks . . . Seem to conjure, when indeed they cheate" (7, 10). Of course the conjuror's claimed authenticity is prostituted and discredited, in that this "true" conjuror has been hired by Brachiano's bounty to serve the aims of sophistic cheaters. All of the false conjurors Brachiano's conjuror complains of (6-20), in a sort of collective Character, are types of the play's scheming protagonists, and share their attributes. They are "Fellowes indeed that onely live by stealth" (17). In his railing, and professional self-righteousness, Brachiano's conjuror presents himself as the type of Monticelso, adept of another faith, who is also self-righteous about his own sins.

The murder of Isabella is much more than pure "spectacle." It is a figure of action satirizing both art and devotion. The conjuror's "strong-commanding Art" (22) has been that of creating the death potion and Brachiano's power to see the effects of that potion. Secondarily it is the power of the artist's portrait of Brachiano, which is a "true" enough imitation of life for Isabella to kiss its lips and imbibe the fatal poison placed upon them.[2] Brachiano must have enough faith in Isabella's devotion to him to know that she will take his portrait for reality and seek to conjure his love to her again magically by kissing it. We recall the "one kiss" Brachiano denies her in II.i.160 as being at last delivered to her here as a kiss of death. Brachiano's curtained picture is positioned as an icon above an altar, and Julio and Christophero, burning perfumes and anointing the picture's lips, are perversions of the priests at the altar, preparing it for the celebration of communion. The communion it parodies represents a death and rebirth originally sealed by the false kiss of Judas. In a sense, Isabella suffers from her fusing of fleshly and spiritual devotion. Her faith is strong because it is blind to Brachiano's implacable nature, despite the evidence of her senses; Julio and Christophero wear "spectacles of glasse" both for the literal purpose of protection from poison and the figurative purpose of representing her (and, morally, her husband's) distortion of vision. We are to see her poisoned kiss literally and metaphorically as well. These black perversions of art and faith make the most intimate act, a kiss sacramental because conjugal, create the death of that intimacy. The conjurer's art is a version of the perspective art used by Flamineo to gull Camillo, and one of many manifestations of the transformation of white into black.

Brachiano's response to his vision appears as a paradox to any moral person: "Excellent, then shee's dead" (24). But it is no paradox to one whose perspective in this scene is that of the devil, parodying God looking down on his work of anti-Creation (it seems reasonable to suggest that Brachiano may at the Red Bull have been here in the Heavens of an upper stage). The commentary of the conjurer, playing the executive Mephistopheles, is most significant. He explains the circumstances, that Isabella would habitually "feed her eyes and lippes / On the dead shadow" (27-28) of Brachiano: as predestinedly dead or damned she has a mess of shadows for her meat, and is almost cruel as a wolf in cannibalizing even his picture with her consuming devotion. The conjuror also emphasizes the presence of Lodovico as a mourner for Isabella, upon whom he did "most passionately doate" (32-33). Thus, with dramatic irony we are made aware that this very murder makes for the deaths of Brachiano and Vittoria, since it gives the banished man both political and amorous motivations for their destruction.

It is to be noted that Lodovico continually appears by reference, as here, or at a distance, as a vindictive shadow himself, waiting to emerge. In a play filled with avengers, he is as the _ur_-avenger, holding back his hand until the end, but whose presence is felt as a potential for ultimate retribution. A Christian interpretation could see the mercy of Lodovico's banishment (rather than execution) as the key to his survival and eventual purgation of corruption. As the play's first scene suggested, he is so far "beyond good and evil" that he does not even feel the need to engage himself with them, and "use" them as the politician would. As a banished man he is paradoxically "pure" enough of involvement in the intrigue to experience from outside the complex circumstances which entrap Brachiano's establishment, and therefore to be hired to resolve their riddle by cutting through the knot of their rivalries.

Next, the Conjurer, referring to his "charmed ground," urges Brachiano in turn to "view Camillo's farre more polliticke fate" (35). "Polliticke" is again an important word here. The first dumb show illustrates corruption of religion, the second of its counterpart, secular policy. In the first art misuses an object of devotion, in the second it misuses an object of war. Whereas the picture of Brachiano is frankly and obviously poisoned, Flamineo creates by his art the stage pretence of an innocent accident occurring to Camillo. It is worth noting here that both Brachiano and Flamineo meet their own fates in manners mockingly appropriate to these they have engineered: Brachiano by a poisoned helmet, Flamineo by direct sword-thrusts following an abortive "staged" murder similar to his vaulting-horse trick.

Brachiano's "T'was quaintly done," as response to the murder of Camillo (38), takes the murder for a work of "art," since "quaint" as aesthetic term is painfully inappropriate to killing. The conjurer's commentary on his own art, analogous as in the previous case to the text beneath an emblem, the dumb show itself, allows the playwright to underline his implications. Camillo, Marcello, and the others are vaulting as part of celebrating their new commissions to fight the Mediterranean pirates, particuarly Lodovico. Vaulting while drunk ("deepe helthes," 40), lends credence to the contention that Camillo's death was an accident. But the scene also presents a parody of warfare; the drunken vaulters seem totally unqualified to launch an actual military enterprise, such as that imagined by the young Giovanni. "Sport" (43) is the weak mirror of war (cf. Brachiano's fatal barriers). The vaulting horse itself mocks the ideal of chivalry; it is an appropriate tool of Flamineo's "vaulting ambition." As we can see from Thomas Middleton's <u>Black Book</u> (1604), vaulting has sexual connotations, associated with brothelry and pandarism, Flamineo's profession. Some of Middleton's knaves are the "race of lusty vaulting gallants, that, instead of a French horse, practise upon their mistresses all the nimble tricks of vaulting;" their mistresses are the "city-horses," that is, the whores, or the housewives, of London.[3] In this sense of vaulting, it is in the sexual warfare for Vittoria, seen as wife or as whore, that Camillo stumbles and falls.[4]

The conjuror's final observations, that the Cardinal and Duke are "come with purpose to apprehend /Your Mistresse, faire <u>Vittoria</u>," and that they are "Beneath her roofe" (48-50), may be, as Lucas says, ludicrously self-evident and forced. On the other hand they lead Brachiano, who has played the observer up to now, directly into the action, anticipating his implication in the following arraignment scene. They allow the audience to see, even before it occurs, the trial of Vittoria for her loose behavior as implicitly a trial for these two murders as well. Since Vittoria is not the actual perpetrator of murder, and Brachiano appears in court only as an insolent spectator, the innocence she professes seems stronger by contrast to this hidden agenda than if her whoredom were actually the only thing on trial.

The conjurer concludes the scene with another commonplace couplet: "Both flowers and weedes, spring when the Sunne is warme, / And great men do great good, or else great harme"

(55-6). As with other moralists, like the Medici brothers, the conjurer pretends not to be responsible for the conditions his homily bewails. But, by cynically equating the amorality of political power with the amorality of natural processes, he proposes a universe pervaded by no grace.

III.i

That section of The White Devil apocryphally designated the third act does have an inherent symmetry of scenes: pre-"trial" and post-"trial" maneuverings flank the famous set-piece of the "trial" itself, as patches of "wilderness" might flank a formal garden; although in this case the formal space becomes itself a wilderness of injustice. The first and third scenes are also analogous to views "backstage," and appear as foils to the "jewel" of the arraignment itself. Their central mover is Flamineo, whose manipulative powers counterbalance Monticelso's magisterial ones, although they are similarly corrupt.

The beginning of the scene forces the juxtaposition of these two characters as politic movers. Monticelso outlines to Francisco (3-9) the strategy of manipulating attendant ambassadors' responses to make the weak, circumstantial case against Vittoria appear more compelling. Flamineo, still under suspicion as Vittoria is, reveals his manipulation by "mirth" of his observers to deter suspicion of him (30-31). Both Monticelso and Flamineo are conscious of the "art" of their actions, and of their audience's subjectivity. They count, for their effects, on the opposite of the "full and understanding Auditory" which Webster, as a manipulator of dramatic illusion, desires.

Monticelso's backstage words to Francisco are self-betraying in other ways. As well as "stacking" his audience with the influential ambassadors, he seeks to destroy Vittoria by making her "infamous / To all our neighboring Kingdomes" (7-8). He is not interested in legal proof of guilt, but in the extralegal judgements of rumor and slander. He depends on the ill-fame he would condemn, on opinion rather than truth.

The interjected quibbling of Flamineo and his lawyer is also purposely inappropriate to a context of justices. "To gull suspition" (31), Flamineo assumes the role of "Fool" that he assumed vis-a-vis Brachiano in I.ii. But by joking that only cuckolds and whoremasters are qualified to judge Vittoria, and making various ribald puns involving both the judge and the defendant, he does point to the truth more forcefully underlined by Vittoria, that her judges are no better than they accuse her of being. In a homiletic metaphor from nature, like the Conjuror's (II.ii.55-6), the Lawyer also observes "For to sowe kisses (marke what I say) to sowe kisses, is to reape letchery . . ." (23-4); this can be taken either as an argument for sexual claustration, or a fatalistic endorsement of sensuality. By this distinction, Vittoria could only be a saint or a whore. But at

Flamineo's self-reflective aside (30-31), the dialogue radically changes tone, introducing a violent fraternal debate between Flamineo and Marcello. The seriousness of this debate is signalled by the transition from prose to blank verse. "Vertuous" Marcello echoes his mother's condemnation of Flamineo as the "engine / To undo my sister" (36). He exclaims "I would my daggers point had cleft her heart / When she first saw Brachiano" (33-34), which casts a mood of violence on his virtue, with its foreshadowing of Vittoria's actual fate and suggestion of his own capacity for violent revenge. Even Marcello can elaborate a paradoxical similitude of love and death.

Flamineo and Marcello engage in a war which is both passionate fraternal strife and a war of words over the naming of things. What to Marcello is "ruine" or "undoing" is to Flamineo "preferment." The dangerous nexus of religion and policy was never more sharply dramatized than here. Flamineo repudiates Marcello's values in martial metaphor, and in so doing breaks from caustic into lyric utterance:

>. . . what has got
>But like the wealth of Captaines, a poore handfull?--
>Which in thy palme thou bear'st, as men hold water--
>Steales through thy fingers. (41-44)

This simile strikes back at its brandisher, in that it applies more truthfully to Flamineo's materialistic dreams of preferment than to the more enduring, though less tangible, ideals of fame and honour to which Marcello is devoted. When most seeming-earnest, Flamineo is for the audience most eloquently defining his own folly, and Vittoria's judges will set this same course in the subsequent scene.

Flamineo compounds his folly by continuing his sermon against his brother's "ambition," ornamenting it with more ornate flowers of rhetoric. In a verbal emblem, he shows the medicinal mistletoe companioned by the "noxious" (Lucas) mandrake, beside the "builder Oke" ("equated by Flamineo with gaine"). Flamineo's observations on the inevitable ill-results of ambition are unexceptionable, except in the context of a Flamineo who has been created as one totally beyond the mingling of mistletoe and mandrake. Harry Bruder finds the "subversion of soliloquy," as practiced here by Flamineo, to be a constant device in the play.[7] Rather than revealing, it conceals and distorts actual motivation. Used by Flamineo, it might better be called the "Machiavellian soliloquy." The politician furthers his ends by proclaiming either moral truths his covert actions contradict, or nihilistic truths that contradict morality altogether. However, as a "politic madman," Flamineo is hardly subverting a convention of self-revelation; his subversion of soliloquy is in this scene the "mad speech" conventional from Ajax through Hamlet. In his speeches here Flamineo rejects the realm of action as one where any gain is ultimately possible--but obviously accepts neither contemplative or spiritual activity as sources of gain as well. His theme is "how shall we find reward?" (51), but he does not admit the philosophical implications of his question. One answer to Flamineo's question is the reward of death he receives at the end because reward has no unwordly meaning to him.

At the point where Flamineo begins to argue that his brother be paid for his ambition by having nothing "When age shall turne thee, / White as a blooming hauthorne" (58-59), Marcello interrupts with one of the few rational and assertive speeches allotted by Webster to a "virtuous" character:

> For love of vertue beare an honest heart,
> And stride over every pollitick respect,
> Which where they most advance they most infect (60-62)

This speech clearly strikes a note of authorial sincerity, and, unusually, is made without irony. Clearly, Marcello rejects the entire previous speech of Flamineo as "polliticke," and has already defined the distance between ethical and political systems. His advice to Flamineo is made so absolute and terse, in contrast to Flamineo's own advisements, precisely to create the sense that it is a truth so self-evident that only a victim of extreme illusion could avoid seeing it. Thus it is not just a verbal arraignment of Flamineo. Its meaning radiates forward to the Medicis' politic behavior in the next scene. Applied to Vittoria, it characterizes her behavior there, where she pretends to be "true to herself," avoiding the politic language that might salvage her "honor."

Virtue, of course, has more faces than Marcello sees. Conceived as "integrity," it has no necessary relation to "chastity." Judging from Marcello's words and his sister's practice, virtue's classical sense is of a higher order than its Christian sense. Marcello pairs himself with Vittoria against Flamineo in terms of their shared integrity, or oneness of mind, rather than opposing himself to Flamineo and Vittoria, as he well could do, seeing them as collaborators in sin. Since Webster gives Marcello little passionate rhetoric, it is hard to believe that he is meant to be perceived as jealous of the alliance between his brother and sister; the most intimate scene between Vittoria and Flamineo is the last one, where they appear as rivals, not as collaborators. Using the hints of his sources, Webster has outlined here the strains placed on the inner coherence of any "upward-mobile" family by the very possibility of preferment. Cornelia's three children could be, in different, less mortal circumstances, those of any gentrified family during a time of aristocracy in crisis. In this family Marcello, taking the role of soldier rather than of courtesan or courtier, has chosen the social role promising preferment which is least likely to compromise his moral integrity or cloud his self-knowledge. We might contrast Antonio, in The Duchess of Malfi, who by the nature of his preferment is forced to exist in a courtly realm, and who, despire his virtu, is denied the strength and assertiveness of Marcello. Unfortunately, also, Marcello's integrity is self-destructive. It is seen by the corrupt as a threat, and he must be destroyed.

Webster breaks the intimacy of the brothers' rivalry by the sudden ceremonial passage of the foreign ambassadors. This intrusion characterizes the role of the ambassadors throughout the play. The Italy Webster dramatizes is fatally self-obsessed, and cannot face outward to engage itself with international issues outside its borders. The presence of the ambassadors puts the intrigues of the families into a perspective of diminution-- as in this scene with the debate between Marcello and Flamineo. In the perspective of Europe, the passions over Vittoria seem almost comically overwrought. The restored quibbles between the lawyer and Flamineo, wherein the latter gives satiric Characters of the ambassadors (68-79) serve the same purpose. Flamineo diminishes them, likening the French ambassador to a pewter knight (a creation of art) and the Spaniard to the claw of a blackbird. This diminution diminishes the status of the observers, who see significant stage-figures as only grotesque miniatures, rather than as the representatives of powers infinitely more significant than Flamineo and his peers. Flamineo's true envy of "movers and shakers" will be revealed later, when he cozies up to the disguised Francisco, hoping some of his black majesty will rub off on him.

III.ii

"The Araignment of Vittoria" has been exhaustively analyzed as a tour-de-force of rhetorical manipulation. Particularly has it been clarified in a central article, by H. Bruce Franklin, which tends to the conclusion that all the participants in it are "on trial" and all are found, in "our" judgement, guilty.[9] By contrast, Dent's influential <u>John Webster's Borrowing</u> deprecates the entire scene as a "dramatic conflict built principally from metaphorical sententiae."[10] However judged, the used and abused rhetoric is a vehicle for presenting an ironic confrontation of intractible personalities, and a commentary on morality and judgement. It is obvious at the outset that Monticelso's court, "located in a consistory, or ecclesiastical court room, in Rome,"[11] is an arena of false judgements. It is an ecclesiastical court making a moral, not legal, judgement, through purely politic, amoral means, for politic, amoral, and illegal ends. The court's workings exemplify the "corruption" which the court is constantly attributing to the defendant, Vittoria. In this arena, "Vittoria asserts what she feels to be her natural identity against the role assigned to her by the court."[12] Brachiano, by attending unbidden and extra-legally, Vittoria, by speaking "plainly," without evasion of the (seeming) "truth"-- both break through the decorum of the court. Their disorder is a critique of the court's false order.

Vittoria initially exercises her power over the court by reducing the prosecuting lawyer's language from Latin to

Latinate English, and finally procuring his dismissal altogether. Her grounds for this are not only his general incomprehensibility, but the desire that the entire "auditory" understand the accusation. This auditory includes, of course the play's audience itself. Vittoria's proclamation that "All this assembly / Shall heare what you can charge me with" (21-22) is an "English" sentiment, rebuking the corruptions in the non-English versions of a native institution. The lawyer's speech is "a casebook study of bad forensic rhetoric," and Vittoria's ridicule of it raises her credit with the audience, as being sympathetic to popular understanding.[13] The Lawyer also becomes allied, via his rhetoric, with Star Chamber proceedings and the civil law, as opposed to Common Pleas and the common law. Vittoria's populistic appeal is of course very politic, if we accept the contention that she is trying purposely to create the impression of being on trial for her life, when she is actually only in jeopardy of her liberty and reputation.[14]

Vittoria is successful in gaining Francisco's agreement to her judgement of the lawyer's "fustian," and Webster's stage direction even has his dismissal of him spoken "as in scorne." But Monticelso's "I shall bee playner with you" (55) prefaces rhetoric that is just as convoluted and artificial--in its hyperbole, not its Latinity--as the Lawyer's.[15] Monticelso declares that his rhetoric's "colors" will be more "naturall" than those on Vittoria's cheeks. But as colored cheeks imply prostitution, so Monticelso's language, figured by painting, is condemned as false by his own metaphor--another example of visual art misused. Despite Vittoria's sharp rebuttal, "You raise a blood as noble in this cheek / As ever was your mother's" (57-58), Monticelso predicts that "proof" will "cry whore to that" (59). Needless to say, an English audience knows that Monticelso's Mother, the Catholic Church, is a whore. Monticelso has directly implied, though, that Vittoria's whoredom is as unnatural as the false colors of rhetoric. She has complexly suggested that her own colors are blushes of modesty, shame's contrary, and that her virtue certifies her newly-preferred lineage (in that sense of "blood") to be as noble as Monticelso's ancient one. Her words may also bear the intimation that if she is a whore, she is no worse than Monticelso's physical mother; this would be a very masculine mode of verbal abuse.

Monticelso defines "proof" as the collective acceptance of a predetermined judgement of Vittoria as "whore," a label which seems to cover a multitude of personality traits. There is of course, a multitude of good evidence, from contemporary theological typologies of whoredom, that Vittoria does have the attributes thereof, and that Monticelso is not distorting her basic nature as an English audience would see it.[16] Clearly, when Monticelso cries, in response to her criticism that he is overstepping his authority as a judge, "your trade instructs your language" (65), he seems to be using the condition of whoredom to represent forcefulness, masculine assertiveness of language. Behind this, he seems to be condemning the freedom from scruple, and from social and moral laws, which Vittoria has assumed, in emulation of the males in her circle including Monticelso himself. Although Vittoria is not self-proclaimedly the seducer of Brachiano--the actual perpetrator of the crimes the tribunal is indirectly trying--and although her role as aristocratic courtesan is not exceptionable in Webster's Italy or his England, Monticelso gives her the "low" attributes of a street prostitude. He himself is, in Protestant terms, a true white devil and prostitutor of spiritual values.[17] His moral hysteria is certainly a response to more than her literal activities with Brachiano. One might say that Vittoria has violated unspoken social order by entering a domain of materialistic politic activity reserved for men, a domain Isabella and Cornelia do not encroach on despite their grievances. These women utter complaints, lamentations; Vittoria, as much as a London roaring girl, issues direct attacks.

Monticelso's continued ad feminam attacks on Vittoria are paradoxically generalized, as though her character escapes him as much as his character of a whore escapes her (105). He first employs Biblical typology on her, comparing her with the ash-falling fruits of Sodom and Gomorrah (65-70),[18] and secondly, "Were there a second Paradice to loose / This Devell would betray it" (72-73), associating Vittoria with Eve as source of humanity's fall--the premier mysogynistic argument.[19] The more appropriate Devil in this case is Monticelso himself, even in the implied skepticism ("were there") of Christ's Second Coming. We have encountered often, from the first scene, this motif of a loss of innocence, a fallen world, human banishment. Monticelso's whole "arraignment" is a betrayal of the mirror of divine judgement that it ought to be, and a parody of the idealized arraignments of sinful Mankind found in the morality tradition. Vittoria addresses the knowledge of this betrayal when she exclaims, like vox populi, "O poore charity! / Thou art seldome found in scarlet" (73-74). The devil is the one who gains preferment when the first principle of Christianity is banished from the realms of judgement.

Monticelso provides, in an overly-wrought periodic sentence, a generalized characterization of Vittoria's sumptuous life "When shee did counterfet a Prince's Court" (78), as being somehow evidence of whoredom. Although the most logical statement, in its structure, that he has made so far, it is speciously so: if a woman parties a lot, she must be a whore, since whores party.[20] Unwilling, or unable, to sustain this style, he abruptly changes his tune, and delivers another generalization, a "perfect character" of a whore (83). Monticelso's character is not perfect, rhetorically or characterologically, since it consists only of a string of affective figures, likening "whore" to various unpleasant aspects of the cosmos. Webster's audience would surely see that this is a "bad" character, as Vittoria does, a character which betrays the folly and ignorance of its creator. It also betrays more about Monticelso's own cosmology and ethics than it does about the condition of whoredom. It

might be seen as an ironic character of his mind. Some of its
similitudes are banally commonplace commonplaces, such as "sweete
meates which rot the eater" (85). Collectively the figures
alternate paradoxically self-destructive human conditions with
those in nature, implying that innocent-disguised-corruption is
a universal condition which harmonizes the universe. In the
natural realm, whores are Russian winters without spring, ship-
wrecks in calm weather, harmony of wedding and passing bells.
In the human realm they are Dutch taxes which extort all means
of livelihood, legal tricks that forfeit entire estates, treas-
uries filled by extortion and empied by riot, counterfeit money
which brings guilt even upon its innocent recipients (almost as
Original Sin does). The natural analogues of whoredom are akin
to the figures Flamineo uses to justify his actions; the human
are all politic crimes, derived it seems from, and similar to,
those described in Monticelso's own black book (Iv.i). Perhaps
most tellingly, whores are worse than dead bodies

>   . . . which are beg'd at gallowes
>   And wrought upon by surgeons, to teach man
>   Wherin he is imperfect (100-102).

In this last irony, Monticelso, clearly sinful in the playwright's eyes, yet speaks for him. The moral imperfection which
led humanity to the gallows is necessary for the surgeons (read
priests, or philosophers) to be able to find out the physical
imperfections of humanity. Seen as physical or spiritual curers,
these new surgeons who practice autopsies will not be able to
rectify the sinful imperfections that continue to lead humans to
the gallows. In the fallen world, with no second paradise to
lose, human nature is essentially and irrevocably imperfect.[22]

    Although Monticelso is potential or actual participant in
the evil practices to which he compares whoredom, and which
illustrate the circularity of self-sustaining vice, which feeds
upon itself, his Character actually constitutes an arraignment
of a world in which there is no hope of redemption, an
a-theistic universe. The lack of proportion between the
Cardinal's language and its object shows his corruption as an
individual, but it also expresses the desperation of anyone
without faith who seeks some "first cause," or principle of
causation, to explain the hegemony of evil. Vittoria becomes
such a governing female Vice in this morality play that Monticelso has established--like one of Dr. Faustus's hot whores, or
his Helen herself. In fact, Monticelso initiates a parade of
the seven deadly sins, all embodied in Vittoria herself: "You
know what Whore is; next the devell, Adultry, / Enters the
devell, Murder" (112-113). Strikingly, Francisco, who unlike the
Cardinal perceives vice in particular, concrete, and not cosmic,
terms, immediately grounds the Cardinal's drama. To him, "Murder"
means "Your unhappy / Husband is dead" (114). Vittoria, perhaps
ironically playing on the secular consciousness of this ecclesiastical setting, gives an immediate Stoic consolation: "O hee's
a happy husband--/ Now hee owes Nature nothing" (115).[23]

Normally, "happy husband" might characterize one who had just enjoyed the sexual favors of his wife. As though ignoring her, Monticelso and Francisco launch into a seemingly rehearsed dialogue, playing with heavy irony on the "accidental" death of Camillo, emphasizing the suddenness with which he lost "motion." Vittoria sees through their obvious implication that she foreknew Camillo's death, and proposes the scenario she would have followed had she planned Camillo's death: overtly and hypocritically mourning, as a true white devil would. To this Monticelso responds with strangely naive-sounding admiration of a highly-valued quality, "O you are conning" (128).

At this point, Vittoria, with <u>actual</u> cunning, turns to do what Monticelso has been unsuccessful in previously, to play the audiences--the ambassadorial audience, and the Red Bull audience beyond them. She will win, following Monticelso's proclaimed tactic (III.i.6), their "approbation," which is worth more than proof. She abandons the "plain" Attic style, and moves to the middle, and then vigorous, persuasive, style of rhetoric, following the prescriptions of Cicero's <u>De Oratoria</u>.[24] She protests that what the judge calls "impudence" is, in her, "just defence." She ritually, "humbly," submits, while at the same time asserting that to defend herself she must break decorum and "personate masculine vertue" (140). This is a very pointed self-description, since "vertue" in the masculine sense has a connotation of chivalric nobility, which her masculine judges lack. Of course Marcello sees himself as possessing this virtue, and Isabella has attempted to personate outrage while overtly expressing her frustration that she cannot personate it in a masculine manner. Part of Vittoria's personation consists of her asserting her willingness to die rather than to plead for her life with Monticelso or any man. The English Ambassador prompts the English audience to respond positively to this personation: "Shee hath a brave spirit" (144).

Vittoria responds to Monticelso's description of her words as "counterfet Jewels" with her most illustrious set speech of the play--often parallelled to the Duchess of Malfi's defiance:

> You are deceived.
> For know that all your strickt-combined heads,
> Which strike against this mine of diamondes,
> Shall prove but glassen hammers, they shall breake--
> These are but faigned shadowes of my evels.
> Terrify babes, my Lord, with painted devils,
> I am past such needlesse palsy-- (146-52)

Accepting the judge's imagery, Vittoria turns it against him by ignoring the "counterfeit," or ornamental, connotations of jewelry, and figuring a covetous aggression (inquisitorial, martial, mechanical, and sexual) against objects of deep value, hidden in the earth.[25] In fact, with "glassen," Vittoria transforms these violent tools into actual counterfeits themselves. She shifts the metaphor, so that falsehood or insubstantiality become attributes of impenetrable darkness, not translucency, of the language, and word-pictures of the accusers, not of their ultimate goals.[25] The "painted devils" she figures as their false imaginations of her, not her actual self as "painted" strumpet. She attributes the "names of Whoore and Murdresse" to the speakers: such are their saints, or fosterers. Unfortunately for Vittoria's persuasiveness in turning these tables, which has given her much repute in our time, Peter B. Murray has shown the pervasiveness of "white devil" in Protestant theology, from Luther on, as the name of a religious hypocrite. The devil, as white, deceives humanity into following him, and makes all humans his instruments. Such deception is the essence of Vittoria's brave words here, not that it is not also that of her judges as well: "Devotion to false values has perverted all Italy to the service of evil."[26]

This defiance of Vittoria has never been truly explored as a paradox.[27] The audience is presumed to know from earlier scenes that Vittoria is guilty of adulterous intent, if not adultery itself, and that her sustained imagery of innocence belies her actions. Yet one must admit that, except for lines 215-20, she never with any semblance of directness denies this charge against her. She constantly transfers the grounds of her innocence to the particular situation of intimidation she faces at the trial. The audience must hold in mind both Vittoria's actual behavior and the machinations of entrapment that furthered her fall. The structure of the arraignment demands a fixed alignment of moral sympathies (especially in its dramatic analogy with morality play structure), which the audience's knowledge makes impossible to sustain without being hypocritical itself. Any sympathy with Vittoria is sympathy for the devil. The trial structure therefore forces the involved audience to experience _inwardly_ the same warfare between politic dissimulation and Christian innocence that occurs on stage; the tendency is to become, through amoral emotional involvement, a collaborator in immoral behavior. The power of the white devil is thus manifested directly in the theatre itself. The arraignment scene thus deliberately creates moral confusion in the spectator; ideally, he or she becomes a little Italy.[28]

The intervention of Brachiano in the trial is a good example of Webster's politic undercutting of an audience's presumed sympathies. Monticelso's impassive response to the defendant's eloquence, just discussed--merely asking her "Who lodg'd beneath your roofe that fatall night / Your husband brake his necke?" (157-8)--is more appropriate to an arraignment, a preliminary examination of an indicted suspect, than any of his earlier utterances. But its inappropriateness as a response to Vittoria's defiance seems paradoxically to make him seem incapable of an meaningful response to her. Brachiano's clear assertion, "I was there," complements this seeming weakness. It seems to be a flash of white honesty that catches the deceptive Monticelso off balance. So does Brachiano's own sustained defiance, which drives Monticelso to a "Ha?" and then to silence. But Brachiano's defiance itself is diabolical, employs Monticelso's own dissimulation of virtue. He was, he says, present to "comfort" Vittoria, out of

> My charity, my charity, which should flow
> From every generous and noble spirit,
> To orphans and to widdows. MONT. Your lust!
> BRA. Cowardly dogs barke loudest . . . (165-69)

Monticelso is accurate in defining Brachiano's charity as lust, even though in so doing he parodies his own corruption of moral language. But Brachiano's rebuke of the judge's definition bears emotional sympathy since it so accurately characterizes Monticelso's own hypocrisy as Christ's representative. By leaving in court, as an ironic "gift," the gown he used as a stool, Brachiano asserts a ritualistic aristocratic contempt, also at odds with the character of a lover of widows and orphans. The gown, given its associations with the love-scene in I.ii, seems to be almost an emblem of lust, mockingly left in the halls of charity. With his final words--his motto "Nemo me Impune lacesit"[29]--his entire intervention can be seen ambiguously as either a chivalric defense of his lady, a symbolic challenge to the Medicis, or a politically terminated act of self-preservation. Monticelso suggests this ambiguity in his laconic observation "Your Champions gon" (187). He would suggest that Brachiano and Vittoria have ludicrously perverted the chivalric relation they seem to be acting out--in their lives themselves, and in Brachiano's specific departure here, since champions do not walk away from the lists. The audience would certainly be justified in seeing Brachiano's action here (as Francisco's Crusader masquerade later) as a parody of chivalry and the moral universe in which it could flourish; there are as many counterfeit knights as counterfeit priests in this play (Giovanni may be the only true knight). On the other hand, Brachiano has taken a direct and deliberate action to cut through the web of illusion created by the court. It could be argued that in relation to the texture of deception in this immediate scene, he does exhibit "masculine virtue."

The web of illusion is repaired instantly, however, in Francisco's own act of politic charity; he offers to overlook the "act of bloud" (Camillo's murder) and to accuse Vittoria only on the ground of "incontinence" (197-98).[30] But he does so on the grounds that Vittoria is not evil enough, she does not have "a soule so blacke," to commit such a crime. He uses as image of such an evil the natural metaphor of vines manured in blood. He carries this Flaminesque comparison out lengthily enough that it seems to apply to Vittoria anyway. Vittoria replies allusively "I decerne poison,/Under your guilded pils" (198-99), applying to her accusers again the imagery of ornamentation, and treating literal poison figuratively.

At this point in the arraignment, Monticelso produces the first "evidence" of incontinence: a letter of assignation from

Brachiano to Vittoria, whose whole contents the Cardinal "shames" to answer. To this, Vittoria provides a rebuttal which would do justice to a Portia, far different from her preceding vehemence: "Temptation to lust proves not the act--/ Casta est quam nemo rogavit--" (207-8). Vittoria is correct on legal grounds, if not spiritual (although temptation does not exculpate either), but her classical authority is suspect--the Latin words are a bawd's in the Amores--and is almost a contradiction of the "temptation" phrase. "She is chaste whom no one has asked (to be unchaste)," but Brachiano has asked her, so she is not necessarily chaste. By spiritual standards, also, temptation can itself be considered sinful, even if it does not result in an act of adultery; one can sin in one's heart. But despite Monticelso's skeptical interjections, Vittoria continues her defense, less legalistically, for sure. In this defense, she uses three different sequential rhetorical strategies. She uses analogy, Monticelso's favorite, asking if he would condemn a river (herself) for a suicide in it (this indicates Brachiano, presumably; but with an implicit glance at Camillo, and with the suggestion of sexual capitulation as suicide, which becomes true for the couple eventually, in a way). She issues a cajoling ad misericordiam appeal to her own innocence ("Beauty and gay cloths, a merry heart, / And a good stomacke to a feast" are her only crimes). Finally, she goes beyond words to the material offer of her goods and properties (in effect, bribing the judge, but even here with irony): "Would those would make you charitable!" (224). This last offer contains its own politic maxim: that greed satisfied can alone breed charity.

Monticelso, in effect, does not "hear" Vittoria's words, any of her appeals, and reverts to a summary of his initial character of her: "If the devill / Did ever take good shape behold his picture" (227-8). Here is a gesture inviting the audience to share this perception--Vittoria as corrupt "art"--a presentation of her self, conjured into sensory form. We are asked to see Vittoria as Spenser's Duessa. The audience, with its higher values and wider perception, is invited by the playwright to perceive Monticelso's staged presentation here as itself a picture of the devil in action, whited by his pretence of exposing the "real" devil behind the varnish of Vittoria's beauty.

As though to emphasize the "art" (thereby falsehood) of such unnuanced absolute characterizations, Webster has the Cardinal present a very specific circumstance of money sent by Brachiano to Vittoria at a particular date (229-30). But this observation reveals how remote from the actual appropriate conduct of a court of law Monticelso's previous behavior has been. The fatal mingling of policy and religion is emphasized here by the abrupt shifts from the manipulation of material evidence to abstract moral denunciation. When Monticelso characterizes this money as "Interest for his [Brachiano's] lust" (232), he leaps from the role of politician to that of priest, and betrays the initiated politician's technique of letting the accused condemn herself in her own words and action. Given the audience's knowledge, it is quite possible to believe that Monticelso's allusion to lust as usury is accurate, that this payment is for sexual favors, making Vittoria in effect the "street whore" that his initial character implied, rather than a courtesan. But by leaping to this statement, Monticelso allows Vittoria to make herself appear victimized by shifting the grounds of righteous indignation to the Cardinal's role in making the statement: ". . . if you bee my accuser / Pray cease to be my Judge, come from the Bench, / Give in your evidence 'gainst me . . ." (232-4). Vittoria makes Monticelso a mirror of Midas (and thereby calls him an ass) by referring to his "intelligencing ears," and challenges him to prove his honesty by his willingness to leave the bench and proclaim his actual knowledge. As he did previously, Monticelso ignores this moral challenge as though it had no real content, and responds by limning in two lines an imaginary drama of extra-legal judgement in the manner of "gilded pills": After your goodly and vaine-glorious banquet, ' I'le give you a choake-peare" (241-2). Monticelso has previously (e.g., 204) identified banqueting and lechery; the pear, as a dessert which is also an instrument of torture, can also bear sexual connotations. This bloody banquet of his imagination is on the surface a representation of Vittoria's previous banquet of hostile words, which will be fatal to her, and of the unswallowable words which Monticelso is about to serve her.

These words consist of a biased biography of Vittoria, equal but opposite to Flamineo's earlier apologia for his own life. Here Monticelso continues the figuration of Vittoria as a work of <u>art</u>. She was born in Venice,[31] is "honorably descended," but Camillo "bought you of your father" (246) and received no dowry in exchange. "Twas a hard peny-worth, the ware being so light" (250). As well as the obvious punning, Monticelso has a deeper purpose: he would imply that Vittoria's marriage is as much whoredom as is the activity that violated the marriage. Camillo paid for her favors under the guise of marriage as Brachiano is doing without the guise.

> I yet but draw the curtaine--now to your picture,
> And came from thence a notorious strumpet,
> And so you have continued. (251-53)

This is a poisoned-word-portrait, revenge for Isabella's, indeed. In this case Monticelso plays the satiric antagonist. There is certainly topical reference to purchased aristocratic brides (Frances Howard or others) in these lines. But Monticelso's assumption is also significant, in that he allows no possibility amid corruption for the existence even of a prior innocence which has been corrupted, nor for any distinction between an individual's inner nature and environment. As he seemed skeptical of a resurrection earlier, here he appears skeptical of a first fall from innocence. The assertion that one's "sale" for money, even if beyond one's power or knowledge to control, exiles one from the garden of virtue into whoredom forever is anti-Christian, the deterministic assertion of the Devil. The example of Mary Magdalen refutes it divinely (see chapter 5). Monticelso can use this assertion to justify his definition of Vittoria as a whore even without having to prove sexual involvement with Brachiano, but it can be used philosophically to justify Vittoria's, or anyone's, continuance in vice, since there is no possible hope of regeneration. This is Lodovico's philosophy in I.i, where he finds mercy and regeneration to be laughable.

Monticelso further "chokes" Vittoria by emphasizing the inevitable pervasiveness of vice: since it is in her whole environment, it must be in her. His ultimate authority for this judgement, beyond the deterministic version of personal history just presented, is that her vice is "ordinary and Ryalto talke" (257): rumor is truth. Moreover, in totally different language "befitting" his station, Monticelso condemns Vittoria almost as a scapegoat for the sins of her entire time (whereas the observer might feel the corruption of her environment to be a mitigating consideration):

> For you, Vittoria, your publicke fault,
> Joyn'd to'th condition of the present time,
> Takes from you all the fruits of noble pitty.   (266-68)

One of the conditions of the time, as the audience has seen it, is the absence of pity, noble or otherwise, most notably in this judge himself. The absence of noble pity *is* precisely the condition of the time which condemns Vittoria. Her "corrupted trial" (269) has been made so by the judges themselves. Most corrupt of all is her sentence, for her supposed corruption, to a "house of convertites" (276). Vittoria, stripping off its euphemistic whiteness, calls it a house of "penitent whoores" (278). The "house" is obviously, as Italianate, a whorehouse. Penitence is the white covering thereof. As the audience will witness in IV.ii, males have easy access, *via* bribery, to its inmates. Brachiano has no trouble stealing Vittoria away from it. More immediately, we can see it as inappropriate for Vittoria, because she is *im*penitent, and her judge knows it. The sentencing of a whore to a whorehouse is a serio-comic emblem of corruption. Of course, for Vittoria, it does have an element of (social, not moral) punishment, in that Monticelso forces her to appear among common whores, rather than in the airy isolation of a courtesan's chambers.

Vittoria's masculine ire in response to this sentence is the very voice of impenitence. It is a paradoxical indignation, though, because she is not the wrongly exiled innocent. One who empathizes with Vittoria would have to feel that her sentence is unjust by virtue of its being just; it is rightful but wrongfully given. Justice ought to be a process, not a static condition. To a certain degree Vittoria is accurate when she ironically cries "a rape, a rape!" (285) and allegorically accuses the Cardinal of "ravishing justice" (285). Rape, as the provocator or ally of whoredom, is applied by Vittoria to the

Cardinal with more than allegorical justice. From her point of view, he has made her into a whore by ravishing the reputation that unsullied justice would sustain. Of course the justice that Vittoria considers ravished would sustain a false illusion of her innocence, and by its very integrity would be a collaborator in her intrigue with Brachiano.

So Vittoria's indignation is as morally problematic as the Cardinal's sentence is. When she (as Isabella before) bewails ". . . womans poore revenge / Which dwels but in the tongue" (294-5), we still must perceive that it was the tongues of the prosecutorial "brothers" that "painted" Vittoria in such colors as to give the sentence its legitimacy. They were corruptors of language whereby the arraignment became so paradoxical and parodic of justice. Actually, Vittoria's own language, in scenes like this one, where she wishes language could be action, is what has colored her as virtuous in the eyes of her audiences. When she curses Monticelso in the manner of her mother, "Let your own spittle choake you" (289), the memory of the "choake-pear" wish gives this evocation of self-destruction a quality of balanced justice. When she prays that Monticelso after the day of judgement be "the same devil" he was before, the epithet seems accurate, as his own spit thrown back on him in the wind. Vittoria's final words also assume a popular, conventionally stoic stance which appears refreshingly unhypocritical, although the context of her immediate "fury" shows that her words are artfully assumed to gain sympathy:

> It shal not be a house of convertites--
> My minde shall make it honester to mee
> Then the Pope's Palace, and more peaceable
> Then thy soule, though thou art a Cardinall--
> Know this, and let it somewhat raise your spight,
> Through darkenesse Diamonds spred their ritchest
> light.   (300-305)

Vittoria's proclamation that her mind to her a kingdom is, similar to Francisco's philosophy uttered in the guise of Mulinassar, is one of a number of suggestions that a stoic alternative exists to the destructive entwining of politics and religion. Its force is weakened by the audience's knowledge of Vittoria's capacity for verbal deception; also, her Boethian transformations of prison are painfully similar to the transformations of reality perpetrated in the dumb-shows and the just-concluded arraignment. "The net effect of the scene is to leave the audience ambivalently desiging the deliverance of someone it knows to be guilty precisely as charged."[31] But does the audience know this so precisely? In another view, Vittoria is definitely the "emotional victor" (but not the moral one?) in the trial.[32] However weighed, Vittoria's "It shal not be . . ." is painful in dramatic context with the realization that what could actually be a redeeming belief is totally the product of its enunciator's temporary subjection. Restored as a favorite, Vittoria will no longer choose her mind for a kingdom.

The insincerity of Vittoria's seemingly admirable defiance is enhanced by the immediate entry of Brachiano, at her departure. It would seem difficult to stage this sequence to avoid the implication of deliberate artifice. Vittoria's seeming frankness balances Brachiano's artful eloquence, greeting Francisco:

> Now you and I are friends sir. wee'le shake hands,
> In a friends grave, together--a fit place,
> Being the embleme of soft peace, t'attone our hatred
> (307-9)

As Flamineo reveals to the audience in an aside, "this is a preface to the discovery of the Dutches death" (313).

As conveyed by the politic murderer, this emblem of tragic reconciliation is tangled with corruption. "Atonement" is a condition impossible in this particular grave--the emblem is a contradiction in terms--just as "noble pity" was denatured of all meaning as a governing value earlier in the scene. If a "friend's grave" is the emblem of peace (and no other thing), peace exists only in the most annihilatory condition imaginable. Nowhere else can it survive on earth. Brachiano's emblem is actually a fit representation of the ultimate evil disguised as good (the "white devil"), and the most unfit emblem possible of peace, whether peace be conceived as a spiritual condition or as secular social harmony.

Brachiano's emblem, representing deception, and used for deceptive purposes, is contrasted to Giovanni's subsequent entrance dressed in undeceptive black, not black whitened by the pretence of friendship and atonement, with open news of Isabella's death. It is interesting to find Giovanni, through honest grief, rather than Brachiano's guile, similarly unwilling actually to name the death; whereas Lodovico, who enters with him, directly states it. Although akin to Brachiano in evil, Lodovico is his opposite in the openness of his acts. It does not seem that he indulges in deception except as a condition of employment by others. Giovanni's frank entrance is contrasted also to Flamineo's preceding aside, which "interprets" Brachiano's emblem for the audience: "it is a "preface to the discovery of the Dutches death," (313-14), and since Flamineo cannot "counterfeit a whining passion" (314) for his patron's victim, he chooses--among other possible roles in response to it--that of a "polliticke mad-man" (319). Flamineo is choosing between alternative counterfeits of true sentiment; Giovanni, imagining true grief around him, manifests his in imitation of his uncle's virtue (321), in fearing to tell of the death, "For I shall make you [Francisco] weepe" (326). Francisco _is_ often taken as truly "weeping" as a result of this interview, and as becoming transformed into a relentless avenger only by the impact of Giovanni's feelings. To J. B. Benjamin, he's not a "true" Machiavellian, but is emotionally "maimed" by the murders and their effects on others.[33]

Giovanni's naïve immersion in the actual sincere emotions of bereavement carries over to his speculations on the meaning of death:

> What do the dead do, uncle? do they eate,
> Heare musicke, goe a-hunting, and bee merrie,
> As wee that live? (331-3)

Giovanni's question is more than a demonstration of his precocity. He addresses the "ultimate" questions of life which almost all the others in his world evade--as people with a purely politic consciousness must. The premises of their world are set forth in the first scene, where Lodovico dismisses any significance in the sort of questions that Giovanni raises here. The dismissal of the possibility of life after death, and the acceptance of death as a final condition, is a mark of banishment from the possibility of salvation.

Francisco's answer to Giovanni's question is itself hypocritical in this context. That the dead "sleep" and will rise only at God's will is orthodox doctrine, but only partial: it refers to bodies, not to souls. Francisco conducts his life, as do others, as though if there is any afterlife it will be the "pagan" one of "eating, etc.," that Giovanni questions. If death has no spiritual significance, if it makes no fundamental changes in any realm except that of the material, then murder can be justified by virtue of its own significance. (It is significant here that Brachiano's killers draw back from this materialism enough to seek to kill him in a condition that will insure his damnation.) Giovanni's question is an oblique condemnation of those who act as though the dead act no differently than the living, and who make no distinction between body and soul. If human death is an inherited punishment wrought upon an originally immortal creation, for which Christ's death conditionally atoned, and if the soul persisting after physical death continues to suffer when damned, or rejoice when saved (depending on one's conduct during the life of the body), death cannot be casually inflicted or suffered.

The absence of some such metaphysical framework weds one to death of the body as the only ultimate or absolute condition. Giovanni, naively interpreting Francisco's analogy of death and sleep--a pagan analogy--wishes himself dead, since he has not slept for six nights. And he wishes Isabella to sleep forever, for she has waked a hundred nights "When all the pillow, where she laid her head, / Was brine-wet with her teares" (340-41). Giovanni's words evoke pathos, "noble pity," for those abused by the faithless, and also parody that faithlessness. His "that I were dead" is a dangerous wish in this context of murder, but is the logical conclusion of the ideology of his elders. Similarly, when Francisco asks, not ingenuously (since in a Christian society love of children for parents should be taken for granted), "Thou didst' love her?" (344), Giovanni replies in disconcertingly physical terms:

> I have often heard her say shee gave mee sucke,
> And it should seeme by that shee deerely lov'd mee,
> Since Princes seldome doe it. (345-7)

This response is also one of "calculated naïveté." Princes (a purposely asexual usage) seldom giving suck is a condition symbolic of the non-nurturing, death-oriented consciousness of the entire Italian state. The imagery of kinds and queens as "nursing mothers" runs throughout contemporary literature, not least as applied to James I. By describing maternal love not in the abstract terms of congratulatory metaphor, but directly as breast-feeding, Giovanni implies that love's real essence is a primal union, pre-verbal, sensory. The word is subject to corruption and abuse if even articulated in a general way--as in Brachiano's protestations of love for Vittoria. By limiting its definition so intensely, Giovanni rescues "love" from corruption. Giovanni's evocation of the breast is also connected with the mode of Cornelia's mother-love. Flamineo, when he breaks the cross-pendant at his mother's breast (V.iii) is breaking with violence this primal physical bond. Brachiano's murder of his wife breaks the bond of love between mother and child even more brutally, in the interest of a lust masquerading as love. The vision of an unquestionable maternal love destroyed in Isabella counterpoints the inquisition of Vittoria, whose non-maternal mannish will defies her persecutors. In a sense, Vittoria is the instigator of Isabella's murder, yet the two women are paired as victims of politic, a-religious male actions, which violate ultimate human interconnections represented by maternality. In this case, both the true and counterfeit coins are debased.

III.iii

Flamineo initiates this scene in as rhetorically paradoxical a manner as before. In this case he begins with the sort of sententious couplet that is usually employed to periodize or conclude scenes. "Wee indure the strokes like anviles or hard steele, / Till paine itself make us no paine to feele" (1-2) is a commentary on the immediate past responses of Giovanni and Francisco to the news of Isabella's death. This gloss is appropriate, yet literally improbable for him to make, since he has not been a witness to the overt grieving it comments on. Its stoic message (with the imagery of hammers carrying on that of Vittoria in III.ii.147-9) is both true and applicable to any innocent observer of the unfolding enormities on stage. But this couplet is also a first expression of Flamineo in his Hamletian role of "polliticke mad-man" (321), and from the point of view of an auditory unsympathetic to his politic mentality, he is here literally insane.

This couplet also incongruously precedes a swath of satirically "low" prose expressing Flamineo's assumed despair over the condemnation of Vittoria, and over the unemployment he pretends will follow upon his master Brachiano's disgrace. The Ambassador

of Savoy urges "comfort" (10) on Flamineo, but he responds with
a multiply ironic conceit--that these honeyed words only pain
his wounded mouth--since he is taking comfort from the belief
of his audience that he lacks comfort. "Comfortable words"
alludes to those which are spoken in the order of Holy Communion
in the Book of Common Prayer, and are taken from four Gospel
passages "all promising Christ's grace to the penitent." The
most honeyed words in the Christian tradition burn Flamineo's
tongue, because he rejects the ultimate premise of salvation on
which Christian doctrine is based.[34]

In his assumed madness, Flamineo also plays (through the
author's manipulations) on the dramatic irony that contrasts the
naïveté of his stage audience to the knowledge of his real
theatrical audience. He attributes to his enemies (who brought
Brachiano down) his own politic-seeming innocence: ". . . In
this a Polititian imitates the devill, as the devill imitates
a Canon. Wheresoever he comes to doe mischiefe, he comes with
his backside towardes you" (15-17)--a mannerism which Flamineo
will actually enact later on, in IV.ii.68.

As a devil disguised as a Canon, Flamineo then proceeds
(19-25) to apostrophize the sins of the time, using language so
stereotyped that it becomes satiric when taken literally--
particularly since the audience knows that to Flamineo such a
moral posture is insane and absurd: "O Gold, what a God art
thou! And o man, what a devill art thou to be tempted by that
cursed Minerall!" (19-21). As well as cursing gold and the lust
for it that overturns traditional dignities, Flamineo predicates
against the traditional dignities of noblemen, who if not exempt
by their station from the rack would reveal under such a torture
their true corruption. Interestingly, but also ambiguously, the
"mad" Flamineo complements the English ambassador's nation for
not selling justice for money--and also, by implication, for not
hesitating to torture noblemen.

As Flamineo continues his tirade, which is somewhat parodic
of Monticelso's wandering character of the whore, he expresses
an idea crucial to the sane meaning of the play: "Religion; oh
how it is commedled with policie. The first bloudshed in the
world happened about religion. Would I were a Jew" (36-38).
Flamineo's Biblical reference is doubtless to the murder of
Abel by Cain. Since this speech initiates a short but delight-
ful exchange with his own virtuous brother Marcello on the
virtues of being a Jew, Flamineo is definitely preparing a
theological parallel with his future murder of his brother.
This context of murder adds meaning to his desire to be a Jew,
since Cain was <u>banished</u> in terms of the Jewish law--not <u>damned</u>
in the manner of Christian punishment.[36] It is probably for
fear of bringing the possibility of punishment into play that
Flamineo opposes the mingling of religion with it. An English
audience would presumably be favorable to this sentiment,
despite the limits of religious toleration in contemporary
England, since the perceived evils of Rome concerned precisely

this commingling, and the previous arraignment scene in the play has just vividly presented Italian law as being the fiat of a corrupt prelate.

But the immediate response to the truth of Flamineo's assertion depends on seeing "policie" in non-pejorative terms as equivalent to "statecraft." In Flamineo's world, policy means corrupt manipulation. The more true religion meddles with the practice of politicians, the harder it is for them to escape experiencing as reality either their sinfulness or the punishment religion allots to it. For this reason, Flamineo's indictment of religion, ironic because there is not enough true religion in Rome to cause any impediment to politicians, is also sincere in that it expresses a real fear of being judged in a religious context, of feeling the "pain" referred to at the scene's beginning.

Flamineo's statement on Judaism, his allusion to Cain and Abel, also applies to the fleeting "brotherhood" he attains with Lodovico in the latter part of this scene. Flamineo and Lodovico, as they initially protest, are brothers in both being Cains--banished or potentially banished men. But Lodovico, by perceiving and articulating Flamineo's corrupt character (especially by naming him a pandar) in a sense redeems himself from this brotherhood and banishment simultaneously with the announcement to him of his pardon from banishment (93-95).

This papal pardon is a perfect example of religion meddling in policy. It certainly does not perform the moral alchemy on Lodovico which Gasparo satirically suggested it would at the beginning of the play. But it does, by licensing Lodovico to avenge Isabella, eventually destroy Flamineo, despite all his policy. It also breaks the diabolical covenant which has just been struck between Lodovico and Flamineo. Marcello, playing the Inducer, has told the audience to "Marke this strange incounter" (61). Both Lodovico and Flamineo have, in ritual asides, sworn to feign politic friendship to "wind" (53) each other. Their harmony, pleasure in each other, and vow to "joyne housekeeping" (72) are thus to the audience pretences on both sides, and their agreement is a stylized paradox of "contrary humours" in accord. They initially insult each other (62-67), and strophically recite the ways in which they will be "unsocially sociable" (73), with physiognomical communication, day-long sleep, and other means of "turning the world upside down." Since each is artfully playing the unsociably social role to draw the other out, there is a certain lack of seriousness to their entire play of humours; nothing they say is really meant. On the other hand, this harmony of falseness is an abstract of the infinitely more diversified false harmonies of the godless society in which they participate. Their "game" is as a moral mirror, actually earnest--when it refers, for example, to the illusion of legality in Vittoria's arraignment. Thus, Lodovico's vow, "Weel never part" (87),[36] and Flamineo's satiric prophecy of eternal union, last only a second. Flamineo predicts that the two will part only when their example has taught all sinners "To scorne that world which life of meanes deprives" (92), but then Antonelli announces that the Pope has pardoned Lodovico, returning him from banishment to human society. In almost the tone of the Divinity addressing a prophet, Lodovico exclaims "Look up againe, / Flamineo, see my pardon" (96-97). If we consider Flamineo and Lodovico as banished, spiritually, in Christian terms, Flamineo is right to be jealous and to protest that "There was no such condition in our covenant" (98). Those who have covenanted with the devil, or at least convenanted together under the devil's patronage outside of human society, have excluded the possibility of pardon, by definition, from the terms of their covenant.

At balance with the seeming divine origin of this pardon is the news that the Pope has signed it only at Francisco's importuning; immediately the pardon is seen as the work of black policy, not of white religion--or of both, commingled. Francisco knows that a pardoned Lodovico will work to the destruction of those who killed his sister. We could say that by acceding to Francisco's suit, the Pope has himself made covenant with the devil and licensed one who considers murders "flea-bytings."

But Flamineo appears to be honestly upset by Lodovico's joyful laughter (97), which breaks the covenant of malcontentedness. If he would be merry, he could at least "Do it i'th like posture, as if some great man / Sate while his enemy were executed" (101-02). This of course describes, if not referring directly to, Brachiano, Flamineo's employer. It is of course quite possibly another calculated hyperbole of the politic madman. But it is also strikingly similar to the posture that Lodovico takes in the first scene, of total indifference to life and death. It seems to me that Flamineo, despite his pose, is meant to be seen as lonely in the banishment from social communion that he has imposed on himself by wearing his politic mask. He has assumed the desperate indifference of Lodovico at the very moment that the Pope's "mercy" has freed Lodovico from that indifference. For all his evil, Lodovico's laugh here signifies a "return to life." Flamineo even pleads with his "brother" to continue to pretend to be a pretender: "Though it be very letchery unto thee, / Doo't [laugh] with a crabbed Politician's face" (103-4). But Lodovico has abandoned the politician's pose, as represented by his unwhited statement, "Your sister is a damnable whore" (105). Unlike Monticelso's accusations, this one, true or false, is a direct statement, devoid of ornament or pretence. Lodovico continues to goad his former brother by parodying the doubleness of the politician: "Looke you' I spake that laughing" (105). Webster has Flamineo for almost the first time at a loss for words: "Ha?" (105). He also puts into his mouth a direct thematic allusion: Flamineo protests that Lodovico had vowed to live.

> . . . Like one
> That had for ever forfaited the day-light,
> By being in debt . . . (111-113)

This is Lucifer's forfeit, but can also be associated with Cain's exile to lands of darkness and incurrence of an eternal debt. Flamineo's reference to Lodovico's "breaking" (115) seems to me not only to refer to the breaking of the Faustian compact with the devil, but to "breaking" from the resolve to live evilly, and capitulating to some element of virtue.

The real breaking is, however, done by Flamineo when he "strikes" (119, s.d.) Lodovico. He has broken the rule of political indirection. He has expressed a non-counterfeit emotion, and thereby his assumed shield of invulnerability has been broken. "If you will not be melancholy, be angry" (119) he exclaims. Lodovico, in this jousting of wills, has proven invulnerable to Flamineo's attempts to break him into some self-limiting declaration, and, on the contrary, has beaten down Flamineo's guard. Once defeated by the commitment of his impulsive blow, Flamineo can be verbally executed by the fatal label "pandar" (124). In IV.ii.51, Brachiano uses the word as a weapon under similar circumstances. Here Lodovico expresses indignation that he has had to take a martial stance against a pandar, and images his fist a Jovian thunderbolt. Self-satirically also, he has his shaking hand an "earthquake" (132), part of the continuing chain of associating human will with natural forces. With sharp clarity, Lodovico understands Flamineo to be of the fellowship of rogues who "are most weary of their lives." Conventionally, such a phrase would refer to those who recklessly incur the hatred and enmity of others, but in context it seems like a sword-thrust of insight into an inner despair which Flamineo's autobiography (I.ii) has hinted, and which will become manifest in his final suicide game (V.vi).

Despite the sharp perception, Lodovico's "shaking" (133) is uncharacteristic. It is wrathful, surely, but he is so mortified by it that it would seem to manifest in him a vulnerability like Flamineo's, breaking out despite his will to mask it. One might find that, totally counterfeited as it is, the momentary brotherhood of Flamineo and Lodovico represents to them a condition of re-integration, redemption from banishment and isolation, which they do not want to admit the desire for. It is necessary for each to break the covenant in order to sustain a long-practiced self-image, but each is inevitably shaken from having touched an experience of communion and of violence in such a short time. Lodovico's resolve to forget it all by drinking wine (134) takes on irony in this connection, since wine can be sacramental as well as profane, and the sacramental drinking of it seals again a covenant with God and a communion of faith with other Christians. Henke's view of the connection between sexuality and spirituality when they are figuratively presented through eating and drinking is relevant here. "The lover is the 'god-eater' who seeks to partake of the vitality beyond reason that is the basis of all life."[37] If sexual union is debased through gastronomical imagery in the play, just as spiritual communion is (here, for example), Webster might be seen as skeptical of both spiritual and wordly consolation.

In any case, the complex byplay between Lodovico and Flamineo here is a fit preparation for the immediately subsequent interchanges between Monticelso and Francisco, whose politic brotherhood is also two-faced.

Chapter V

Whoredom

Mary Magdalen is the First Whore, in the Christian tradition, the "Original" in the Renaissance sense, of the other particular women of later time who sell their bodies.[1] She has passed down to them her problematic nature as one who was converted from extreme depravity to consuming faith. As the Geneva Bible annotates the scene of Christ's "Noli me tangere" in the garden, "Because she was to muche addicted to the corporal presence, Christ teacheth her to lift vp her minde by faith into heauen, where onley after his ascension he remaineth."[2] Mary Magdalen is the World, Flesh, and Devil; yet her transformation to faith in Christ, because so extreme, represents the radical possibility of spiritual enlightenment being accessible to anyone, even the one most consumingly devoted to the World, Flesh, or Devil. In the many traditions of her companionship with Christ, Mary Magdalen stands out for her opposition to exclusionary doctrinalism; it is because she has known sin so deeply that she can show such understanding of sinners, such a flexibility that the other apostles, particularly Peter, are hostile to her.[3]

I suggest that to an auditory of the seventeenth century, even one as lacking in understanding as Webster's, the presence of a whore on a stage, or an evocation of the condition of whoredom, would suggest and be associated with Mary Magdalen, even if it did not cause viewers to recall any particular events of her Scriptural life. In The White Devil, Vittoria's contradictory qualities, as accused whore, are a direct expression of the problematic doubleness of the Magdalen of tradition, and this doubleness can be found in the stage whores, her sisters, who appear in earlier plays. The one crucial element in her similarity to her prototype is left out by Webster, however, and this is the root of his own ambiguous treatment of her: unlike some of her predecessors, there is no conversion in her life. That when she is sent impenitent to the House of Convertites, or "house of penitent whores" as named by Monticelso, her Peter, she is converted only from anger at her lover to submission and silence, is an indication of the quality of Webster's parody of the Magdalen tradition. In the House of Convertites, at the deathbed of Brachiano, confronted by Flamineo in her study--and even, at first meeting, confronted by her mother in a very different garden from the one where Magdalen confronts Christ--she is offered situations ritually appropriate for conversion. In every case, Vittoria glides through them untouched by the signals they are sending her.

Contrary to these <u>potentially</u> sacred situations are the actual profane spaces, types of the whorehouse, within whose bounds an unrepentant Magdalen can operate freely, and where the virtuous may be trapped, if they dare to enter. Such a space is the actual House of Convertites, or the "Appoticaries summerhouse" (II.ii.202) of feast and lechery where Brachiano supposedly first meets Vittoria. The profane space is one of self-indulgence, but it is in proximity to the bed, which is the most profane space of all; the bed of sin is at the center of the House of Convertites, and its wages are the bed of death on which the poisoned Brachiano expires. Figuratively, the poison is the whore herself.

One of the earliest English presentations of Mary Magdalen can show us an original profane space in clarity. In the Digby <u>Mary Magdalen</u>, staged in the round, with Mary Magdalen's father's castle (initially) in the center, the King of Flesh, on his Stage of Flesh, conspires with Sloth, Gluttony, and Lechery, to lure Mary from her castle. It is on the stage of the World-- the World being the original profane space--that these Vices collaborate with Satan "To entyr hir person by the labor of Lechery, / That she at the last may come to helle."[4] But the place in the Digby play which has the most obvious heritage in Webster's time is the "Tavern" in which Mary is seduced, by wine, to fleshly sin. In the Digby play, of course, since Mary must be seen as <u>originally</u> innocent and good, and misled in the city (here Jerusalem, not Rome or London) by outside agents, she is as much a victim in her sin as in Curiosite, the "frisch new galaunt" she entraps in the tavern. In fact, like Vittoria's no-longer-fresh duke, Mary's galaunt is the collaborator of Lechery in the fall of Mary. He lives "in the world" only, defining his identity by his clothes, buying silk for his "constant lady," to whom he is presumably constantly inconstant.

The tavern is, as always, the antitype of the church, but its identity cannot be separated from that of the man and woman who make it the ground of lechery. Morally and spiritually Mary's clients, beginning with her first one, collaborate in her sin by their willingness to be seduced; when she falls, multitudes do likewise, so their salvation depends on her. In a sense, she carries her profane place with her, and wherever she goes, is it.[5] Her body is the Temple of Flesh. Thus her conversion is more difficult of achievement if and when it occurs, than others, because she must almost literally become a new person. It is interesting to note how well Vittoria expresses this mode of the Magdalen's existence; in the courtroom, in the House of Convertites, after the removal to Padua, corruption surrounds her and derives its justification from her presence. One of Webster's points may be that in Vittoria's Italy, or his England, there is no person or milieu that could be immune to infection by the whore's travelling presence, none that could overawe it.

It is significant that the places in the Digby play which are most clearly opponents of the tavern, and most capable of affecting the whore's condition, are places where Mary can be in solitude, free from the inter-enticement of other beings. One is her "arbor," where she consoles herself at the beginning. The other is the wilderness, where she eventually lives as a hermit, and where she is privileged to view the heavenly Jerusalem, having escaped from the earthly. It is worth considering Vittoria in the light of this Magdalen who, as a condition of conversion, must ultimately separate herself from the World of other humans for the extent of her mortal life, since the mark of her profession is so deep in her body, and ineradicable. Vittoria's devotion to the World is never altered by events or environment. The only time we can imagine her in solitude is in the final scene, when the World in the form of Flamineo rudely interrupts what may have been devotion, although Webster ironically conceals from us whether the book she holds is a worldly or a spiritual account book. In any case, her "arbor" here is easily invaded. And, at this time, while using the word "soul" more than once, the unrepentant Vittoria remains devoted to the World, clearly conceiving of only two realms, "that which was made for man / The world . . . "and "that was made for devils /Eternall darkenesse" (V.vi.63-65).

Lewis Wager's Protestant and didactic Life and Repentance of Mary Magdalene (1567),[6] which focuses on the same early episode in the legendary life of Mary treated by Thomas Adams (see below)--the supper at the home of Simon the Pharisee, where Mary washes the feet of Jesus--does not offer profane places, but adds circumstances to her identity. Wager's Magdalen is a young woman already married, too young. Infidelity is the ringleader, followed by Pride of Life, Cupidity, and Carnal Concupiscence, of the jolly fellows who invade her castle to draw her from fidelity. It is almost possible to see the masks of these jolly fellows on the faces of Flamineo and Brachiano, as they seduce Vittoria in her young husband's garden; although, of course, as has been suggested, Webster takes care to prevent Vittoria from having much original innocence and primal fidelity. Actually, the Bianca of Middleton's Women Beware Women is a more complete parallel to Wager's Magdalen, except that she is too pure at first.

When Wager's protagonist is first seen by the audience, "tryfling with her garmentes," she is not innocent in the sense of purity, but she is innocent in terms of the naïveté in the dissatisfaction with her respectable lot. She is shallow-minded and worldly, cursing (her tailor) in low language ("Nowe a mischief on his dronken knaves eare") for making her ill-fitting clothes. Wager clearly emphasizes that the sin of whoredom her tempting Vices lead her to is not merely sexual indulgence, but the even graver violation of the sacrament of marriage: "Of all bondage truely this is the ground, / A gentlewoman to one husband be bound." Again we can see a Magdalen theme in Vittoria--

the violation of marriage, and more indirectly, the unbinding of family ties based on that sacrament.

The *carpe diem* argument is greatly used by Wager's Vices, and it leads to another interesting development. Mary agrees that the time of youth has no long permanence, and Infidelity follows up on this by urging her, once her youth as a whore is past, to "play the baude."/"This is the order, such as wer harlots in their youth / May use to be baudes evermore for a truth." Anticipating the achievements of Shaw's Mrs. Warren, Infidelity sees Mary as able, with the "honest possessions" her bawdy-house clients have left her, to live in high estate, by oppressing her tenants, taking fines, and practicing usury. He proposes here a social order, grounded on whoredom (akin to the underworld of crime in Monticelso's black book, discussed in Chapter VII below), which can lead to as much worldly success as moral enterprise can, and also one which involves branching out into many other evil enterprises. All these evils are, by implication, rooted in whoredom. This vision of whoredom is, we realize, that of Monticelso's characters of a whore in III.ii; but since Webster surrounds Vittoria with all kinds of other vices clearly not literally originated by prostitution, this association only adds irony to, rather than in any way confirming, the Cardinal's assertions.

Although Wager's Justification and Love, heavily abstract figures, dogmatize Mary Magdalen's penitence, her forgiveness and conversion, at the home of Simon the Pharisee, in terms of a doctrinally sanctioned process of conversion, Christ himself finds in her *actions* ("gestures") rather than in any abstract process, the manifestations of true faith. Christ rebukes Simon for inviting him to dine only "to shew your rechesse and treasure," whereas in each of her "gestures" Mary has turned Simon's house into a sacred place:

> At this womans synne you do greatly grutche,
> As though your selues were iust, holy, and pure,
> But many sinnes are forgiuen hir, bicause she loued muche.

Mary has had the possibility of sainthood fulfilled in her, and thus every woman of her calling is potentially capable of a more pure Christian life than the "average" Simon's, precisely because she has risen so far from a previous low condition. A more extreme transformation is possible for such a one than for the lukewarm faithful. Another theme of her conversion, expressed by Wager's Mary herself, is that she offers hope for even the most depraved sinner, whose "knowledge of sin" might otherwise lead him or her to the suicide that is the end result of spiritual despair.

Although Mary Magdalen does not appear in her own persona significantly in later Elizabethan and Stuart drama, whores bearing her physical and spiritual mark are everywhere. I think one reason for their popularity, beyond the sheer titillation they provide, is the inner spiritual drama that the prototype of Magdalen allows them to suggest. How can we be certain that any soul is truly lost, and any individual irrevocably "evil," if those who bear the heaviest weight of sin can be pardoned and altered totally? The whore creates a _frisson_ of unease by so tightly combining her physical, sexual reality and her spiritual potential. Vittoria is intriguing not because she actually conforms to Monticelso's character of a whore, but because she can be, essentially, a whore (of the courtesan class), without possessing the attributes of his character. Who can directly impugn her faith? Who can deny her sinfulness? This moral ambiguity is shared by many who figure in the category of whoredom. Juliet's Nurse is bawd for the girl she has raised from infancy, yet she shares the romantic glow of the passion whose fulfillment she furthers. In its haze of idealized love, _Romeo_ _and_ _Juliet_ remains a play modeled on the experience of the medieval Magdalen into whose father's house enters the World in the person of a gallant, not named Curiosity, and his male companions.

In the decade before the performance of _The_ _White_ _Devil_ many dramas presented characters who acted out the archetypes of Magdalenic whoredom. The Jacobean whores do seem to fall into the two modes of our Magdalen plays. One is that of the lady of original rectitude, whose whoredom consists of her seduction by Infidelity from a marital bond, to licence, with various degrees of resistance to, or redemption from, this seduction. The other is that of the professional whore, whose profane place is not a violated marital house or bedchamber, but the bawdy house, her natural place of business. Two plays of 1603 can illustrate this division.

As Darryl Gless has elaborated,[7] the monastic life whose chastity is the polar opposite of whoredom (and to which Magdalen finally returns) became to the Reformation a manifestation of "spiritual whoredom," through its hypocrisy and its supposed placing of works (the World) above faith. In _Measure_ _for_ _Measure_, Isabella's nunnery--and the realm of absolute values in which she believes as a novice--is _prima_ _facie_ a sacred place directly balanced against the whorehouse of Mistress Overdone and her companions. But to Shakespeare's non-Catholic audience, the nunnery is the whore of Babylon's bawdy house; Mistress Overdone's house is at least the resort of honest, unwhitened devils. Elbow's "honest" wife has tempted to follow Magdalen's path there, however: "if she had been a woman cardinally given, (she) might have been accused in fornication, adultery, and all uncleanliness there" (II.i.80).

The pun on Cardinal/carnal is just one indication of Shakespeare's actual equation of nunnery and whorehouse. The Magdalenic progress from whorehouse to nunnery cannot represent a valid spiritual ideal. Most fulfilling, in _Measure_ _for_ _Measure_, is the partial progress to a morally mixed state. Isabella moves downward from spiritual whoredom to noble marriage; her brother Claudio and cousin Juliet move upward from the House of Lechery (in Claudio's case it is a prison), to marriage likewise. And Mariana moves "laterally," as it were into public acknowledgment of a consummated marriage. Mariana's "moated grange" might be considered as a place of assignation that actually contains the paradoxes of this middle state: it is used as both whorehouse and temple. The profane union it permits sacramentalizes the more profane earlier condition, in which Mariana is basically a "whore" (by Angelo's own definition).

Whatever the Duke/Friar's much contested typological identity, the role he plays in Act V of <u>Measure for Measure</u> is, in Magdalenic terms, that of Christ. In Shakespeare's striking inversion, though, it is the male "customers," or would-be customers of unmarried women (Angelo and Claudio), who are condemned, and then pardoned. The Duke's words to Barnardine (himself, admittedly, an unrepentant criminal) express the terms of pardon in the context of the Magdalen story:

> Sirrah, thou art said to have a stubborn soul,
> That apprehends no further than this world,
> And squar'st thy life according. Thou'rt condemn'd;
> But for those earthly faults, I quit them all;
> And pray thee take this mercy to provide
> For better times to come. (V.i.485-90)

To apprehend no further than this World is the root of sin, and also source of a potential for salvation. If you do not yet know God, or of God, you have yet to learn of the Spirit, and cannot deny Christian truth knowingly. Mary Magdalen does not know of her sin until she learns of the reality of something beyond this World, and of herself as spirit as well as body.

In this context, even Webster's ecclesiastics cannot define Vittoria's whoredom as a sin except in terms of this World: whores are winters, taxes, bells, and dead bodies. Vittoria herself, though, refuses stubbornly to see any further, and at her death knows not whither she goes. Brachiano's capricious condemnation of Flamineo for fratricide seems to relate likewise to the ambiguous condition of Christian mercy in the face of a world-limited vision. That Flamineo must renew his "lease" on life each day against a condemnation to death appears as an act of mercy meant to teach the possibility of a reality beyond this World. In the light of this reality the actual condition of life in the World can be understood as being universally that of a loan. If this is Brachiano's mercy, it does not teach Flamineo or anyone else, including its promulgator, to provide for better times to come. We might be tempted to see the Rome and Padua of <u>The White Devil</u> as like Shakespeare's Vienna without his redemptive Duke; the entire city would become a profane place, the city a house of physical and spiritual prostitution. In Protestant terms, this is what Rome, any Italian city, or Italy itself, actually is, and throughout his play Webster suggests this identification.

The second drama (among many) which presents whoredom particularly in a Magdalenic context is Dekker's and Middleton's The Honest Whore (parts I and II). Though there is much changing of course in the ten long acts of these two plays, and much shifting between the particular concerns of the two collaborators, the fate and condition of Bellafront, the "honest whore," dominate the other intrigues. Representatives of all classes and conditions frequent Bellafront's profane house, and are affected by her moral condition.

The plays are filled with spiritually-connotative language relating to the Magdalenic identity of whoredom. Those who condemn Bellafront without reflection use the whole repertoire of attributes employed by Monticelso in his "characters." Bellafront's own father is typical: ". . . a Strumpet is one of the Deuils Vines; all the sinnes like so many Poles are stucke vpright out of hell, to be her props, that she may spread vpon them . . ." (part II, I.ii.105-107). In one of her intriguing debates with the noble Hippolito on the merits and demerits of whoredom, Bellafront herself (by this point converted), describes her first tryst with "Curiosity" as a scene in hell itself, and her bed and room as the ultimate profane space:

> My bed seem'd like a Cabin hung in Hell,
> The Bawde Hells Porter, and the lickorish wine
> The Pander fetch'd, was like an easie Fine,
> For which, me thought I leas'd away my soule . . .
> (part II, IV.i.356-59)

This vision of whoredom as an infernal sacrament is of course contradicted in the two plays by the emphasis on Bellafront's moral conscience. The very fact that the tables can be turned, and the once-whore becomes the condemner of whoredom against its praiser, the noble Hippolito who originally tried to "save" her, dissociates her as individual woman from the condition she once was in. And the activities of all the other characters, from her self-righteous father Orlando to Hippolito himself, with his nostalgie de la boue, and the prosperous merchant Candido, prostitute to his own vision of Perfection--all these emphasize the idea that whoredom is a potential condition of sinfulness in any person of any trade.

Bellafront is of course the streetwalker, not the courtesan that Vittoria is, and a comparison of the plays cannot equate the two women. Vittoria's debates with the Cardinal, for example, are similar only in form, but not in content, to Bellafront's debates with Hippolito. Vittoria is the creature of her situation, and acts courageous in the interests of self preservation; Bellafront, of a much less privileged station, can conceptualize issues and problems, and speaks to them as much as to her own condition. Unlike Vittoria, she can see beyond the

World, and this vision allows her eventually to escape the tyranny of her condition. Yet the anticipation of The White Devil in language and circumstance of The Honest Whore is striking. The most overt anticipation is in the use of Bridewell at the end of the second Part as a climactic and ultimately profane place; it is the same place as Vittoria's "House of Convertites," but revealed in much more provocative detail as the prison specializing in "the Bawd, the Rogue, the Whore" (part II, V.ii.44). As the Master of Bridewell says,

> . . . Some it turnes good,
> But . . . some going hence,
> Are (by being here) lost in more impudence.
> (part II, V.ii.257-60)

Such latter effect is, presumably, Vittoria's. This Bridewell presents its inmates who are "Past shame: past penitence" (V.ii.301) as particularly affecting the costume of virtuous wives. So Dorothea Target and Penelope Whore-hound dress and act as a bride and a citizen's wife respectively, and drive the audience to ask what actually distinguishes their condition in madness from the sanity of real brides and wives. Or, conversely, as another whore, Catyryna Bountinall, ridiculing Mistress Horsleach, the Baw'd's, claim to honesty, asks, "burnt at fourteene, seuen times whipt, sixe times carted . . . and yet you are honest? Honest Mistris Horsleach, is this World, a World to keepe Bawds and Whores honest?" (V.ii.374-378).

   As The Honest Whore, like The White Devil, uses whoredom to question the distinction between virtue and vice, so it initiates other images and themes involved in The White Devil. When Bellafront seeks to marry Matheo, who originally corrupted her (cf. Angelo and Mariana, Lucio), redeeming whoredom by marriage, she pleads:

> Matheo thou first madst me black, now make me White as before; I vow to thee Ime now
> As chaste as infancy, pure as Cynthias brow.
> (part I, V.ii.439-41)

It is notable how ineffectual the marriage of Brachiano and Vittoria is in restoring any such primal innocence. The exchange of jewels, as it relates to sexuality and infidelity, as in The White Devil, I.ii, is evoked by Infelice when she feel Hippolito is acting the role of Brachiano:

> This very purse was wouen with mine owne hands,
> This Diamond on that very night, when he
> Vntyed my Virgin girdle, gaue I him:
> And must a common Harlot share in mine?
> (part II, III.i.49-53)

Throughout the play Bellafront's condition, like Vittoria's, is associated literally and figuratively with "prodigall feasts" (part I, II.i.437). And throughout, violently contradictory visions of Bellafront's nature, as of Vittoria's, continually provoke an observer's value-judgements. To Hippolito, in his first debate with Bellafront, "You have no soule" (part I, II.i. 322); to Bellafront, her Bawd is "our sexes monster," a "course deuill," and "Gossip of hell" (part I, III.ii.30 ff). And, while to Hippolito, Bellafront is "the diuell, . . . a woman, in mans shape" (part I, IV.i.122, 26), the audience is asked to repudiate Hippolito's respectable authority and empathize with this devil when she resolves to be "new borne," to fly "From this vndoing Cittie":

> A woman honest first and then turne whore,
> Is (as with me) common to thousands more,
> But from a strumpet to turne chast: that sound,
> Has oft bin heard, that woman hardly found.
> (part I, IV.i.196-99)

In the early years of James I's reign, a remarkable number of plays--of which the above are just representative examples--focused on this condition of whoredom, either that of the professional prostitute, the subsidized courtesan, or the Christian spouse or virgin fallen into sin--and any combination of the above. One might find in this focus the reflection of national anxiety at the loss of a rule whose unassailable virginity symbolized order and security, and at the growing anxiety over the lack of purity of her successor's regime. Perhaps the anguished questioning of the true nature of whoredom in these plays responds to a fear of national abasement and prostitution to other powers that might ensue if England changed, deprived of Astraea's guidance. These topical urban whores seem allied to the allegorical Whore of Babylon of Catholicism (dramatized in Thomas Dekker's 1607 play of that title). There was a fear of the real possibility that Duessa would lead the Red Cross Knight astray. In effect, England could become a profane space and become Italianized--Italy being the dwelling place of the Whore of Babylon.

So the social "fall" into whoredom, and the spiritual "fall" accompanying it as emboided in the type of Mary Magdalen, took on new topical meaning as dramatized to express each other at this time. Measure for Measure presents this connection in its balance between an Old Regime of mercy and a temporary New Regime of false justice, wherein whoredom enters the highest seats of power. The Honest Whore presents a similar insecurity, in questioning, as The White Devil does, whether the real whores may be those who name others "whore." Similarly, with less profundity to be sure, Webster's plays written with Thomas Dekker, Westward Ho and Northward Ho, present a bawd (Mistress Birdlime) and a whore (Doll) seeking to lure respectable bourgeois housewives into lewdness. The Dukes in Measure for Measure and The Honest Whore preside over moral and social restorations, but in Westward Ho, the inviolate wives remain, with their husbands, isolated in the profane city, where Mistress

Birdlime's rule prevails: ". . . there's more resort to this Fortune-teller, then of forlorne viues married to old husbands, and of Greene-sicknesse Wenches that can get no husbands to the house of a wise-Woman. Shee has tricks to keepe a vaulting house vnder the Lawes nose" (V.iv.253-7). Between Mistress Birdlime's vaulting house and Flamineo's vaulting horse falls not much of a shadow.

Chapter VI

Third Movement: ". . . Strange fowle, from this foule nest."

IV.i

Francisco and Monticelso conspire together in what comes across as a conspiration of devils. "Webster has made Monticelso [especially in this scene] at once the perfect victim of the white devil that Luther describes and the perfect white devil himself."[1] Francisco presents himself as the revenger of outraged innocence, and the scene's first words, in their poetry, evoke the condition of, use the language of, innocence: "MON. Come, come by Lord, untie your foulded thoughts, / And let them dangle loose as a bride's haire" (1-2). The condition he compares with Francisco's confidence is really that of the moment when innocence is lost, and the bride shares her bed-chamber with her lord for the first time--a moment which Isabella has recalled (II.i) in her attempts to woo back her husband.

When Francisco unfolds his thoughts, it is in consciousness of the murder which has ultimately contraried this innocence ("Your sister's poisoned," 3). Francisco's unfolding of his thoughts is an expression of false innocence, since in doing so he disavows the desire for revenge (4-5). In one view, of course, this is not hypocrisy but reluctance: his decision for revenge is "intensely tragic . . . because he shows a deep sense of social and religious conscience."[2] In another, he "maintains a distanced, mocking attitude toward the revenge . . ."[3] It is true that he does also disavow the aim of going to war against Brachiano, supposedly because of the crimes that will be "Committed in the horred lust of warre" (11), and its imposition on his "poore subjects" (8). I suggest that what the audience might consider a moral and responsible position here is really just rhetorical self-exculpation. War itself, as, say, Giovanni presents it, is not inherently evil; what _is_ horrid is the war of lust. But these scruples are mere cover for Francisco's actual thoughts, which are in accord with Monticelso's protest, "What, are you turn'd all marble" (6). To avoid bloody action, the Cardinal seems to say, bespeaks insensitivity and lack of feeling. It is true that Francisco's disavowal of war is carried through. But it is avoided not from compassion; rather, in view of the modes of evading war that figure earlier in the play, out of cowardice, fear of overt commitment, and devotion to politic ideals. We have just witnessed Flamineo disconcerted and demoralized by his own individual act of war against Lodovico. War and policy, no less than religion and policy, are dangerous when commingled.

Monticelso expresses the politician's principle of war evasion, ironically, in martial metaphor: "We see that undermining more prevailes / Then doth the Canon" (15-16). He elaborates this advice with a similitude espousing deception in a manner contradicting his condemnation of Vittoria's deception in the arraignment. He perverts a traditional symbol of warlike nobility: the lion (diminished to a cat) plays with the innocent mice deceptively, then pounces when they least suspect. Certainly such is a cowardly lion, corrupted by policy. Francisco plays the subtle lion in pretending to disavow Monticelso's advice. "Free me, my innocence, from treacherous actes . . ." (25) is a prayer that is not intended to bear fruit, particularly since Francisco cannot be said to possess any innocence to which he can appeal. This prayer, is the immediate preface to his request to see Monticelso's "black book" of all the notorious Roman criminals. It is bolstered by two metaphoric expressions of virtuous innocence and the self-destructiveness of treason: Francisco will be a "safe vallie," not an "aspiring mountaine"; treason, like a spider, is caught in its own web. Both of these are "answers" to Monticelso's deceptive lion, but not evidence of his disavowal of deception. He wishes to see the Cardinal's black book to "Passe away these thoughts" (30). Most immediately "these thoughts" are the figures of virtue which he has just uttered.

The Cardinal's black book, ". . . though it teach not/The art of conjuring, yet in it lurke/ The names of many devils" (36-39). Monticelso as a politic necromancer is in a sense more dangerous than Brachiano's real conjurer, as the company of human devils is a more imminent threat than any diabolical spiritual forces. The Cardinal is, in effect, the commander of the seven deadly sins, and his enumeration of his "army" of criminals (48-69) in his book is meant to contrast to his enumeration of the vices of whoredom. He may be more of a white devil than Vittoria, in that he commands actual criminals, whereas she can only represent abstract, verbally presented sins. The criminals in Monticelso's book either have equivalents in the play's characters, or else are "white devils" in the nature of their activities. As well as usurers, lawyers, and politic bankrupts, Monticelso shows his book containing pandars (such as Flamineo), pirates (such as Lodovico), and divines (such as himself). Ironically, he does not elaborate on the last category: "I slip them o're for conscience sake" (64). Obviously Monticelso's conscience is a black one. Even to a fellow devil he would not reveal the identity of those of his own profession, particularly since he would presumably have to list himself in his book.

Francisco's response to this "generall catalogue of knaves" involves spiritual parody. The black book is referred to as though it were a Bible. He would have Monticelso "fould downe the leaf" (69), not at a striking verse, but at the passage on "Murderers," and asks to borrow this "strange Doctrine" (69). Doctrine is an apt characterization, since the actors in the book are apostles of the politicians' doctrine. When Vittoria is viewed perusing a book at the beginning of the final scene, the audience will recall the Cardinal's book, and wonder what doctrine she is actually perusing.

Francisco also speaks with strong (if purely authorial) irony when he compliments the Cardinal:

> You are a worthy member of the State,
> And have done infinite good in your discovery
> Of these offendors (71-73)

Since these offenders are the heart of the state, there is infinite good in their discovery to a State governed according to their principles, since it can use them to further its aims. "Discovery" in reference to underworld figures refers to the unmasking and by implication, the removal, of the evil members of the state's body (see chapter 7). Francisco's discovery involves the census of certain valuable citizens, as it were the servants of the state. The "Oh God," with which he compares the knaves and extirpated wolves signals ironic exaggeration of false piety, and, of course, makes the situation of valuable criminals topical, since the wolf problem is specifically English, literally and as a moral metaphor. When Monticelso finally leaves, Francisco gives him a doubly ironic adieu: ". . . report / You have left me in the company of knaves" (79-80). Since what follows is a long revenger's soliloquy, Francisco has been left humorously with a book of knaves, but seriously, on the literal level, with himself as knave.

When left alone, Francisco initiates a long audience-informing soliloquy (81-143), which constitutes the remainder of the scene. Herein he speculates on the origin of the Cardinal's list as compiled by a "cunning" _nouveau-riche_ Judge ("lately skipt / From a Clerkes deske up to a Justice chaire," 82-3), to advance himself through the conviction of those "poore rogues" (87) who cannot afford to pay him a bribe. Francisco morally condemns this hypothetical individual, who is given Flaminesque attributes, and sympathizes with the impoverished rogues, in an ambiguous expression of _noblesse oblige_. It seems that the commercialism of the bribery he suggests here appears to be the basis of his moral judgement: it lacks both the subtlety of politics and the honesty of overt criminality. In contrast, regarding those knaves who can pay off their judges, My Lord [Monticelso] he winkes at them with easy will, / His man growes rich, the knaves are the knaves still" (90-91). The satiric harmony of this non-terminal couplet expresses Francisco's satisfaction with the idea of order sanctioned by the prelatical wink, which allows all three estates described to flourish.

Francisco's ideal state, seemingly, is a dystopia where one corruption complements and feeds off of another. He exemplifies this harmony in action by describing the "use" he will make of the book. His exclamation, "That in so little paper / Should lie th'undoing of so many men!" (96-7) is again studiedly ambiguous. Such an exclamation from the homilist would lament misused regal power, or specifically the criminal powers of those on the list, or the power of Francisco to use the criminals' powers. Francisco's version of it seems more a neutral exultation and wondering at the harmonies of microcosm and macrocosm of crime. In a self-parodic way, he imagines himself as the commander of a criminal army. In another version of perverted martial virtue, he believes his courtesans on this list could "lawndresse three Armies"--that is, serve them sexually, as camp-followers, or cripple them, if opponents, with the pox (this ignoble sexualization of war will recall Giovanni's earlier idea of paying his soldiers with the hands of widows). In ironic self-distancing, Francisco adds to the martial parody:

> See the corrupted use some make of bookes:
> Divinity, wrested by some factious blood,
> Draws swords, swels battels, & orethrowes all good.
> (99-101)

Francisco's characterization of Monticelso as a misuser of knowledge is as well a self-characterization. In the homilist's posture ("See!"), Francisco is actually pointing the finger at himself. <u>His</u> "factious blood" raised against Brachiano's house will be let by purely metaphoric swords and battles--<u>i.e.</u>, the politic cunning, the contrary of actual war, with which he will employ the Cardinal's book.

Here, as throughout, there is no strong personage in existence who can speak without his irony Francisco's commonplaces--no one, that is, except the audience itself. Since Webster provides no Kent or Horatio to exemplify the value-system his protagonists violate (Giovanni is too seldom on stage to do this consistently), he forces the audience to fill the void by throwing its own conscience into the action. The witness to the play has no choric surrogate to express his/her indignation. But the engagement this technique draws out is always defeated by the characters' inability to express any sense of remorse, any change of attitude, or any hidden virtues, which might validate the expense of energy or attention on the audience's part. The result, in such scenes as this, may be experienced as a sense of the futility of active virtue, or an almost intolerable indignation at the blind persistence of vice.

Francisco immediately follows his homily with the decision to "fashion my revenge more seriously" (102). His revenge will be initiated through the corrupt use of the Cardinal's corrupt book, with "fashion" implying the amoral aesthetic of revenge as a work of art. In pungent self-revelation, Francisco has difficulty even remembering what Isabella--the cause of his revenge--even looks like:

> Let me remember my dead sisters face:
> (Call) for her picture: no; I'le close mine eyes,
> And in a melancholicke thought I'le frame
> Her figure 'fore me (113-116)
>   Enter Isabella's Ghost

This picture reminds the viewer of an earlier picture--that of Brachiano, whose lips killed Isabella. Francisco has a humorously contrary use for Isabella's picture: not as an object of devotion, but as a secular guide to her features. His non-attachment to the one of his blood whose death he is scheming to revenge is emphasized by the self-conscious "putting on" of melancholy, and his arrogant misattribution of her ghost to the powers of his own "imagination." As he observes her ghost, he outlines a Platonic theory of art: "by the quicke Idea of my minde . . . I could draw her picture" (109-110). As a materialistic Machiavellian, Francisco sees the "Idea" as a creature of his own mind, not a transcendent entity, and he associates the painter's art with a belief that transcendent reality has material origin:

> Thought, as a subtile Jugler, makes us deeme
> Things, supernaturall, which have cause
> Common as sickeness. 'Tis my melancholy . . .
> (111-113)

Francisco's melancholy as contradictor of supernaturalism might be applied to the militant secularism of the other characters; for example, Brachiano's conjuror is his servant, and he deals in natural powers only. Francisco's theory implicitly justifies supernatural events as merely forms of "artistic" manipulation of objects of the material world. Yet the tone of his comments suggests a veiled fear of being in the presence of what he rejects intellectually, of some power that is beyond his control.

Webster's ghost here is very restrained, considering the author's exaggerated reputation for machinery and spectacle. Its silence and departure on command almost ask the disturbing question of whether it really is not just a creature of Francisco's imagination. But its presence betrays chinks in Francisco's self-created philosophical armor of invulnerability:

> How cam'st thou by thy death?--how idle am I
> To question mine owne idleness . . . did ever
> Man dreame awake till now? . . . remove this object--
> Out of my braine with't! what have I to do
> With tombes, or death-beds, funerals, or teares,
> That have to meditate upon revenge? (114-119)

The moralist's answer to Francisco's last question would be "everything to do," since these objects represent the ultimate vulnerability of living creatures, and if revenge could ever be established as an ethical activity, they would be its source and justification, not extraneous details. But even more telling for Francisco's unity of mind is the solipsism of "idleness." Momentarily Francisco is forced into the self-division created by self-judgement, since idleness becomes oppressive enough, and like enough to guilt to need to be ordered away. For a moment its presence is beyond his politic control.

At the ghost's departure, Francisco helps to exorcise its power over him by ironic self-ridicule: "States-men thinke often they see stranger sights / Then mad-men" (121-22). An audience might turn this irony against Francisco, perceiving statesmen *as* true madmen. Francisco's ghostly sister here (as Flamineo's ghostly Brachiano later) implies by her presence a supernatural sanction for revenge. Francisco's will to revenge exists prior to, and seems unaffected by, the apparition. He endorses Reginald Scot's Protestant skepticism of the spiritual reality of rhosts. They are figments of a melancholic imagination.[4] So we find a politic Italian parodying Protestant skepticism of Catholic supernaturalism by holding the skepticism without its Protestant grounding in Grace and determinism. His subsequent statesmanly dismissal of the ghost, immediately followed by his writing a politic love-letter to Vittoria, tells us indirectly how little morality there is in his revenge. He does not "see" his lost sister with emotion. He expresses little love or bereavement. His revenge becomes the object of his passion, and its own justification, an act of will in service to nothing beyond itself.

The gratuity of Francisco's revenge is expressed in his characterization before the fact of his "waighty businesse" as a "Tragedy" (124) in which he, the artist, will inject the "idle mirth" of his pretended love for Vittoria. Francisco is evidently the kind of dramatist whose excessive use of comic relief Webster disapproves. The content of his feigned letter to Vittoria is self-congratulatory: "I am so us'd to frequent flattery, / That being alone I now flatter my selfe" (129-30). This solipsism also accords with the unconditioned freedom of his revenge. Francisco might be alluding to Shakespeare's Richard II and his mirror: self-justifying action is blind, and destructive of the world which the actor, looking only into the mirror, cannot see. Francisco's revenge takes off from a dark side of stoicism, which he will whiten later when in black disguise at Padua. Vittoria's "my mind to me a kingdom is" is ethical as a defense against destructive action, but not, as Francisco articulates it here, as a justification for it.

Francisco, finally, in a homiletic couplet, characterizes his methods, politic and self-justifying, in an opposition of mind and body: "He that deales all by strength, his wit is shallow: / When a mans head goes through each limbe will follow" (135-6).[5] The mind leads and enables the body. Francisco errs in his definition of the mind and its domain, although his metaphor, suggesting sex, birth, and covert theft, could have a disturbing psychological truth. But staking all of life on wit, seeing the whole body as subject to the head, is a misreading of the individual's relation to society; in the state as body, all members work together. Francisco's unbalanced world-view is shared by other leaders of society until the problematic succession of Giovanni, who contains, as much-grieved Prince Henry did, a balance of body and mind.

IV.ii

The "House of Convertites" is an unusual space in Jacobean drama, its identity being inherently satiric of one of the most conventional spaces: the whorehouse. The original narratives described by Boklund have Vittoria sequestered in a "monasterie of Nunnes," so it seems likely that Webster did not originate this space and its name.[5] But he may have recognized the implications of the "monasterie" when likened to the familiar identity of London's Bridewell, the workhouse for sexual offenders which appears in such plays as The Honest Whore (see above, ch. VIII).[6]

As the House is introduced to us, with Flamineo cajoling its Matron concerning Brachiano's access to Vittoria, we might almost imagine an allusion to Measure for Measure, where Lucio gains less ready access to Isabella in her nunnery. Certainly this House with its impenitent population plays on the English assumption that Catholic convents are literally or figuratively houses of prostitution. The initial stage business emphasizes this connection: the Matron is complaisant both in arranging Brachiano's assignations and in passing on to Vittoria the communications of his pretended rival Francisco. The staging suggests this access is so open that, despite Francisco's servant's urging of "all care and secrecie . . ." (8), Flamineo can overhear and intercept Francisco's letter two lines later. The letter's anticlimactic naivete' as a vehicle for seduction, compared with Francisco's self-congratulatory cunning in drafting it, comes to seem like cunning again when Brachiano responds to it with jealousy. Of course, knowing the letter was meant to be intercepted confuses the issue of its tone and Vittoria's access. In the long run, the letter's naivete seems to be calculated, a black whiteness, since without it the suggested abduction of Vittoria which it contains would not have appeared viable to Brachiano, and the abduction is precisely what Francisco aims at.

Brachiano's and Flamineo's discussion of the letter are full of the bawdy and common speech that has filled all scenes in which Flamineo plays the role of pandar. "Who sent it?" Brachiano asks, and Flamineo ridicules him: "as if a man /

Should know what foule is coffind in a bak't meate / Afore you cut it up" (24). Brachiano responds "Ile open't, were't her heart." This imagery foreshadows Brachiano's jealousy, and also associates food and sex with acts and conditions of death: the lovers' ends are almost predetermined by the attitudes this language betrays.

The sonnet by Francisco, which Flamineo reads aloud, is itself allusive to things important to Webster but presumably not in the consciousness of the writer of the letter. Francisco presents himself self-consciously as an old man: January wooing May. He begins by comparing Vittoria with a vine now unpropped by a tree (Brachiano), which recalls Vittoria's dream of him as the graveyard Yew. His second quatrain expresses the resolve to "uncharme" (an oft-used word) Vittoria's imprisonment and lead her to Florence "where my love and care / Shall hang your wishes in my silver har" (33-34; cf. III.i.59-60). Presumably Vittoria is again imaged as a jewel, an ornament to Francisco's age, but the meaning of the figure is, as Flamineo sneers, "equivocal." Will Vittoria be an object of attention, or an exploited ornament to age? Francisco's poem concludes with courtly hyperbole so inappropriate to a Machiavellian's pen that it is obviously satiric: "And all the lines of age this line convinces: / The Gods never was old, no more doe Princes" (39-40). Flamineo exclaims ". . . teare it, let's have no more Atheists / For Gods sake" (41-2). That princes age is sadly true, but their lack of control over their own mortality is one thing that contradicts their assumption of total control over their lives and the lives of others. Flamineo might be seen as perversely right in qualifying as atheistic an assertion that Princes are as immortal as, and therefore not ultimately subject to, Gods; although simply to assert the mortality of the Gods, as Isabella seems to in II.i, would seem more directly atheistic. But his exclamation betrays fear, as in III.i when he pits "advancement" against age in his angry dialogue with Marcello. Age is one human quality no politician can control.

Brachiano's rant in response to this letter breaks decorum in bearing no proportion to the letter's content, particularly since Flamineo's satire has discredited it already. It undercuts any remaining belief in the depth of his devotion to Vittoria, which his solidarity with her during the arraignment might have revived. In his jealousy Brachiano calls her what his enemies on stage have continually called her--"Whore,"--and Flamineo what the audience has continually been led to call him--"Pandar" (51). In effect, Brachiano is parodying the false accusations of the arraignment, where he has shortly before been an indignant spectator.[7] Brachiano appears to be capable of resolute action only when he is "backed into a corner," and as a response to being challenged or victimized by circumstances or individuals. Here he creates a significant crisis in his relation with Flamineo by rebelling against the indirect power that Flamineo has attained over him, and over Vittoria as well. We might see Brachiano as being preyed upon by brother and sister, and sometimes of becoming half-aware that, in our contemporary language, he is "being used."

Brachiano initiates his assault on Flamineo by affirming Flamineo's identity as his "dog" (we might note that Cecil was James I's "beagle"). ". . . Doe you brave? due you stand mee?" (53) Brachiano asks with menace. Flamineo's power exercises itself unprotested when it takes the disguised form of empathetic encouragement. The "brave" and "stand" evoke a martial mode of opposition which Brachiano will not tolerate. His "Would you be kickt" (54), also canine-allusive, connotes usually a general chastisement or disciplining. Flamineo, who favors cudgelling trees to make them bear fruit, chooses to interpret it literally, and responds "Would you have your necke broke?" (57). This is of course a reference to Camillo's end, but also figures as a direct threat to the master in whose service Flamineo originally did the killing. He implies here that his murder was ultimately his own free act, not one which was accomplished through, and sanctioned by, the power of Brachiano. This cloaked suggestion that, since the first murder was Flamineo's own choice, he also might choose to murder his master, evokes Brachiano's most loaded rhetorical question: "Do you know mee?" (58). Few, if any, of the characters really know any of the others, save perhaps sexually, and certainly this ignorance, resulting from self-concealment, is the source of destruction. But, more directly, Brachiano means "know" in the sense of Flamineo's understanding his rank, position, prerogatives--his public self. Flamineo parries this query through a technique similar to his previous ones: he calculatedly misreads Brachiano's word, and gives it the religious sense an unpolitic audience would find in it. He takes on, in so doing, the theistic attitude he actually rejects:

> O my Lord! methodically.
> As in this world there are degrees of evils:
> As in this world there are degrees of devils.
> You'r a great Duke; I your poore secretarie.   (59-62)

Flamineo evokes "degree," which is precisely what Brachiano has been talking about, but in the terms of spiritual hierarchy. Specifically, he implies that he and his master are ultimately equals, since one's ultimate status is spiritual. The quibbling Catholic (versus Protestant) theology which mitigates sins by giving them different degrees of seriousness, and different powers of mitigation through penance, is tacitly analogized by Flamineo to the social degrees which Brachiano is appealing to in putting his servant in his place. Flamineo's final line here, therefore, which agrees with Brachiano's view, caricaturally stereotypes their respective social degrees as "great" and "poor" and invalidates them by the statement of shared evil which precedes it.[8] Webster's audience, which might be forced to agree with Flamineo's implication that spiritual status takes total precedence over social status, also has to face the fact that this is a statement made by a devil, with a purpose that denies the primacy of the spiritual. Certainly, by not defining which of them is the greater devil, Flamineo could be saying that in the kingdom of devils <u>he</u> is the great duke and Brachiano the secretary. Webster's text often leaves it doubtful whether or not an audience is expected to perceive whether one character has actually heard or apprehended the words of another. In this case, Brachiano appears to back off (implying that he has understood his secretary's tortuous threats), with a face-saving martial metaphor from his naval past: "Pandar, plie your convoy, and leave your prating" (64).

Flamineo, in response, returns to his role as servitor, his pandaric actions, and his prating. He pretends fear that Brachiano will destroy him, as Polyphemus saved Ulysses only to be devoured last. This is a deceptive allusion, for it was little Ulysses who eventually destroyed "great" Polyphemus. Brachiano, as well, "would dig turves out of my grave to feed your Larkes" (67). This line recalls line 21--the fowl coffined in baked meat--and seems to go beyond its immediate dramatic purpose, as others of Flamineo's incongruous bursts of "poetry" have. It describes a familiar condition--the seeming ideal rooted in death and dissolution, which is the prior reality, and which discounts all possibility that the ideal can actually exist. While speaking in such mock obsequiousness Flamineo, the Pandar, walks backward leading Brachiano to Vittoria, an action which identifies him as a devil.

Brachiano's confrontation of Vittoria with Francisco's letter, which follows, is a beautiful re-inactment of Vittoria's arraignment by the Cardinal.[9] In the arraignment, Brachiano appeared as Vittoria's indignant defender. Here he makes the same false accusation of whoredom that Monticelso did, but it is for her imagined betrayal of the relationship which has already made her a whore in the judge's eyes. Brachiano presents similar epistolary evidence and similarly prejudges the defendant without giving her a chance to respond. To him now, Vittoria is "A statelie and advanced whore" (77), and he already "sees" all the love-letters in her Cabinet. He sees her in the jewel-imagery of the arraignment as "the dev<u>i</u>ll in christall" (89), a conventional locution for deception.[10] If this arraignment of Vittoria is to be seen as a diabolic "inverted ritual" (of an already inverted one, the arraignment), Brachiano's ultimate characterization of himself, as part of another kind of ritual, though hyperbolic, takes on a special significance:

> Thou has lead mee, like an heathen sacrifice,
> With musicke, and with fatall yokes of flowers,
> To my eternall ruine. Woman to man
> Is either a God or a wolfe (90-93)

Brachiano's classicizing emblem of himself as bull, deceptively honored sacrificial victim, betrays the Christian language; in it, "eternal ruine," Brachiano's ultimate Christian fate, is reduced to a material pagan sacrifice. Brachiano's

eternal ruin is really due to the paganism of his ideology and
faith, of which this speech is a high example. Brachiano's
power to parody rituals derives from his inability to see any
higher reality that they can represent or embody. His
momentary valuation of Isabella ("O my sweetest Dutchesse . . .,"
100) is a function only of his emotional disequilibrium, as is
his (true to the audience) judgement that "I was bewitch'd; /
For all the world speakes ill of thee" (102-3). This is the
direct inverse of his resolve, when courting, to elevate
Vittoria above the valuation of the world (I.ii).

The irony of Brachiano's position is that he achieves a
moral vision only as a product of temporary "madness," in which
his natural faculties are blurred--here, by jealousy, in V.i by
poison and the fear of death. Similarly, God is named only for
His name to be taken in vain:

> VIT.   . . . You did name your Dutchesse.
> BRA.   . . . Whose death God pardon
> VIT.   Whose death God revenge
>   On thee most godlesse Duke.   (105-8)

These prayers of the faithless both call on a divine judgement
which if taken seriously would inevitably damn them. Each wants
to exempt him/herself from a punishment by a God whose reality
their actions continue to deny; they are both "heathen."
Vittoria proceeds to "arraign" Brachiano as she herself has
been arraigned, and as Brachiano in II.i brought Isabella before
his own bar of judgement. Vittoria's long (109-129) accusation
can easily be experienced as in part the release of frustrated
rage against those who sentenced her to the House of Convertites. It is also "special pleading," as practiced by her
accusers. If Brachiano has "stain'd the spotlesse honour" of
Isabella's house, she has collaborated in the staining. If
Brachiano has "preferred" her to "this incontinent colledge"
(very different from Flamineo's University of Padua), she belongs
there, even if the process that brought her there was corrupt.
But these accusations flow into a self-directed resolve to reject
him. The very force of this resolve makes it seem desperate and
uncertain, not assured. Vittoria's imagery for freedom from
Brachiano is amputation ("Weeping to heaven on crutches,"
124),[11] and death ("tosse my selfe / Into a grave . . ."). Her
gesture of renunciation also seems to express the opposite:
"She throwes her selfe upon a bed."

Brachiano's response is so stylized that it reeks of a
similar insecurity: "Vittoria! My dearest happiness!
Vittoria!/ What doe you aile my Love? why doe you weepe?"
(131-2). As Vittoria! is his death-cry later also, it seems to
bear a fatal weakness that complements his bravado. Brachiano
is mastered by Vittoria, and here he seems to confirm Francisco's judgement on the witless strong ones. Calling him
"foole," Vittoria echoes the view that his "greatnesse hath by
much oregrowne thy wit!" (146-47). "What dar'st thou doe, that

I not dare to suffer,/ Excepting to bee still thy whore?" (147-8). Vittoria actually calls herself here for the first time what she denies being, but only as function of asserting her invulnerability to the Duke. Her defiance is strangely inappropriate to his pleading (not threatening) stance: "Will you heare mee." Quite possibly it demands stage positioning that would parody the listening and hearing of the wooing scene between them (I.ii). Here, as in I.ii, Flamineo takes upon himself the role of pandar, despite his being named such in contempt by both of the lovers. In a monologue of reconciliation, which demands a staging of quick shifts from one addressee to another (152-64), he in turn chastises his sister and makes light of her rage to Brachiano. Probably the text implies a staging wherein he seeks to draw their hands together, for Vittoria rejects his plea: "Let us renew right handes" (172). In any case, this plea would be suspect as a pledge of permanence, in the light of Brachiano's earlier inverted marriage ceremony (II.i), which it echoes.

The animal psychology which Flamineo applies to his coaching of Brachiano's reconciliation renders suspect its sincerity ". . . be not like / A ferret to let go your hold with blowing" (170-71). So does Brachiano's vow that neither rage nor wine will "make me commit like fault." This vow is hard to take seriously, given his history as a vow-breaker, and given that only rage or wine, conditions of unreason, are considered as possible reasons for breaking it. The vow jars with Flamineo's appeal to Brachiano's "penitence," and his arguments that in jealousy, "Best natures doe commit the grossest faultes,"

> . . . as best wine
> Dying makes strongest vinnegar (178-80)

"Lying" is suggestive here. Moreover, Flamineo's naturalistic simile is subtly contradictory of what it pretends to illustrate. Vinegar is the final state of Flamineo's wine, not the fault that produces a better wine (wine dying into vinegar might be considered in harmony with the play's other allusions to the Crucifixion as betrayal; if so, Flamineo is in this context also speaking a truth which he consciously denies). More directly to the intrigue at hand,

> A quiet woman
> Is a still water under a great bridge.
> A man may shoot her safely. (183-5)[12]

Presumably once shot (by a boat or a gun) the quiet woman is left behind. Vittoria perceives, with the audience, the duplicity of Flamineo's rhetoric. Yet her "O yee dissembling men!" (185), laying men bare in a word, is also coyly accepting, and virtually signals her own resignation from the battle; as rebellious, it also dissembles.

Flamineo's reply is laden with suggestions: "Wee suckt that, sister, From womens brestes, in our first infancie" (185-6). As with Giovanni's thoughts on his dead mother, and Flamineo's encounter with his mother in the fratricide scene, the reference to nursing presents a sense of ultimate betrayal of a relationship basic to human nature. In this reference, Flamineo, thinking of the infancy of the world, is theologically accurate with respect to original sin--although he doesn't allow for redemption therefrom. But dissembling as a primal sin seems specifically to be attached to Flamineo's consistent rejection of maternality, his disavowal of his own childhood as a condition of dependency (this contrasts to Giovanni's nostalgia for it, as in III.ii.345-7). The breastmilk which Princes seldom suck, which connotes virtue and the sustenance of life, turns to vinegar, as comfortable words do, in Flamineo's mouth. Women, as the source of either spiritual or worldly deceit, absorb the guilt for all deceit from out the souls of men. Flamineo seems to equate treachery with the female nature that is primal, at the very sources of life.

Despite this destructive assertion, Vittoria becomes increasingly submissive to Brachiano's demands. "Am I not low enough?" (188) she asks, referring both to the abasement of her feminine nature by Flamineo's comment, and her "falling" again into psychological and sexual submission to Brachiano. We recall the play on wearing his jewel "lower" in I.ii. With her "I'll speake not one word more" (194), she does become literally silent for the duration of the scene, and the gloating romantic commentary of the victorious pandar, "Hee's a sweet armefull," (197), indicates clearly a staging of the lovers embraced in reconciliation, exchanging kisses. Vittoria's last words indicate a submission directly at odds with her persistence in the arraignment scene.[13] Here Vittoria has been verbally mastered and reduced to silence; "Womens poor revenge / . . . dwels but in the tongue" (III.ii.294-5). Silenced, Vittoria has no power. But she has been mastered by words also. The dissembling company of males uses only these weapons, as in the archetype of verbal deception, the conquest of Troy:

> Couple together with as deepe a silence,
> As did the Grecians in their wodden horse.
> My Lord supplie your promises with deedes.
> You know that painted meat no hunger feedes. (202-4)

Flamineo's true pandaric heritage is revealed in this allusion. Verbal dissembling allowed the horse its entrance, and the silence within had the purpose only of deception. The horse is a work of "painted" artifice which subverts the frankness of martial action. What Flamineo really means by "deeds" is that Brachiano should marry Vittoria--and that such a "deed" will end his own hunger by attaching him to wealth, as much as it will allow freedom to Brachiano's hungry lust. Referring to the fulfillment of love as an ultimate act of deceit, it betrays before the eyes of the audience the shallowness of the love which the audience may be seeing simultaneously in the dramatic emblem of a deep and silent embrace on the stage. Vittoria and Brachiano love in the same atmosphere of satiric irony as to Shakespeare's Troilus and Cressida (brought together by Pandarus). The allussion here also makes a myth of the plan subsequently outlined (211-223) to spirit Vittoria, like Cressida, out of her "city" and to Brachiano's seat at Padua.

Although Brachiano's plan for the rape of Vittoria (and her family) is formulated in a satiric context, with the implication of predestined disaster, it still represents a "breaking of the web" of prior actions. Brachiano takes a vigorous initiative in escaping the magnetic pull of Rome, literal and symbolic center of corruption, and characterized by Flamineo as "Barbarie" (206). Brachiano's resolve, fulfilled through dissimulation (Vittoria disguised as a page) is a parapeteic moment: he publicly proclaims his alliance with Vittoria's family ("I will advance you all," 222), and defies the Medicis' assumed hegemony over private and state-affairs. Brachiano also becomes a "traitor to his class," a noble outlaw, self-banished from the center of power. Despite his crimes, he is an "innocent" in assuming that geographic removal can somehow distance him from the reach of his enemies' plots. There is no sanctuary possible in this realm, which is one of its greatest horrors. The strangers Brachiano will receive into the sanctuary of his own domain, demonstrating the secure landholder's ideal of hospitality, will actually be the dissembling Hellenistic Romans he has taken refuge from.

It is appropriate that at this moment of newly-launched action Flamineo should break the tempo by reciting one of his long, seeming irrelevant, school fables. This one is of the Nile crocodile, relieved of painful tooth-parasites by a small bird; the crocodile resolves to close its jaws on the bird to conceal his failure to reward it for his services. The bird, however, has a "prick" on its head, which forces the crocodile to open its jaws, whereupon the bird flies away safely.

Brachiano applies this fable to Flamineo's feeling that he has "not rewarded / The service you have done me" (236-7). Flamineo, satirizing his own similitude as it "hold s not in every particle," says Vittoria is the crocodile, cured by Brachiano (no doubt, with his "prick"). But his parable is dissimulation, since as consistent allegory it must require the threat of vengeance by himself or by Vittoria for this lack of reward (the "prick," therefore, may connote, as well as lust, the sword that might resolve the situation lust has created).

The "perpetual silence" (231) the crocodile plans for the bird between its jaws is like the treacherous silence within the wooden horse; it is also a "bloody prison" (234) such as the room where Vittoria and Flamineo encounter death by sword. Flamineo's parable can apply to any escape from a treacherous imprisonment caused by a naive assumption of benevolence in nature or in human nature. It can apply to the situation of the young Giovanni, who, interestingly, is a little bird in II.i.128-129. Flamineo's fable is thus, I would argue, purposely over-elaborate. Breaking the momentum of Brachiano's active resolve with its passive words, it foreshadows the verbal treachery which will, later, sabotage his plans permanently. It characterizes Flamineo's discordant nature, implying inner division at the moment when accord and unity are most necessary. It implies dissatisfaction at the point of greatest promised satisfaction: "I will advance you all." It describes a redemption out of keeping with Flamineo's ethic, and in such a "barbarous" setting that its inconsistency with the Italian world is strongly emphasized. As "politic madman," Flamineo adds an ultimate antagonistic touch in characterizing this speech as calculated artifice, based on extremes of loquacity and terseness--a protean "varying of shapes" (246) that will prevent people from giving him a graspable identity. Of course, he apopthegmatizes, "Knaves do grow great by being great mens apes" (247). So, as a self-proclaimed knave, he sees Brachiano's behavior as spontaneously mad, like his own; his rise is based on aping what is implied to be a will too "varying" to bring off its plans successfully.

IV.iii

The public scene of the Papal election is really a "private" scene.[15] It is certainly meant to complement the arraignment scene, as a set piece of pageantry, with foreign ambassadors as a chorus implying its portentiousness. But for logistic and thematic reasons it is literally a "conclave" (2), which the audience experiences from outside the walls. One of its purposes is "to emphasize the claustrophobic conditions out of which the new head of Christendom emerges."[16] The secrecy of the Papal election is symbolic of the covert, politic nature of Catholicism itself. That the atheistic Lodovico has the job of insuring the election's honesty by searching entering food-dishes and the like for bribes, is humorously expressive of this. Point is added when Lodovico himself accepts the bribe sent by Francisco to overcome his Christian scruples about murdering Brachiano. Lodovico is the corrupt "matron" to this House of Convertites.

The victory of Monticelso in the election seems, precisely because we do not witness it, suspect rather than above suspicion, by virtue of its secrecy. It is hard to avoid associating the smuggling in of letters to the Cardinals with the smuggling in of Francisco's letter to the House of Convertites, with an aim of deception in both cases. The Vatican and the House are tacitly equated as whited sepulchres, seeming places of refuge, or exile, from the world, yet actually sites of the most Wordly behavior.

At the outset, with Lodovico's description of the attendant ambassadors and their religious emblems, the witness is presented with the whole Christian world as being intent on the outcome of the Papal election. The contrast between this international attention and the new Pope's first concern with the amorous intrigues of Brachiano and his company is bathetic, and provides a negative comment on the statesmanship of the Papacy. But it also tells us that Webster's story is not meant to be only of local or "private" significance. The actions in the play can represent the tendencies of all Catholic-dominated culture, whose corruption threatens the moral order of the world.

It is also significant that the ambassadors present at this particular ritual all represent quasi-religious orders of knighthood--from the Knight of Rhodes to the Knight of the Garter--rather than secular governments. I would suggest that these spectators represent a lost ideal, a time when religion and policy were not contradictory or mutually destructive. Webster's Italian world stands for all fallings away from this ideal everywhere in his time. Knighthood is characterized by martial piety, the perfect fusion of sacred ends and secular means. Giovanni would fit into this chivalric company, whereas Francisco, the politic noble, is its exact opposite, except when he puts on the white disguise of the black knight to deceive Brachiano.

It has been noted that Lodovico's searching of the dishes entering the Vatican (20-29) could be an allusion to the sending in of message-or poison-laden pastries and baked meats to the imprisoned Sir Thomas Overbury, with whom Webster was connected. Although the information on this ritual conveyed by the English ambassador, as well as his subsequent discussion of the claustration, can function in the play purely as topical allusion or local color, it is so lengthily evoked as to become almost metaphoric. This is particularly true when the Cardinal Arragon appears on the "Tarras" (presumably the upper stage) to announce that Cardinal Monticelso has been elected Pope. To the viewer who "knows" Monticelso from his past in the play, his elevation seems to be a final confinement, or imprisonment, in a moral or spiritual sense: the man who holds the black book has been established as the supreme power. The corruption of Monticelso's election is also suggested by the news that the Cardinals have "given o'er [up] scrutinie and are fallen/ To admiration" (39). Scrutiny is balloting, and admiration is the "Adoration," which according to the treatise of Bignon, Webster's source, "is not esteemed by many, so lawful and available as scrutenie: because by meanes of contentions, and partialities, there may be some fraude or violence committed therein, in that the weaker side may be drawne to Adoration by the example of those more mightie."[17] This manipulation of the weak by the strong is precisely the _forte_ of the Medicis. The Latin of Arragon's announcement, and of the populace's response ("_Vivat sanctus Pater_ Paulus _Quartus_," 48), enhances the sense of entrapment, subjection to a decision arrived at in contempt of the vernacular world. To any Protestant, the Latin of religious ritual conveys the sense that the common person is being hoodwinked.

Vivat suggests the opposite of its meaning of new life. As at Vittoria's arraignment, and later at the death of Brachiano, the Latin represents a perverted ritual.

Webster's conjunction of entrapments and escapes is timed to create dramatic irony. Immediately on the populace's "Vivat," a servant enters, announcing to Francisco "Vittoria my Lord--". . . Is fled the Citty--" (49-50). One may note the mocking echo of v's in Vivat and Vittoria. Vittoria's flight, Francisco reveals in soliloquy to the audience, after feigning outrage, is as calculated as Monticelso's election seems to have been: ". . . 'twas this / I onely laboured" (54-55). Since the Whore metaphor for Catholicism was so commonplace, it is not an exaggeration to consider that "To marrie a whore" (59) as Brachiano will, is what Monticelso by his election has done figuratively. Thus the private flight of Brachiano from the House of Convertites parallels the public emergence of Monticelso as Pope from the Vatican. This union of private and public affairs is emphasized by the subsequent emergence of Monticelso "in state" (63), both remitting the sins of those gathered in public and privately attending Francisco's news of the escape. Monticelso's first act of his Papacy responds to Francisco's private business by pronouncing excommunication against Brachiano and Vittoria:

> Wee cannot better please the divine power,
> Than to sequester from the holie Church
> These cursed persons. (68-70)

The prior Pope's liberation of Lodovico contrasts ambiguously to this negative liberation of his future victims from their Catholic communion. Of course, to the Pope, this is no liberation but a confinement, a sequestration from Christian liberty. But the excommunication is politically a banishment, as well, from Rome (73). That like the play's first banishment it totally lacks for its subjects the Christian meaning it has for the audience is ironically emphasized after Monticelso has left. Francisco asks if his hireling has "tane the sacrament" to murder Brachiano, and Lodovico replies "With all constancie" (75-76). Lodovico's figurative communion here is diabolical, and "inverted ritual" leading to the faithful commission of a mortal sin. But it is also the communion of Monticelso, from which the lovers have been banished, since the Papal banishment is what enables the murder of Brachiano.

The subsequent dialogue between Monticelso, who has reentered, and Lodovico, following Francisco's departure, tangles the thicket of duplicity even more. In a way it is a private ritual in direct contrast to the Papal election. With leading questions, the Pope, as confessor, induces Lodovico to acknowledge his intent of murdering Brachiano; as a confessor, the Pope prescribes penance. Lodovico appears to be swayed by the arrival of a payoff of a thousand crowns from Francisco-- Judas being bribed for a betrayal. But this scenario is blurred.

In IV.i, Monticelso, who here feigns ignorance of the revenge plot, has been covertly urging Francisco to take this very revenge, as an "underminer." And Lodovico's posture has been so aggressively amoral up to this point that both his confession and momentary penance seem to have the same qualities as his deceptive courting of Flamineo in III.iii. I would suggest that the "white devil" figure applies to this entire exchange, as it did to the dual dissimulations of Flamineo and Lodovico in III.iii. The holiest and unholiest of men are communing while playing antagonistic roles, and the audience is meant to perceive both that they are feigning and that each is aware that the other is feigning. Monticelso's actions in this scene, and his disappearance from the play subsequently, are often taken as a sign that he has renounced the bloody work of his brother.[18] "As Francisco loses himself in pursuing revenge, Monticelso finds himself by abandoning it."[19] But it should be noted that all of the known sources of Webster's play also drop the new Pope at this point.[20]

The Pope begins his examination of Lodovico by inquiring why Francisco worked so hard to secure his pardon from the prior Pope, a question that easily suggests its answers: so that he might be employed in his criminal vocation. Lodovico feigns, in response, innocent speculation:

> Italian beggars will resolve you that
> Who, begging of an almes, bid those they beg of
> Doe good for their owne sakes; or't may bee
> Hee spreades his bountie with a sowing hand,
> Like Kinges, who many times give out of measure;
> Nor for desert so much as for their pleasure.   (85-90)

With subtlety, Lodovico parallels Francisco's charity with that involving extremes of power and impotence--Kings and beggars. This calls to mind the arguments over rule and servitude between the devil and his secretary in the previous scene. There may also be the suggestion that beggars exist because of the misplaced (or withheld) bounty of kings. But both beggars and kings, in Lodovico's analogy, profess to ask for or do out of charity what is actually done out of cupidity. The beggars "use" the appeal to soul-health to play on donors' guilt when they gather alms. The kings pass off as bounty what is actually self-indulgence--"pleasure"--which has no relation to merit in the recipient. Webster is allowing the antagonist of his own probable Christian ideals to express a moral judgement of hypocrisy. But he has Lodovico do so in a veiled enough manner to call from Monticelso the same seemingly-naive exclamation that he delivered to Vittoria: "you're cunning" (91). He follows in language which has become iconographic in this play, and with a tone of curiosity rather than censoriousness, "Come, what devill was that / That you were raising" (91-92).

When Lodovico states a satirically obvious falsehood, that Francisco has been consulting him about a horse, the Pope replies with (feigned?) indignation at his evasion: "O, thou'rt a foule black cloud, and thou do'st threat / A violent storme" (102-3). This particular storm-imagery constitutes an accurate prophecy of Lodovico's future, but he twists it with an equally accurate rebuttal: "Stormes are i'th aire, my Lord; I am too low to storme" (103-4). Beyond the double sense of "low," Lodovico's response is accurate in two ways. He is in the pay of "higher" ones (e.g., Kings); but also, the momentum of events, the condition of the time, creates a stormlike power of collective evil that no individual will can withstand. "Stormes are i'th aire," and humans are fatalistically bound to be blown in whichever direction they are going.

In this context of exculpatory wit, Lodovico's decision to satisfy the Pope's curiosity, and suddenly change roles--"I come not to you as an Intelligencer, / But as a penitent sinner," (110-11)--appears as an obvious deception. We will remember that in the Pope's black book the generations that come first are the Intelligencers. In our ignorance of what postures or intonations might have accompanied this covenant between Pope and murderer on Webster's stage, we can still gather that the mock-confessional situation, as a universally accepted mode of conveying Intelligence, is operative here.

Lodovico's "confession" is that he is "sworn" to avenge Isabella's murder, for the reason adumbrated in I.i.43-44: "I did love <u>Brachiano's</u> Dutchesse deerely; / Or rather I pursued her with hot lust . . ." (114-15). This would appear to be again a self-satiric justification for a gratuitous or suborned act. There is little other confirmation of Lodovico's passion for the "faded" Isabella. The supposed motivation of betrayed love, as well as the delicious equivalence of dear love and hot lust, emphasizes the false "art" of this entire confession scene. Lodovico is parodying Brachiano's own situation of murdering the husband to attain the wife. Lodovico is ridiculing fundamental truths as well--for example, the basic opposition of love and lust--with the same energy that the Pope is pretending to affirm them.

In response to this confession, the Pope delivers a homily similar to his speeches to Vittoria. He even uses Puritan imagery: "Do'st thou imagine thou canst slide on bloud / And not be tainted with a shameful fall?" (121-22). He evokes the "Eugh-tree" rooting in graves. He calls up, and echoes, Gasparo's satiric advice in I.i:

> Instruction to thee
> Comes like sweet showers to over hardned ground:
> They wet, but pierce not deepe (125-26)

He leaves Lodovico to his "penitence," which may "conjure" the devil from his breast (130). To the Pope's questions Lodovico could but answer "yes" in favor of sin, since he does prosper from graves, and is hardened to instruction. But, by using conjuration where he should evoke Christian purgation, the Pope implies he is himself hardened against Christian truth. If this ritual has been an "inversion" of confession--one of Hurt's three inverted rituals in the play--it would have to be assumed that as Lodovico's confession is parodic, so is this homiletic rebuke to him by the confessor.[21]

    Lodovico's resolve to renounce his sinful intent because it is "damnable" (131) appears to be as faithless as the sermon he has just been subject to. Not only does his resolve last for a mere few seconds, but it is also motivated by Lodovico's expecting the Pope's "suffrage, by reason / Of Camillo's death" In other words, he expected spiritual reward, or at least toleration, from the new Pope for having contributed to a murder which he assumes was in the Pope's interest. Lodovico's unregeneracy flowers in his disappointment that the Pope did not reward him for murder. It is even more evident (perhaps too evident, in a stylized Morality symmetry) when Francisco appears and bribes Lodovico with a thousand crowns, pretended to be sent from the Pope, to accept the "position" of his intelligencer. To the audience, one irony can be that the Pope's spiritual and the Duke's temporal bribes have the same immoral purposes, and are valued alike for what they promise him materially. But Francisco's deception, besides serving his own purpose in covering his tracks, plays ironically with Lodovico's own innocence. It leads him to the false conclusion, which yet confirms his own philosophy, that the Pope was the source of both spiritual incitement to virtue and material incitement to vice. So Lodovico's conception of the Pope as a perfect white devil is in this incident false, but is based on a deception by Francisco which is itself the act of a white devil. Soliloquizing on his deceptive view of the Pope, Lodovico is himself a white devil in appearing to denounce the hypocrisy of the Great, while concluding eagerly "Now/ to th'act of bloud . . ." (153).

    Lodovico likens the "modest forme of greatnesse" created by "Art" (used here to describe the Pope's imagined deceit, actually Francisco's art) to that of "Brides." At "wedding dinners" they are seemingly queasily modest at the "wanton jests," yet secretly in their thoughts they are rehearsing the "hot and lustfull sports" of the marriage night. Greatness is defined, for Lodovico, as the ability to be falsely innocent, yet his sense of his own greatness seems to have different premises: "there's but three furies found in spacious hell; / But in a great mans breast three thousand dwell" (154-6). The more of hell Lodovico can materialize on earth, the more hell fills him, the "greater" he will be. Lodovico remains striving for a true definition of evil. His metaphoric bride--who might conjure up Vittoria, a much more sullied bride--is hypocritical in imagining lust while practicing chastity. But one who practices both vice and virtue, and one who practices only vice and pretends to no virtue, are both incarnations of evil closer to this play's experience. Compared with his own desire to embody the most extreme evil, Lodovico's bride might seem to be his own imagined deal, conjured up but rejected: her lust is safely contained within the embrace of lawful marriage.

V.i

Depending on their actual positioning, "A passage over the stage of Brachiano, Flamineo, Marcello, Hortensio, Corombona, Cornelia, Zanche, and others" suggests an emblematic grouping of a parade of the doomed, collective passengers on a ship of fools.[22] By blood or household attachment, all of these are in a sense "banished" or fallen from the center of power; they wait, unknowing, to be demolished. There is irony therefore in Flamineo's initial exclamation:

> In all the weary minutes of my life
> Day nere broke up till now. This marriage
> Confirmes me happy. (1-3)

Since Brachiano's household is moving into darkness, Flamineo is a "gull" of circumstances, if we are to assume his happiness holds no cynicism. He is at last allied by blood to his master and presumed source of advancement. But his diction, like his situation, is ambiguous. In a dark lifetime of self-pity day may finally break, but it also may "break out"; or founder, as a ship--of fools--may.

A signal of the "breaking up" of Brachiano's alliance is the credulity of Flamineo in the presence of Francisco disguised as a Moor--a literal white devil. He uses strangely laudatory language in describing Francisco as a "goodly personage," "experienc't / In State-affares." Presumably, Flamineo has not read _Othello_, so he is not suspicious of one who has by report "serv'd the _Venetian_ / in _Candy_ . . ." Flamineo is also credulous reporter of the state of the disguised Gasparo and Lodovico, who present themselves as wordly--yet ascetic--Knights of Malta. Flamineo's description recalls immediately the representatives of Orders at the Papal election, and their idealized nature. In Flamineo's thumbnail biography, the disguised Lodovico and Gasparo are former Courtiers of Hungary, who defected into the "strickt order of Capuchins" (16), but finding that order _too_ strict, left it. "Troubled in conscience," they eventually found a happy medium in the Knights of Malta. That this history is drawn out so long would indicate that it makes a special point. These Knights, as the real ones of IV.iii, are not only unusual in being moderate and not extremists, but they have, in Flamineo's words "commedled religion with pollicie" (III.iii.37) in terms of the highest ideals. They are midway between the court and the cloister, with the body serving the spirit, but with neither denied. In actuality, these Knight murderers are white devils, their virtuous pretence serving a diabolical end; they have commingled world and spirit in a perverse and inverted way. The apparent admiration of Flamineo for all three conspirators suggests a fatal weakness for virtue, which is new in his character, maybe the symptom of his debilitating "happiness," a weakness which foreshadows his downfall. This admiration closely precedes his fatal recourse from political manipulation to direct action--the murder of his brother, itself foreshadowed by his blow to Lodovico in III.iii. 119--which also puts him in jeopardy.

Flamineo seems even to admire an attribute of "Hard Penance" (24) in the false knights, which the attentive observer would consider a politician ought to recognize immediately as a subterfuge necessary for maintaining a disguise: "They have vowed for ever to weare next their bare bodies those coates of maile they served in" (23-24). Again, virtue is mocked, but there is also a profound mockery of the martial ideal represented by the young Giovanni, and a prediction of Brachiano's hard penance when he dons his poisoned helmet.

Flamineo's new posture here is that of observer, outsider, rather than politician or pandar. He is excluded from the intimacy of "Mulinassar" and the Knights with Brachiano, and this banishment plays interestingly against the foreignness he describes in the trio, as in the disguised Francisco, who has a "deepe contempt/ Of our slight airy Courtiers" (34-5). The audience can share this contempt, while at the same time having this contempt both for Flamineo, who perceives it, and Francisco, who expresses it. The commonplace Flamineo concludes by attributing to Francisco may be taken with similar irony: "Glories, like glow-wormes, afarre off shine bright / But lookt to neare, have neither heat nor light" (38-9). Agreeing with this, as applied to courts, we can perceive how Flamineo lacks this very discernment, in not perceiving the Moor's glories to be deceptive.[23]

Brachiano lacks this discernment also, as he immediately enters with the Knights, praising their service against the Turk, a service as useful as a credit card to the possessor. Brachiano regrets that the "vows" of the two Knights have forbidden them acceptance of his bounty (see IV.iii.88), but accepts their wish to hang their swords in his chapel, an act emblematic of the crusader's mingling of war and faith. In view of Lodovico's discussion with the Pope in the previous scene, his self-abnegation as a disguise for ultimate corruption harmonizes with his relationship to Francisco: Francisco is paying him bounty to pretend the rejection of all worldly reward.

When alone, the conspirators "imbrace"--a sort of kiss of peace, affirming their sacramental pledge to murder. Lodovico protests, despite his ingenious role, that Francisco's plan for murder both lacks artistic originality and does not insure Brachiano's spiritual as well as physical perdition. Gasparo sees that Brachiano "could not have invented his owne ruine, / Had hee despair'd, with more proprietie" (64-5), and that therefore the planned murder will have damning spiritual effects analogous to those that would afflict the spiritually-despairing suicide. But Lodovico wants the plot to be "ingenious" and unprecendented, so that it might be cited, like a Biblical event, as a prototype or example ("mirror") for future murders. He imagines situations that might have a more immediate spiritual effect on Brachiano: for example, the poisoning of his racket's handle so

> That while he had bin bandying at Tennis,
> He might have sworne himselfe to hell, and strooke
> His soule into the hazzard! (70-72)

Lodovico's concern for Brachiano's damnation seems at first incongruous, since he has been distinguished for his own total rejection of a spiritual, let alone moral, dimension in life. But we could also see that, beginning with the very first scene, Lodovico has been on the cutting edge of the issue of a political viability for a Christian order in the world. Like a comrade from another time and place, Flannery O'Connor's Misfit, he has been challenging God, through the extreme sinfulness of his actions, to make His divine immanence manifest in retribution. He might be "absolute for" Brachiano's spiritual, as well as physical death, on the chance (cf. Pascal) that God might proclaim an unquestionable presence. Lodovico's emphasis on art is evidence of this motivation: the artist is the lesser God; in the absence of his Model, he must create the world in his own image, and Lodovico's image is the opposite of God's.

It is almost amusing to find Francisco dissatisfied with his own art of revenge, for contrary reasons; in his case it is too ingenious. Francisco is a vicarious soldier. He is not immediately enthusiastic about Monticelso's politic theory of undermining (IV.i.15-23): ". . . this revenge is poore, / Because it stealls upon him like a theif" (77-8). He fantasizes a Roman scene of taking Brachiano in pitched battle and leading him in triumph to Florence. Lodovico assents (seriously?) to this act of imagination, but elaborates it in a parody of Brachiano's earlier vision of himself as a Pagan sacrifice wreathed (IV.ii.90). The parody becomes an amoral emblem:

> . . . crown'd . . . with a wreath of stinking garlicke,
> T'have showne the sharpnesse of his government;
> and rancknesse of his lust (81-83).

Lodovico's morality is bathetic, since garlic does not have supreme connotations of evil. The dis-ordered public and private goernment of Brachiano compares favorably with the anarchic lack of government that Lodovico, as pirate and assasin, represents. As often, "Flamineo comes" (84), here ending the ethical speculations of the assasins, and their words apply also to him, since the theme of the subsequent exchanges will be lust.

In this period of exchanges, Marcello plays the role of catechizer and moralizer that he did in III.i. As Abel, Marcello exudes self-righteousness as insistently as Flamineo does cynicism, and in a sense becomes the satirist's satirist. The particular object of his moral indignation is Flamineo's intimacy with Vittoria's black servant Zanche, a relationship Webster introduces here directly for the first time. Like the relationship between Othello and Desdemona, or Tamara and Aaron, this attachment is seen as inherently "against nature." Symbolically, it is an alliance with the devil, as Marcello says (85), and as Flamineo does not hesitate to admit.

A twentieth-century consciousness can well see Flamineo's defiance of racial stereotyping as a redeeming attribute, in contrast to the sanctimonious racism of Marcello. A psychologically oriented perceiver might feel Flamineo is taking revenge on his master for having to play the pandar to his _amours_, by conducting his own _amour_ embarrassing to the community. In Renaissance terms, Zanche bears on her skin the devilish mark that Vittoria is felt to bear inwardly; as lover she is the mirror of Vittoria in a condition beneath garments of whiteness or blackness. But Webster could be asking the audience to agree with Marcello that Flamineo is toying with an ultimate sale of himself to the devil, physically, since he does not know the spirit. Flamineo protests "I doe not conjure for her" (3), and in bawdy wit suggests that the devil of phallic sexuality is present in every male: it takes no cunning to raise the devil "for heeres one up allreadie, / The greatest cunning were to lay him downe" (89-90). Marcelle "interprets" Zanche to Flamineo as the morality figure a contemporary audience might "see:" "Shee is your shame" (91). Yet, as is his rhetorical custom, Flamineo insists on interpreting his remark in a naturalistic context: women stick like burs.

At this point Zanche spies the black-faced Francisco, and exclaims on him as a "Country-man" with whom she resolves to speak "In our owne language." One who interprets Zanche as "Shame" will see that the dramatic irony of this self-deception is limited: both do come from the same spiritually lost country, and both speak the same language of deceit.

Responding to Flamineo's queries about the "iron daies" of his military service, the disguised Francisco appears to be an almost purposeful reminiscence of Othello and his seductive memories of service. But here Francisco uses modesty as a stratagem (modesty considered by Marcello as excessive "stoicism"), to evade an answer. It is intriguing that Marcello should consider the stoic stance unfavorably. In view of his reprobations, and his martial profession, he probably is seen as identifying stoicism with weakness, or lack of commitment to action or ideals. In view of his imminent murder, we might feel that _real_ stoicism would be the most viable position to take in this atmosphere of instability. Francisco does take up on Marcello's philosophical word, and phrases in his own terms an idea of his equality with, and thereby freedom from, the need to flatter and impress, Brachiano. He and Brachiano, as differently placed bricks (presumably in an edifice), are still all "made of one clay" (106). This is true in contrary senses. If "degree" is accepted as real, Francisco in his ducal public identity is Brachiano's equal, and as a fellow murderer he is his moral equal, as he would be even if his public identity were inferior. In the other sense, his argument takes up from Flamineo's own discussion of equality with the Duke (IV.ii.60 ff.): there may be hierarchies of devils, but all diabolical humans are equal in that they are servants of the devil. The actual portée of Francisco's brick analogy, if it were in the mouth of a non-hypocritical preacher, is that of the Bible: all flesh is clay or grass. In the light of the democracy death imposes, the only degree of substance is spiritual degree. Flamineo understands, and ridicules, this basic meaning: "If this souldier had a patent to beg in churches,/ . . . hee . . . would tell them stories" (112-13). Flamineo, the impoverished scholar, can see in Francisco only the archetypal begging soldier, but his imagination turns him into a preaching friar.

In response to Marcello's profession of a soldierly vocation, Francisco delivers a second homiletic speech, also grotesque in context because of its fundamental truth. This one is on a popular subject of the time, the "miserie of peace." "Onely outsides are then respected"--as to say white devils flourish most in peace, since their habitat, the Court, becomes the martial field. The colossus of the court is a pygmy when on the field. This character of the time is directly applicable to the play's dialectic between soldier and court-politician, and Francisco is a perfect example of the latter. In fact, since he has just been discussing this issue in his own persona (79-80), he could be considered obsessed by the implications of the act he is about to commit. It is not a question of guilt, but of "degree:" by comparing colossi and pygmies, Francisco makes a very Flaminesque point about the relativity of truth--and he wins Flamineo over with it--but he also expresses a form of self-judgement and questioning. Proclaiming a vision of himself as a pygmy may interfere with the exultation in others' views of him as a colossus.

As the "minion" of a Cardinal, says Flamineo, one may do "the devill knowes what vilanie" (122), says Francisco. As this dialogue progresses, the accord of mutal congratulation between Flamineo and Francisco comes to echo that between Flamineo and Lodovico in III.iii. To the audience, the former couple may seem similar in values and in their ability to preach against their own villainies, though Francisco is pretending to greater virtue.[24] But this perception clashes with the total difference between them in actual social position. Webster plays subtly on this dramatic irony. Francisco compares pigeons in harvest time unhunted "because they belong to the Lord of the Mannor; whilest your poore sparrowes that belong to the Lord of heaven they go to the pot for't" (127-29). This emblem of social injustice as a misery of peace is mock-populist and anti-aristocratic, its sparrows and Lord of the Manor evoking New Testament parables.

Flamineo, whose whole aim is to become a pigeon before he meets a sparrow's fate, does not oppose this application of their discussion, but redirects its message as a vehicle for "polliticke instruction." The Duke has promised a pension to "Francisco," but since he is a "great man," Francisco must be satisfied only when he has it in hand. Obviously this advice to Francisco is Flamineo's advice to himself, and mirrors his own condition.

Flamineo "covers" for this politic advice by continuing with a traditional complaint, more in Francisco's vein, against the limitation of subsidy to soldiers who have given their limbs in wars, in this case against the Turk. Such partial philanthropy Flamineo describes as "miserable curtesie" (136). Flamineo is still describing himself in this picture, since the unrewarded soldier and the unrewarded scholar are so alike as victims of society that each can figure the other. Yet it is true that in this interchange Flamineo has slightly shifted his role and now pretends to being the "discoverer of abuses." This is of course another mask that his protean nature (IV.ii. 244) wears, but it is in keeping, as a departure, with the next major movement in this scene: the "wonder" of Flamineo in love.

Of course Flamineo's lady is the "Witch" (148) Zanche, and an unspoken purpose of their strange encounter is to serve as a foil for the relationship of Brachiano and Vittoria. Webster is employing a romantic comedy convention of great currency: the servants of the lovers couple in a love-plot slightly burlesquing the main intrigue. Webster even burlesques this situation: the servants' love is a union of sin, both metaphorically and literally, in the mingling of black and white blood. The noble union it mirrors is inwardly corrupt, and morally offers no contrast to it. In fact, again Zanche's external blackness can simply represent Vittoria's inner blackness, and the secretary is the shadow of the Duke. The evil in this relationship is but a distillation of that in the lovers' whole entourage, as shown by the fact that others do not recognize the relationship as evil. Only Cornelia and Marcello share the audience's presumed a priori condemnation of it. Of course, as in V.vi, it is hard to know how much of Flamineo's professed feeling is false. Webster himself is using their byplay to set up the intense irony of Zanche "innocently" turning from Flamineo to fall for Francisco, in his Moorish disguise, since he is of "her complexion." This is another example of one white devil deceiving another into innocence.

Flamineo's first justification of his "love" for the "Witch" Zanche appears possibly flippant: ". . . shee knowes some of my villainy; I do love her, just as a man holds a wolfe by the eares . . ." (148-50). Their love is based on shared villainy, consisting of the dangerous intelligence Zanche might betray if crossed, and the intimacy of intense hostility. Flamineo's love can be manifest only through what the audience experiences as the antitheses of love. Further, Flamineo

confesses that he made some "darke promise" (an obvious pun) of
marriage to Zanche, and he constantly flees from the promise as
"a frighted dog with a bottle at's taile" (155). Surely there
is an element of humor in this incongruity--Flamineo casually
confessing an apparently desperate alliance. But, unlike
Brachiano the one pursued in love, Flamineo is metaphorically
and seriously "promised to darkness," from which, like all
unrepentant sinners, he cannot escape. All his quibbles possess
a quality of jeopardy, endangerment, loss of self-direction.
When Zanche recalls to Flamineo his "oathes" (reminiscent of
Vittoria's and Brachiano's broken promises in the House of
Convertites), Flamineo disavows them as being relevant only to
their moment of utterance: "Lovers oathes are like Marriners
prayers, uttered in extremity . . ." (170-71). Professions of
love and faith are non-binding phenomena subject to the mutability of nature. Yet Flamineo recognizes the possibility of
jeopardy calling forth a temporary commitment. He compares
drinking, as a similarly unselfcontrolled situation: "drinke
drawes on protestation; and protestation drawes on more drinke.
Is not this discourse better now then the morality of your
sun-burnt Gentleman?" (175-77). Flamineo here is contrasting
his atheistic naturalism to the stoicism of the disguised
Francisco. In this contrast he sketches an endless cycle,
wherein all "protestation," taken as avowal of allegiance to an
absolute, is a product of literal or figurative drunkenness,
wherein reasoning faculties and self-knowledge are drowned.

Flamineo's ethical relativism is harmonious with Francisco's in a sense, but Francisco draws an absolute conclusion--
that there is ultimately "no difference" between individuals, if
external circumstances are considered. Flamineo sees a constant
changing of circumstances, from which a fixed truth can never be
abstracted. As for love, Flamineo seems to see it as one of
many momentary and ultimately "unreal" states. In illustration
of love's transience, his exposition of it is interrupted by
Cornelia's violent entrance, physical attack on Zanche, and
denunciation of her as a whore and a bird of prey: "Is this
your pearch, you haggard? flye to'th stewes" (178). At
Flamineo's outraged response, Cornelia abruptly leaves, in a
sequence of entry, sudden blow, and exit that is "exactly and
ghoulishly parodied by Flamineo in the murder of Marcello."[25]
Immediately her abrupt blow creates an alliance between Flamineo
and Zanche, which is further enhanced by Marcello's "You're a
strumpet." This has the same power of the Cardinal's naming
Vittoria a whore, and Brachiano's naming Flamineo a pandar. As
Marcello's physical and verbal attacks on Zanche heighten,
Flamineo also becomes more overtly violent[26] and less politic in
his language, to the point that he implies, and Marcello takes
up, the challenge of a duel with the other to vindicate his
honor and attachment to Zanche.

This swift sequence of action and reaction illustrates
perfectly Flamineo's philosophy of mutability. In this case,
the equivalent of drunkenness is anger, but the protestation it

finally draws forth, the resolve to duel, appears to the audience as a confutation of that philosophy. According to it, it should be a passing fancy, not a commitment, But Flamineo leaves the stage before he is in a position to renounce it as such. Of course, the forthcoming fratricide does perform this renunciation.

The alliance of Flamineo and Zanche may be difficult for a modern audience to accept, no less than is the more profound one of Othello and Desdemona. Our consciousness may demand empathy with Flamineo in his defense of a black woman's honor and of his right to marry her (Marcello: "Shee brags that you shall marry her. Flamineo: What then?" 186). Flamineo's "I am of age" (190) appears even more irrefutable an argument in our time than it may have been in seventeenth century romantic drama--at least where it referred to an alliance between white lovers. Marcello's hysteria seems also to undercut his martial identity, ringing Freudian tones of dark sibling rivalries and sexual jealousy.[27] Certainly Marcello, in an oath, refers directly, as Cornelia has before, to the archetype of such rivalry, that of Eteocles and Polynices:[28]

>   Now by all my hopes,
> Like the two slaughtred sonnes of _Oedipus_,
> The very flames of our affection
> Shall turne two waies. (197-200)[29]

Surely Webster wants to avoid simplifying Flamineo; by having him directly attacked by the "virtuous" brother here, he gives him, as a victim, complexity. In this exchange Flamineo does not appear to act as a white devil. His family, already implicated in Vittoria's "whoredom" and its chain of sins, seeks to sustain a pretence of virtue, while their chief mover appears to be openly entertaining a socially and morally degrading alliance, as if to make fun of the very marraige he has worked so hard to attain, and which has made him so "happy." Here, if anywhere, we might be justified, nonetheless, in seeing the moral tables turned, and the saving remnants of the righteous revealed as tyrants of virtue.

But if Flamineo is to be perceived as a consistent character, it may be more appropriate that he be considered a laughing _provocateur_ here, using his love, as he did his pandarism in I.ii, as a weapon of revenge against his family. Marcello declares "war" on Flamineo, presenting himself as the scourging satirist ("I'le whip/This folly from you," 192-3), with a sense of righteousness that adds personal insult to the injury of his public success as a soldier. O'ertopped by his younger brother, Flamineo expresses a wished fantasy in the form of a curse: "I do suspect my mother plaid foule play, / When she conceiv'd thee" (196-7). Marcello perceives this outburst as a disownment of brotherhood, almost a paternal disownment as well, in that Flamineo is elder son in a fatherless family. As Marcello is close in feeling and values to his mother, and like Giovanni acknowledges and reverences motherhood, Flamineo's words are to

Chapter VII

The Black Book

Monticelso's "black booke," containing "The names of all notorious offenders / Lurking about the city" (IV.i.33-34) transports him for the duration of its exposition from Rome to London. He becomes the chronicler of rogues and vagabonds, in effect, of the "underworld." His prototype is the actual magistrate Thomas Harman. Harman's famous, much-plagiarized <u>Caveat or Warning for Common Cursitors, Vulgarly Called Vagabonds</u> (1566) first listed (alphabetically) the actual names of all notorious offenders lurking about the country in his time.

The currency and popularity of rogue pamphlets, most derived from Harman, at the time <u>The White Devil</u> was first presented, would have clued an audience instantly to the generic topicality of Monticelso's black book. This is particularly true since the phrase "black book" was euphemistic for a rogue pamphlet; members of the audience might have read two related works with the phrase in its title: Robert Greene's <u>The Black Book's Messenger</u> (1592), meant to be prefatory to his neverwritten <u>Black Book</u>, and Thomas Middleton's <u>The Black Book</u> (1604). The pamphlets most closely tied to this section in Webster's play are those of Middleton and Dekker, associates and collaborators of his, whose own topical London play, <u>The Roaring Girl</u> (1608) similarly incorporates rogue-gazetteer and glossary material, from Dekker's <u>Belman of London</u> and <u>Lanthorne and Candlelight</u>.

Two elements of London underworld literature stand out in Monticelso's description of his own black book: the diabolic analogy (the underworld as hell), and the nocturnal setting (rogues work their tricks at night, and, as it were, on the night side of life). But the contemporary underworld exposés depend on a <u>quality</u> of realms: a world of light and honest dealing is being undermined by the social (and, metaphorically, spiritual) forces of darkness. Webster's <u>whole</u> realm is suffused with darkness, however, and almost everyone in it is diabolical. To the accustomed audience, a chronicle of rogues implies a battle between the semi-allegorical forces of good and evil; in Webster's ironic treatment, both sides are in darkness, and diabolism is universal. The differences are only of degree.

Inserted at this moment in Webster's play, when Italian society's chief movers and great men have already been confirmed as dark and evil, Monticelso's black book therefore plays him as a sword, severing his most intimate bond. His response is an equally deep sword-thrust of words, as an ultimatum and challenge that permanently disowns his own brotherhood with Flamineo: "Those words I'le make thee answere/ With thy heart bloud" (200-201). Marcello's challenge to Flamineo foredooms his own destruction, since he is too honorable to subvert battle with treachery. He tells his attendant "beare him my sword, / And bid him fit the length on't" (203-4). This gesture is consonant with the etiquette of duelling--to insure that the combatants' swords are of equal length--but it innocently assumes that Flamineo is as honorable as he is. That Flamineo will run him through with the very sword he sent to insure fair play is an act of ultimate treachery, but it might also be considered a "fitting" retribution for Marcello's innocent blindness to evil.

Zanche, alone on stage, makes advances to Francisco in his Moorish disguise, with an ironic aside: "I neere lov'd my complexion till now" (206). This exclamation is interesting as an insight into Webster's view of a black person's psychology. Zanche apparently perceives a separation between her "self" and her color, and is discontent within her own skin. Complexion can also be temperament, and she can be experienced as loving one of an equally diabolical temperament. But Francisco is not really of her complexion, and here plays the white devil to her deceived black eyes. The deception is underscored by his rebuffing her love on grounds of his age, expressed seasonally ("Spring at Michaelmas") in the same figures that he used to dismiss his age in his deceptive love-sonnet to Vittoria. Zanche parries his hypocritical protestations ("I have vowed never to marry," 210), by offering to sell herself to him by way of her rich dowry. She analogizes the dowry to the presents sent with ambassadors to bribe princes' favors; thus, according to Monticelso, was Vittoria sold to Camillo, "better loved for [her] dowry than [her] virtue." The corruption of public affairs can be equivalent to the corruption of private love, and Zanche brings the two together by offering as her dowry "Intelligence" of, presumably, Brachiano's household. Thus this shadowy wooing, based itself on false premises, will be advanced by way of betrayal of the couple whose initial affair was first based on betrayal.

a role of ironic understatement, tinged with satire. What we have already seen is much worse than what is now to be paraded before our horrified eyes. The quality of irony is pointed by the tribute Francisco pays to the Cardinal for his virtue (Francisco has just asked to borrow the black book for his own black purposes):

> I do assure your Lordship,
> You are a worthy member of the State
> And have done infinite good in your discovery
> Of these offenders (IV.i.71-74).

To this hypocritical praise Monticelso answers drily "Some-what, Sir." Now, the authors of most rogue pamphlets sincerely or in pretence courted the image Francisco projects that of "benefactor of the state," discoverer of abuses, bringer of dark acts to light. Their self-image is that of healers of a wounded civic body. Harman, speaking as a Justice of the Peace, can claim credibility in this aim. When, he says, the rogues "indecent, doleful dealing and execrable exercises may appear to all, as it were, in a glass,"[1] there will, through new vigilance of Justices, sheriffs, and other authorities, be an "amendment of the commonwealth" in all areas. "Then shall this famous empire be in more wealth and better flourish, to the inestimable joy and comfort of the Queen's most excellent Majesty . . ."[2] Similarly, Robert Greene, in his <u>Notable Discovery of Cozenage</u> pretends to be the <u>honnête homme</u>, exposer of vice: "I am English born, and I have English thoughts, not a devil incarnate because I am Italianate."[3] He continues

> Seeing . . . such a dangerous enormity groweth by
> Cony-catchers to the discredit of the estate of
> England, I would wish the Justices appointed as
> severe Censors of such fatal mischiefs to shew
> themselves <u>patres patriae</u>, by weeding out such
> worms as eat away the sap of the Tree, and,
> rooting this base degree of Cozeners out of so
> peaceable and prosperous a country, for of all
> devilish practices, this is the most prejudicial.[4]

Thus Greene combines imagery of natural and spiritual corruption, both working underground, to characterize his rogues, and, also as Webster does, defines them by "degree."

The persona of Dekker's rogue pamphlets is the "bellman," who leads the reader into the night's "wilderness where are none but monsters,"[6] and casts his lantern's light to reveal and hold them at bay until cock-crow: "When all other men do rise / Then must I shut up mine eyes." His 1632 edition of <u>Lanthorne and Candlelight</u> dedicates his "discoveries" to the Justices of the Peace of Middlesex: "He is a true Justice that can search the disease to the bottom, and has medicines to cure it; and such are you."[7]

In this context of justifying discoveries of rogues by pamphleteers as instruments whereby civil authority and the law can uproot them, Monticelso's "discovery" is a very ironic instrument. Monticelso's rogues are discovered in order to become instruments of authorities for subverting authority. Not enemies of the magistracy, those in the Cardinal's black book are part-time employees of it. Francisco's valedictory "If any aske for me at Court, report / You have left me in the company of knaves" (IV.i.79-80) is witty not just because of its reference to the book of knaves, but because it is literally true; and those at Court are likewise knaves. Francisco, speculating on the identity of the complier of the black book, "honestly" discovers it to be a Judge himself, who will use it as a modern enforcer would, demanding payment to avoid inclusion in it.

Obviously some of the corrupt use of the Cardinal's black book depends on its <u>not</u> containing the same degree of underworld figures that other rogue pamphlets did. Beginning with Audeley's <u>Fraternitie of Vagabonds</u> (1561), a basic format for English rogue pamphlets was a taxonomy of villains and/or their villainies, by type and degree. Audeley lists them in "orders" and "companies," suggesting military or heraldic hierarchy; Harman lists his types of vagabonds by "degree" from higher to lower, paralleling the social hierarchy of the civil commonwealth of daylight. Dekker's rogues are in Regiments and Squadrons. <u>Martin Markall, Beadle of Bridewell</u> (1610) creates an entire <u>mundus alter et idem</u>, with its own topography, towns, orders of society, and a Grand Jury of rogues which indicts Dekker's Belman for libelling rogues. It is called the land of "Thievingen." Monticelso's black book, as he and Francisco summarize its contents, also catalogues the underworld as a dark mirror of respectable society's order, but his rogues are not entirely "outsiders," literal vagabonds with no support system in the society of light, living in another world. All of Monticelso's devils and knaves are patronized by, and do service to, "legitimate" members of society. Put another way, they do not undermine the commonwealth because they steal from it, but rather because they have corrupt commodities that legitimate society values enough to pay them for; they are even the basis of its self-perpetuation, to judge from the role they play in the survival of Webster's great men.

So Webster parodies the premises of rogue pamphlets not only by showing the actual evil of the "legitimate" authority that traditionally prosecutes the rogues, but also the actual legitimacy of those traditionally prosecuted as evil. Rather than with the Rufflers and Upright-Men of Harman's hierarchy of criminals (these are cashiered servants, soldiers, and the like, who rob under the guise of begging for charity), Monticelso begins his hierarchy of rogues with Intelligencers, hired <u>by</u> those in power to spy on their peers. His hierarchy, reading downward, includes pandars (like Flamineo), pirates (like

Lodovico), all of whom have aristocratic associations; middle-class politic bankrupts, wife-pandars and usurers; white-collar lawyers and divines. From this "generall catalogue of knaves," Francisco chooses the one category not inherently sanctioned by some form of legitimacy--murderers--for further study, and eventual employment.

So Webster uses the conventions of the rogue pamphlet to reinforce his portrayal of an entirely corrupt society; the dualities of light and dark, virtue and vice, underworld and this world are applied to an actual realm monochromatically dark, vicious, and diabolical, and the conventions of duality take on an ironic presence. This manipulation can be made clearer if it is related to a recent, and widely read, pamphlet, Dekker's Lanthorne and Candle-light. Or, The Bell-mans second Nights walke (1608).

This work is an elaborated sequel of his original Belman; it was to be followed by further elaborations and amended editions. The structuring conceit of Dekker's work is the diabolical visit to the earth from hell, a widespread situation, given popularity and wide currency by Thomas Nashe's Pierce Penniless. Although the section on sins of daylight, which Dekker added to the Belman in 1612 as "O per se O" and is more a catalogue of rogues in the manner of Harman, blurred the diabolical visit as a governing situation, Dekker displayed it fully in his neglected 1612 play, If this Be not a Good Play, the Devil is in It. In Dekker's conceit, the general court sessions in hell are broken up by the disconcerting news that the belman's light has been interfering with diabolical dealings on earth, and the messenger Pamersiel is sent to counteract his revelations by creating more sins in the city. Dekker's Court in Hell is paradoxical in a way; there sinners, such as those represented in the Cardinal's black book, are given infernal punishments: "The courtier is sued here and condemned for riots. The soldier is sued here and condemned for murders . . . The citizen is sued here and condemned for the City-sins (their wives for pride and servants for stealth)."[8] On the other hand, the devils are the very instigators of sins. Dekker's devils practice entrapment. This vicious cycle, even though it is not necessarily meant to be taken with dreadful seriousness, has its earthly analogy in the behavior of the great in The White Devil, especially as the arraignment of Vittoria provides a court-scene engineered by devils. The "vicious cycle" in The White Devil can flourish--until the rise of Giovanni at the end--because no representative or embodiment of a realm other than the World and the Underworld exists to intervene in the cycle.

Another deterministic and pessimistic conceit shared by Dekker's pamphlet and Webster's play is that of the diabolic disguisement. Pamersiel instigates vicious behavior by putting on the garb of different trades and social roles--initially he is "translated into an accomplished gallant with all accoutrements belonging,"[9] and he implicitly, if not directly, disguises him self as other urban and rural villains later. Eschewing all allegory, Webster still manages to imply with persistent epithetization as "devil" of all the characters (two examples among many: I.ii.246, of Vittoria, and V.iii.103, of Flamineo) that their outward human shape is the "accoutrement" only of their actual devilish natures. It can be said of Vittoria, as Dekker says of the horse-courser (changing the pronouns), "Neither steps he upon the Devil's stage alone, but others are likewise actors in the selfsame scene and sharers with him . . . of these ravens there be sundry nests, but all of them as black in soul as the horse-courser with whom they are yoked in conscience."[10]

In the cycle of sins, and the devilish disguisement, ideas, as well as in the whole tenor of their works, Dekker and Webster both seem to have the appearance of fatalism, and if their works are to be taken at face-value, faithlessness. There is no presence of a book of the godly to vie with the black book of the vicious. The Belman is a narrative device, not an actual character with virtuous attributes; and if Giovanni is Webster's belman, he is, as Lodovico says (V.vi.287-89) of the same blood as his diabolical uncle, whose diabolical disguise his light of virtue could not see through. Dekker goes so far as to say that the "most part of men" are "by the sorcery of their own devilish conditions transformed into wolves [a favorite Websterian figure] and, being so changed [are], more brutish and bloody than those that were wolves by nature . . ."[11]

It is hard to find in this stance any hope for human betterment, unless the reader assumes that the statements of the earth's moral conditions are deliberately hyperbolic, and places Dekker's pamphlet and Webster's play in the context of "prophecy," as Jeremiads. But neither Dekker nor Webster implies the threat of divine retribution. In fact, it is intriguing to find Dekker's Belman, the only representative of any kind of light in his work, gaining his information about the villainies Pamersiel has uncovered in a scene very similar to the one wherein the Cardinal shares his Black Book with the Duke. Meeting the Belman on his way back to hell, the devilish messenger mistakes him "for some churlish hobgoblin, seeing a long staff on his neck, and therefore to be one of his own fellows."[12] It is upon "questioning with him how he had spent his time in the City and what discovery of land villainies he had made in this Island Voyage," that "the mariner of Hell opened his chart which he had lined with all abuses lying either east, west, north or south,"[13] and it is the copy he has made of this map that the Belman reveals to the reader in Dekker's pamphlet. So even the Belman has to become a devil, in the view of the other devil, in order to gain the moral awareness of evil. These scenes of confidential sharing of dark knowledge, Dekker's and Webster's both, can convey a double message. They do allow the audience to feel itself in a morally privileged position, as witness to the secret map of all abuses; but they also convey the sense that the complete picture of evil in the world is so carefully hidden and inaccessible to the virtuous that no individual or institution with virtuous intent could gain the knowledge necessary to make the world white again.

Chapter VIII

Fourth Movement: "The bed of snakes is broke."

V.ii

Cornelia is strategically a "minor" character in terms of the number of scenes she is allowed in <u>The</u> <u>White</u> <u>Devil</u>.[1] Although she is lamentative and choric, it is necessary to Webster's purpose that not too large a choric constituency of virtue be found in his Italy. Therefore, he presents her as monitory as the beginning of the play, and as lamenting an ultimate fatality at the end, but not in process, where her worlds could, even in failure, mitigate the disaster her family meets. Ophelia, her model in her madness, is much more persistently present. Since her family follows Brachiano on his pilgrimage from Rome to Padua and destruction, one is led to feel she is the creature of her childrens' wills, despite her condemnation of them, and in contrast to other ambitious matriarchs in drama.

Cornelia is first seen as Flamineo's most violent and outspoken opponent (I.ii.205), where she already prophesies her house sinking to ruin. In V.ii she is, in a macabre way, the imitator of his own madness in Act III, except, of course, his is dissimulated and hers, presumably, real. In both roles she is more perceptive than anyone else of the inner truth of external events, and in both cases she shakes Flamineo's solipsistic invulnerability as no one else can. To the degree that Marcello shares her values, and is intimate with her, Flamineo's fratricide in this scene is the closest he can get to a matricide he does not have the will or courage to commit. As well as this transference, jealousy of Marcello and fear of his mother's undeceived view of him might be seen to motivate the murder, although Dent sees the whole event as entirely "unintentional," and Flamineo's distraught response to it leading to his "disintegration."[2]

The preparation for this tragedy is Cornelia's entry with words of intimate concern for Marcello, since she has heard rumors of the impending duel. Her compassion immediately establishes a mood of frank concern and love which has previously found no voice in the play. It is certainly a love directly contrary to that voiced between Flamineo and Zanche in the preceding scene. To Marcello's evasions, Cornelia queries, with unconscious irony considering his innocence, "Will you dissemble?" (4). Marcello is incapable of dissumulation. His hiding the proposed duel out of "tender concern" for his mother is directly negated by the instant and unexpected sword-thrust, which

Flamineo accompanies with the single, neutral sentence "I have brought your weapon backe" (14). Webster's stage-direction "Flamineo runnes Marcello through," accompanying the sentence, gives no clue as to whether the act is to be perceived as deliberate or spontaneous and unpremeditated. In fact, it is striking that this one speech is one-third of Flamineo's entire utterances in the murder scene. The connotation of his uncharacteristic silence, as well as of his uncharacteristic direct action, may be that he has gone beyond the words with which he usually laces and justifies his actions. His will has preempted his wit; possibly he is to be considered, as Dent contends, to be appalled for once at his own nature.

Flamineo's silence is more emphatic in view of the heightened rhetoric of other witnesses to the deed. In one of Webster's more overt uses of symbolism, Marcello is given before his impalement a query to his mother: "Was not this crucifix my father's?" (10). He continues,

> I have heard you say, giving my brother sucke,
> Hee tooke the Crucifix betweene his hands,
> And broke a limb off (11-13)

Fast upon Cornelia's response, "Yes; but 'tis mended" (13), Flamineo enters and stabs his brother.[3]

If this crucifix is, as it seems, around Cornelia's neck, and Marcello refers to it as "this," staging would require them to be very close together, Marcello holding the crucifix, when Flamineo runs him through. The implied staging would emphasize the physical intimacy of Marcello and Cornelia, and Flamineo's "distance" from them, almost as though he were stabbing both of them, certainly as one who is banished from their union. Thus, as well as its obvious prophetic value, placing Flamineo in the position of a Judas, a typological Cain, abusing the symbol of New Testament sacrifice, the cross also connotes maternality and paternality. It was the gift, as children are often considered to be, of the father to the mother. Marcello's murder is a violation not only of humanity's _spiritual_ inheritance, but of the _natural_ life-prinicple of generation, of some inheriting from fathers through the agency (vessel) of mothers. Marcello and his mother can figure, in posture and inconography, the Son and his mother, in the mode of the _pieta_, and also the nursing relationship, the most sacramental natural act of union between generations. The conjunction of cross and sword at this moment demonstrates ironically the truth of Flamineo's comments on the dangers of mingling religion and politics, and provides an intense emblem of this mingling, as wrongly conducted, which pollutes all aspects of life in the play. The real, and archaic, orders of Crusading knighthood (parodied in the "Knights of Malta," etc.) do not break the cross when they wield the sword.

So Cornelia's "mended" is a false hope. The breaking of the cross, a type of the original sin that banished humanity miraculous environment of the Gospels, where the dead are called to life for God's sake. Even when she acknowledges the physical reality of his wounds, her "His bleeding inward will kill him" (34) can be taken metaphorically for the self-consuming grief of those who discover the death of the Hope of the World.

Amidst all this vain hope in rebirth, Cornelia's devotion takes a surprising turn. In the face of empty and conventional comforts ("Your kindest office is to pray for him," 41), distracted Cornelia uses Flaminesque language, ". . . you shall put us both into one coffin" (37), emphasizing the body of the dead, but also the possibility of sharing the death of the virtuous one and rising with him redeemed. This is the course of faith so extreme that Everyman's companions rejected its challenge.

Webster's skill in stage-movement is again manifested by Brachiano's entrance at this point, in the armor which will be his own coffin in the next scene. He is accompanied by Flamineo as his servitor. Unknowingly, Brachiano is witnessing a prophecy of his own doom. With the implied entrances of Lodovico and his crew earlier, we are now allowed a very ironic tableau of all parties to the subsequent murder, including the victim, as spectators of the present one. Brachiano's query of Flamineo, "was this your handy-worke?" (45) is ambiguous, although the word exudes the irony of understatement. In II.ii, paired politic and martial murders were experienced as artistic "handy-work" by a complacent Brachiano. Here, similarly paried murders, politic and martial, done for revenge and not the pretence of love, have an even more negative sense of "art" attached to them. Flamineo's response is also ambiguous: "It was my misfortune" (46). This seems to be the ultimate statement of self-banishment from human community--for a murderer to describe his act as an act of Fortune against him. Webster complicates Flamineo's self-isolation here by having Cornelia perform a similarly absolute act of self-sacrifice. Lying to cover up her detested son's murder, she denies his hand in it, accusing the onlookers who do not heed her calls to revive Marcello. In a sense she is ultimately right, since we can consider Marcello the victim of his society, wherein the virtuous cannot survive; he himself did issue the initial challenge to the duel. Cornelia also turns her self-sacrifice into action. "Shee runes to Flamineo with her knif drawne and comming to him lets it fall." This rejection of revenge under the most extreme provocation stands outside the texture of the play's values. It is a submission to an absolute ethic and rejection of the strongest possible wordly temptation to violate the "law of kind," shedding the blood of one's own family.

Brachiano, addressing Cornelia (as "Mother," describing her actual relation to him now, but also suggesting her generic identity here), receives a lying response from her to his question about Marcello's death. She has Marcello the aggressor, implying that Flamineo killed him in self-defense or with just from felicity in the infancy of the world, can be "mended" only temporarily by continual, renewed expiatory sacrifice, in the imitation of Christ. There is no absolute redemption. Flamineo's punishment for this act is to live in a condition representing humanity's: dependence on daily reprieves from a daily condemnation to death. But Flamineo himself is ultimate unregenerate. Killing his brother is a natural fulfillment of his initial, original childhood sin of breaking the cross. His resolve to go to "sanctuary" (see the bitter use of "sanctuary" in Ford's *Tis Pity She's a Whore*) resounds violently. Although he might achieve it literally, ultimate spiritual sanctuary is unattainable by this exile.

Marcello, in his death speech, alludes with understanding to the crucifix's prophecy. He says that "There are some sinnes which heaven doth duly punish, / In a whole family" (22-23). While this describes his own family, as well as the classical vision of tragic retribution represented by the house of Oedipus, his words also suggest the primal sin of the family of humankind. It seems there is a congruence between Adam's universal, and Flamineo's topical, overreaching. "This it is meaning both the act and its retribution to rise / By all dishonest meanes" (24-5). Marcello's final words are a monitory commonplace:

> Let all men know
> That tree shall long time keepe a steddy foote
> Whose branches spread no wider then the roote.
> (25-7)

It is hard not to see this tree as an Edenic one, as well as to associate it with other trees in the play, particularly the yew tree which grows in graveyards--gardens of death after the Fall--and whose spread is associated with the life of the senses. Marcello's tree is half-personified. It defines conditions of restraint and non-presumption in the individual, and the collective order of a society, state, or family.

Cornelia's response to her son's death is a disbelief, which, as in Lear's incredulity over Cordelia, is a dramatic convention. But Cornelia's insistence on life in the presence of literal death is, in the context of this play, also an act of that faith which is starved or absent in politic consciousnesses. Its exception, and analogy, is Isabeella, whose faith causes her to worship Brachiano's portrait, and keep alive his dead love. Flamineo is involved in both of these love-breakings. Cornelia's faith is expressed in the protestation "here's no body shall get anything by his death" (30). This is both a cynical and a naively idealistic assertion. The gratuity of the act, at least as it first appears to the audience, is consistent with the values of a society which devalues life, although Cornelia herself partakes enough of her society's values to accept the naturalness of killing someone for gain. Her "Let me call him againe for Gods sake" (31) suggests the provacation: ". . . hee fell with's head/Just in my bosom" (64-5). Her merciful treatment of Flamineo has no more effect on him than the Pope's merciful justice had on Lodovico. And, as the page says with limpid clarity, "This is not trew Madam" (66). The realization comes that Cornelia is using her own politic means to save Flamineo's life, which he has jeopardized by his impolitic action.[5] Cornelia cannot escape a compromise of her integrity. Even one absolute for virtue to the greatest extreme is forced to use some form of corruption to sustain that virtue.

Brachiano's response is unconsciously self-destructive. He perceives that Cornelia is lying, and will not grant Flamineo an absolute pardon. Rather he forces him to "beg" his life as an absolute dependent. He grants him "a lease of your life" (73), and Flamineo must receive a new pardon at the end of each day. This is an extremely moral punishment in that it does imitate in law humanity's existential condition under a Christian dispensation. It also rebounds on the lawgiver, since this will prove to be the last day of Brachiano's own lease on life. Flamineo's reply is perhaps meant ironically, but nonetheless appears as a concession to Brachiano's absolute power: "At your pleasure. / Your will is law now . . ." (75-76). Nothing could be further from the truth.

Simultaneously with these speeches, "Lodovico sprinckles Brachiano's bever with a poison." So that in the moment when he is prescribing a lease on life, and gaining a concession of the absoluteness of his will, Brachiano's life and will are doomed. The motivation he gives for condemning Flamineo is also impure. He will keep Flamineo "in awe" for "braving" him before (IV.ii), so this just condemnation is really as well an act of personal revenge.

This scene ends with the first and only speech from Brachiano's murderers. In calling for his beaver, Francisco interprets, aside, "Hee calls for his destruction" (79). As a murderer, Francisco is the most inappropriate speaker of a homiletic epitaph on Brachiano--: "The last good deed he did, he pardon'd murther" (82)--and also he is inaccurate, since we have experienced no good deeds to Brachiano's credit before, and a pardon for Flamineo is, in effect, a bad deed.

V.iii

The murder of Brachiano at the barriers integrates motifs developed in the preceding actions. Certainly, the barriers, as stylized combat become "art," represent the same ceremonial mirror of warfare that the vaulting horse did, and Camillo's murder receives retribution here. In both cases clear action is perverted to politic ends, although the action itself is an inadequate game-playing, mocking actual warfasre. Also in symmetry, it is poison on the real Brachiano's face that causes his death, while in II.ii poison on his painted face has caused his wife's death.

It is not clear whether stage directions imply that the barriers were on stage or not, at least at the original performance. Probably the detail of "first single paires, then three to three" implies stage-combat. If so, the "barre" (9) as on stage, with Vittoria by it, makes a dramatic pun on the court-room of Vittoria's arraignment before the bar in III.ii. Here there is a court of actual life-and-death judgement.

Brachiano's slow dying provides a number of speeches wherein he can ring changes on a new awareness of his world and his past, now that he is across the bar of life. Almost immediately he addresses his "strong heart" elegaically: "There's such a covenant 'tweene the world and it, / They're loath to break" (15-16). This is a profane covenant, the opposite of the Christian one. Devotion to the "world" rather than the "spirit" has led Brachiano into many evil actions. Having broken his covenant with God, breaking his covenant with the world would be the only way of redemption for Brachiano. But he does not see the "world" in this light. Instead, he yearns to offer "infinite worlds" to Vittoria, who, in his vision, is a "good woman" (obviously she contrasts to Cornelia who has just been seen by the audience as a true "good woman" in Christian terms).

Brachiano's admonition to Vittoria, "Do not kisse me, / for I shall poison thee" (27) is a clear recollection of Isabella's death, its contrast to that kiss underlining the symmetry of this retribution. More, Brachiano *is* "poisonous," and has already poisoned Vittoria with his passions. His reflections in this environment disconcertingly combine conventional deathbed piety and "pride of life." He wonders, having "given life" to so many condemned men (as his "lease on life" to Flamineo), "have I not power / To lengthen mine owne a twelve-month?" (25-6). The assumed power, and the spiritual ignorance giving rise to the question, are in the Marlovian tradition of the transcendent man who lives so deeply in the world that he cannot see its bounds. Brachiano's "given life" is particularly presumptuous, since the audience's experience of him is as a giver of death. His next speech is more difficult to interpret. Responding to Francisco's dark "Sir bee of comfort" (29), Brachiano seems stirred, by the stoic connotations of "comfort," to launch into a stoic contempt of death speech: "O thou soft naturall death, that art joint-twin / To sweetest slumber . . ." (30-31). The extreme conventionality of this "character" of death casts doubt on its speaker's sincereity. The Duke is opposed to stoicism (V.i.103), and despite the natural "distraction" of his dying, he seems to give this expression of yielding almost the quality of parody. Shortly afterward, leaving the stage, he exclaims ". . . let no man name death to me, / It is a word infinitely terrible--" (40)--not "soft and natural."

A modern witness might consider that Brachiano has broken through artifice to be "authentic," in eschewing "painted comforts" (I.i.50) for the confession of actual terror. Brachiano's terror is certainly due not only to the fear of death at this moment, but also to the awareness of the deaths he has created, and the eternal death which, if Christianity speaks truth, will devolve on him in retribution for these murders. On the other hand, if this *is* a redemptive and god-fearing attitude in Brachiano, before he lapses into total distraction (83), the stoicism he seems to parody is a valid attitude towards death, which contrasts, for example, to Cornelia's failure to accept it. This attitude, ridiculed by Lodovico when Antonelli proposes it to him (I.i.44-50) is ultimately embraced by the final victims in V.vi, including Lodovico, and may partly ennoble their ends.

It seems that the very presence of the community that Brachiano's position has fathered around him makes the quiet discipline of an acceptance of death seem almost absurd. To Vittoria's "I am lost forever," Brachiano responds "How miserable a thing it is to die, / 'Mongst women howling" (38-39). The spontaneous, yet traditional, expressions of mourning, such as those Cornelia exhibits, seems to suggest to Brachiano an imagined future state in hell, surrounded by howling spirits (cf. Vittoria in line 182, "this place is hell"). The presence of Lodovico and Gasparo also suggests the actual presence of hell, as they are wearing, presumably, the hooded and death-suggestive garb of Franciscans (in Flamineo's punning identification, they are of the Order of the Duke of Florence, a most deadly Order).

Flamineo, restored by the dramatist to his former garrulity as satiric observer, emphasizes the condition of Brachiano in his own hell, alienated from the full experience of his own dying by the presence of his entourage. He sees Brachiano as an emblem, illustrating the "solitarinesse . . . about dying Princes" (41). He parodies Brachiano's exclamation on mortality (24-27): "As heretofore they have unpeopled Townes; divorst friends . . . where are their flatterers now?" (43-44). The Flatterers (of which Flamineo himself is the clearest example) "are but the shadows of Princes bodies, the least thicke cloud makes them invisible" (46-47). Flamineo suggests that the Flatterers, et. al., become insubstantial to the Prince, who needs them no more and seeks only solitude for his dying; in their insubstantiality the flatterers become almost like the ghosts of the dead themselves. Likewise, the Prince, dying, is of no use to the flatterers, who therefore desert him. In a subsequent dialogue (47-66), Francisco, playing the innocent (and still, we remember, a Moor) draws Flamineo into confessing this second source of Princely solitariness to be most true for him, in his own disappointment at his lack of monetary reward for his flattery. As Brachiano's "shadow," Flamineo, of course, grieves only over the damage done to his own advancement. At the same time, he is willing to censure the Duke under the guise of being a bad "States-man" for being more interested in cannon-balls than human lives.

This dialogue is interrupted by Lodovico, who comes to report on Brachiano's increasing "follie" and "brain-sicke" language, which includes babbling of "Battailes and Monopolies, / Levying of taxes" (69-70). These are aspects of governance which, evidently, Brachiano can stoop to only when out of his senses. Flamineo fulfills the tenor of his preceding dialogue by responding "There's some good lucke in that yet" (79) to the news that Vittoria has been named guardian of Brachiano's estate.

The entrance of Brachiano, "presented in a bed," allows Webster to provide such a mad-scene as his contemporaries, and be himself, seemingly loved. The stage-directions read "These speeches are severall kinds of distractions and in the action should apeare." As often in such scenes, here the madman speaks with the sanity missing when he was sane. Brachiano accuses his audience of secular state-crimes, and resolves to be "mine owne Steward" (86). He takes a universal blame upon himself (87), for "was't ever knowne, the divell / Raild against cloven Creatures?" (89-90). Implied is the recognition that both he and his auditory are "of the devil," but since it is inappropriate for the devotees of the devil to chide their own kind, he will rail against himself. "Cloven creatures" can, of course, describe those who are hoofed, and humans in general, with their two legs. Flamineo, a cloven creature, black himself, never hesitates to "Chide blackness," and other devilish characters do likewise, so Brachiano's premise is false, but he is almost unique in following its conclusion and, as Cornelia does, blaming himself. In his subsequent mad-speeches, Brachiano's distorted vision does see those about him as they really are; his perspective for once corresponds with that of the audience, as he perceives the diabolical shapes beneath the seeming-human exteriors.

This distracted speech of Brachiano is a crucial passage, for here a moral vision is drmatically realized, one which is like in nature, but opposite in meaning, to Monticelso's character of a whore or Francisco's knaves. Brachiano does not stop at "social sins" in his enumeration. He sees the devil working through the social acts of those around him, and their essential spiritual depravity. In this condition, Brachiano is his own "conjuror"--he sees across metaphysical, not only physical, distance. and thereby gives full richness to the play's titular metaphor. The "Politian Florence" (93) is a dog or fox, and Brachiano such another. Brachiano sees the devil in full regalia, with pins in his codpiece (98-103)--another grim version of the sexual jewels pinned on Vittoria in I.ii.[7] He wonders that the others present can see only "nothing." He sees Flamineo--as Flamineo often sees others--in a static emblem:

> See, see, <u>Flamineo</u> that kill'd his brother,
> Is dancing on the ropes there; and he carries
> A monie-bag in each hand, to keepe him even,
> For fear of breaking's necke. (110-113)

The neck-breaking naturally refers to Camillo. Flamineo's true state of spiritual peril, dangling above the fiery abyss and sustained only by a fatal balance of purely material objects, Brachiano realizes more strongly than he does his wife's. But Vittoria is seen as a white devil literally, her hair sprinkled with Arras powder, "as if she had sinn'd in the Pastrie" (119). The climax of Brachiano's vision comes when Lodovico and Gasparo appear "in the habit of Capuchins," to provide last rites, with candle and crucifix. To the English audience, the Capuchins would be inherently great devils. In culminating Brachiano's parade of devils, they bring together his visions and reality from the audience's perspective, in a single image. As the others surround Brachiano and participate in the inverted deathbed ritual, the audience can see Brachiano in hell, literally "surrounded by devils." Even though his death agony has provided him a momentary vision of truth, this vision has no redemptive power within the play. It has merely allowed us to witness the loss of his soul in a condition of awareness of that loss, which may make the suffering greater.

The crucifix held by Lodovico and Gasparo, the mock "Churchmen," will recall Cornelia's broken crucifix, and the entire ritual can be considered a "breaking" and perversion of faith. Vittoria's exclamation on the crucifix "O hold it constant, / It settles his wild spirits; and so his eies / Melt into teares" (132-4) presents a false perspective; Vittoria pretends to see a redemptive breaking of wildness into humility and submission, but Brachiano's tears are of remorse, if anything, not of penitence. In any case, the constancy set forth in Vittoria's words is broken by the false recitations of the counterfeit Capuchins. The Latin phrases they utter in the public death-scene are orthodox enough (135-46),[8] urging Brachiano, in martial metaphor, to fortify himself against the enemies of his soul. But once the assembly has been urged out by them, in the interest of "private meditations" of the Capuchin's "order" (that is, the order of murderers), they invert orthodoxy. They curse him, and consign him into the arms of the enemy of his soul ("Devill <u>Brachiano</u>, / Thou art damn'd," 150-51), in a parody of the Commendatio Animae, which traditionally follows the offering of extreme unction in Catholic ritual.[9]

To an Anglican or Puritan audience, Latin ritual is itself diabolical; we may recall the Papal scenes in <u>Dr. Faustus</u>. Webster plays on his murderers' doubleness by having their diabolical Latin of the public ritual be "white" in content, and their straight-forward English of the private ritual be "black." Since the damners of Brachiano are themselves damned, for even more crimes than he has committed, it is hard to believe in the validity of their judgement of him. They are even less qualified to consign Brachiano to hell than the Cardinal was to sentence Vittoria to a House of Convertites. Still, their choric judgement, like that of the Duchess of Malfi's masquers, is to be seen as an ultimate crime-killing the soul, the hope of salvation, along with the body. By condemning Brachiano, the killers condemn themselves even more than before in the eyes of a Christian audience. And, in a sense, their own evil defeats itself. They identify themselves to their victim (166), in order to have the satisfaction of Brachiano's suffering by knowledge of their deception.

But their revelation revives Brachiano enough for him to cry "<u>Vittoria</u>! <u>Vittoria</u>!" That final cry is complex and ambiguous. It could well indicate a revived hope, and a reaching out to the crucifix. The re-entry of Vittoria at these words might suggest this. Certainly, as an isolated cry, her name can take on its generic meaning of "victory," this relating to the imagery of the murderers' Latin incantations, where Brachiano is in war against the devil. But whose victory is it? More likely hers, or the devil's, than his own. Brachiano could also be felt to be calling upon the cause of his fall, and his cry could resound as a judgement upon her. The implications of his cry somewhat depend on whether Brachiano is presented on stage as actually hearing and understanding the damning words of his murderers. At his cry, Lodovico responds, with irony, "O the cursed devill, / Come to himselfe againe!" (17071). If, therefore, he is unconscious before, the purpose of the murderers' denunciation would have to be a communication with themselves--a venting of spleen--or with God, and not with him; perhaps they are to be considered justifying their murder as an execution deserved. If Brachiano cannot hear their words, his cry for Vittoria cannot be considered to express an awareness that he has been damned. I tend to feel the murderers' words are meant to sink into Brachiano's consciousness somehow, not to be just a revelation to the audience of their state of mind. That Brachiano must be killed a second time, having risen from the dead with the cry of victory on his poisoned lips, signals a failure of the attempt to kill his spirit (such a rebirth is mocked by Flamineo shortly before his real death in V.6). The murderers themselves remain, at least on the surface, unaware of the true nature of their act, or of its probable failure in the damnation Lodovico has so yearned for. They appeal to "charity" in clearing the chamber for the final suffocation of Brachiano, and Lodovico compares his practice favorably with that of the mercy-killing of charity hospital inmates. Lodovico's final gesture is called by him "a true-love knot/ Sent from the Duke of Florence" (175-6), even here parodically referring to the love-letter to Vittoria that sent Brachiano on his road to Florence and doom.

The staging of the next dramatic moment is disconcerting. Vittoria immediately enters with Flamineo and Francisco, exclaims "O mee! this place is hell" (182), and leaves the stage again. Although there is artifice in this swift entry and departure, there is also the connotation of "truth to life," because of spontaneity found in Flamineo's fratricide and Cornelia's attack on Zanche. Because Vittoria's pronouncement is so isolated and unadorned it comes across as "true," as the most complete and accurate definition possible of "this place," which can be the space where Brachiano dies, Padua, or all of Italy itself, if not the world.

Vittoria's exclamation also stands out as accurate in contrast to the subsequent philosophizing of Francisco and Flamineo, who apparently feel free to weave speculations on the murder at length while the tableau of dead Brachiano, surrounded by his killers, stands before them. Flamineo reflects cynically on Vittoria's grief ("There's nothing sooner drie than womens teares," 189), and bewails the "end" of his "harvest": Brachiano has given him "nothing." The grim reaper has reaped Flamineo's future with his master. With "white" disingenuousness the disguised Francisco speculates that "this was Florence doing" (193). Flamineo elaborates on this speculation by distinguishing--again--between the "killing strokes" of the "Machivillian" (Francisco) and the "waightie" strokes of the "grosse plodding slave" (193-96). The Machiavellian is successful because his strokes come from the "head." Clearly Flamineo is ambivalent; he regrets the murder but admires it as a work of art.

This ambivalence continues through Flamineo's further thinking. He ironically sympathizes with Brachiano's doomed reputation, now he is dead: "Miserie of Princes, / That must of force bee censur'd by their salves!" (204-5)--he himself being, of course, one of the censuring slaves. He comes out with another tentative conclusion, relating to his earlier dialogue with Francisco in V.i, that, therefore, "One were better be a thresher," or, presumably, slave, although "thresher" connects with "harvest," a few lines back, and therefore, with death as the real leveller. Flamineo's final speculation is on speaking with Brachiano again, even though he is dead. " I cannot conjure," he says (211), which is, in some senses of this oft-used word, a lie, but he swears that if prayers or oaths have any effect, he will speak with him, even in the depths of hell. If Flamineo's ambivalent feelings bespeak a "losing of control" in him at this point, so does this resolve, since he does not think to refute its prophecy that he will soon go to hell, will "bee blasted" (215), by the "Excellent Lodovico!" (215) who steps forward to be addressed at this very prophetic moment.

What Lodovico introduces to Flamineo at this moment is his "infernall" (220) lover, Zanche. Francisco's address to her is powerful: "You're passionately met in this sad world" (223). This seems to imply that her entry is positive or redemptive, as it brings back life-affirming concerns; but, in a Christian perspective, passion is the cause of sadness in the world, and her presence can only make it more sad. What Zanche comes to tell is a fairly obviously fabricated "dream," as though in

imitation of the dream Vittoria tells, and she overhears, in
I.ii, of Francisco sneaking into her bed at night. Francisco
chooses to pre-empt her dream by inventing a similar one about
her, and the two exchange, strophically, details of their
imaginary dreams in the way that Flamineo and Lodovico exchanged details of their imaginary "housekeeping" in III.iii.
Here, Lodovico takes on the role of satiric commentator to this
"strange encounter." Saying "Marke her I prethee, shee simpers
like the suddes A Collier hath bene washt in" (248-49), he in
effect calls her a white devil. Zanche then reveals to Francisco, as Mulinassar, the "intelligence" which is, as she
believes, her dowry: the poisoning death of Isabella, and
"damn'd <u>Flamineo's</u>" actual responsibility for Camillo's death.
It is this news that Lodovico greets with "The bed of snakes is
broke" (256).

Of course, this revelation plays on much dramatic irony.
The intelligence is not news either to the audience or to those
on stage; in fact, only Zanche can experience it as news. But
it is also the open, "white" articulation of a fact that has
been assumed continually, been a motivator of a chain of
deception and destruction. This is probably what Lodovico means
in his exclamation: the murders have been publicly described
and acknowledged. On the one hand, dissimulation is no longer
as necessary as it was after this statement, but it also gives
heightened necessity for a "final solution": the extermination
of the Coromboni, and their black familiar. Therefore Zanche's
intelligence has the further irony that in confessing it on the
hope of bringing passion into her life, she seals her death
warrant and brings more sadness into the world.

The frankness of Zanche's intelligence is itself hypocritical. She, also, parodies confession: "I sadly do confesse
I had a hand/ In the blacke deed" (257-8), and, "urg'd with
contrition" (260) she confides her plan to rob Vittoria to
furnish her imagined flight from Padua with her Mulinassar. This
plan is characterized by Lodovico as "Excellent penitence!"
(260). It is parodic of the flight of Brachiano and the stolen
Vittoria from Rome; it is even more a product of illusion. The
further erosion of politic successes is represented here in
Zanche's total obliviousness to the folly of her plan, or to
the deceptions under which she herself labors. There is also a
parody of the materialism that governs politic lives: Zanche
believes that all the money she will steal will defy the proverb,
and will "<u>wash</u> <u>the</u> <u>Ethiop</u> <u>white</u>" (270), not thinking of the real
nature of her blackness in the minds of others.

It is true that on her departure (momentary), Francisco
exclaims "why till now we knew not/The circumstance of either
of their deaths" (273-74), but this is an ironic quibble. They
"knew" the <u>perpetrators</u>, but not the circumstance. Francisco's
observation allows Lodovico the strange statement "Why now our
action's justified" (276). This is a curious defense from

someone whose reputation is that of obliviousness to all values. Francisco seems to consider it a true, and not an ironic, expression, for he replies with protest, "Tush for Justice!" (277). The _ex_ _post_ _facto_ appeal to justice is no more valid than the absolute dismissal of it. But Francisco crowns his dismissal of justice with his own self-justification. The murderers' acts (past and contemplated) have "purged" the disease of the state, and "the fame / Shall crowne the enterprise and quit the shame" (279-80). Francisco uses the traditional tyrant's excuse for his tyranny, one which echoes down the centuries. Politic action is an evil necessary to restore order, however much it may violate the principles on which order is founded. He even acknowledges the "shame," not recognizing that no fame can acquit shame, since fame is wordly and amoral. The Christian commonwealth cannot survive unless its rulers are guided, as in the chivalric ideal, by shame and fame, in the sense that its accomplishments must be grounded in, and limited by, a moral code.[11]

V.iv

This scene is summarized, in its three movements, by Flamineo in his concluding soliloquy:

> . . . the disgrace
> The Prince threw on mee; next the pitious sight
> of My dead brother; and my Mothers dotage;
> And last this terrible vision of Brachiano   (138-41)

These climaxing encounters separate Flamineo from all sources of support or reassurance outside himself. He is drawn into a sharing of Brachiano's final condition of "solitariness," experiencing as a social condition the self-reflectiveness that has characterized his language throughout the play. Flamineo is paradoxically forced away from his role as satiric commentator and politic manipulator by the consequences of actions he has taken or induced in those roles. At the center of the audience's concern, and the play's action, from the time he murders his brother, he has no personal center or governing self-image necessary to sustain that position. He has not possessed any sustaining illusions, as for example Shakespeare's Richard II has, which can fill his awareness in this condition of deprivation and can give a tragic cast to his situation. The banishment from court, from family, and (in acknowledging Brachiano's ghost) from his own politic materialism, in this scene, leave him "naked." Needing an antagonist by whom to define himself, he turns against the only survivors--his sister and her servant. In resolving, as he does at the scene's end (142-3), to gain Vittoria's wealth, or kill her, he is pitting himself again against his own blood, and also against the source of whatever assets or preferment he has possessed. His resolve is in effect a resolve to suicide; he will precipitate a final annihilation of his family, in a way a suicide of society, since the family is to society as the individual is to the family, a basic and necessary constituent. Flamineo's destruction of his sister will be a counterpart to and consequence of Francisco's avenging of his, which is similarly destructive in the long run, but more frequently justified, in terms of fame or honor, in Renaissance morality.

Giovanni's initial rejection of Flamineo is itself symbolic of a family restored through the son's maturation. Giovanni's counterpart in virtue, Marcello, no longer exists to restore his family, and Flamineo's "restoration" has been its opposite. Flamineo begins the scene with one of his allusive fables. He does not think Giovanni "sweet," as Gasparo does, but sees him as the peacock sees the eagle, "fairer" than he, were it not for the eagle's talons. Flamineo's allegory is true to his politic philosophy, in which power plays the role that beauty is due. It is also true prophetically, and with dramatic irony, since Flamineo will soon feel the "sweet" prince's talons. Applied to the whole play, eagle and peacock certainly do figure the martial ideal and the corrupt courtly spendor that has usurped the martial ideal and the corrupt courtly spendor that has usurped it. As in Cymbeline, the eagle relates to the restoration of royalty from corruption and banishment--as Prince Henry would restore Elizabethan values clouded in Jacobean decadence.

But Flamineo misjudges Giovanni's adulthood. He says his talons will grow out "in time," but this time is immediately. In absolute contrast to his father's, Giovanni's first word to the parasite are words of dismissal: "I pray leave me Sir" (9). Giovanni is both martial and politic in that he does not, even in wrath, "engage" himself with Flamineo. Flamineo is exiled. Exile is merciful to Lodovico, whose realm is action, but is terrible to the would-be politician, whose realm is intrigue, and who needs to be present in court to flourish.

Flamineo responds by attempting an obviously misguided seduction of Giovanni through appeal to his new power. He is now "ith saddle" (18), and "by himself." The appeal may also allude to the vaulting horse and barriers incidents: those in the saddle are most likely to fall off and break their necks. Giovanni's response is terse, stern, and, interestingly Protestant:

> Study your praiers, sir, and be penitent,
> 'Twere fit you'd thinke on what hath former bin--
> I have heard griefe nam'd the eldest child of sinne.
> (17-19)

As well as parodying in its single line (19) Flamineo's elaborate secular allegories, Giovanni casts Flamineo's entire condition into a context where all the forces Flamineo evokes and believes in (e.g., talons) have no value in themselves. Giovanni's three-line sermon is also somewhat of a rebuke of the elaborately figured sermons of other hypocritical representatives of moral order and abusers of language, such as the new Pope. As Flamineo says to this, "he threatens me divinely." Giovanni assumes that the most substantial threat to Flamineo must be spiritual, not material. In so doing he upends the assumptions of all his materialistic peers, first articulated in the initial scene. "What hath former bin" is not merely the recent secular history, wherein Flamineo's sins are writ, but the Christian history of falls from the original Edenic state. In Protestant terms, we are all guilty and children of sin, and we all suffer thereby. Flamineo is living proof of this, having been engaged, both as tempting devil and fratricidal Cain, in reinactments of the world's first crimes. The Christian consciousness empathizing with Giovanni's words might see their very expression as a step towards restoring the fallen world of his time and place.

Flamineo's bantering response to Giovanni is ambiguous. Certainly "I am falling to peeces already" (21) makes fun of the seeming insubstantiality of Giovanni's thunderbolt, yet it also suggests how little Flamineo has expected such a reply. Flamineo lets his own imagination lead his response into the conceit of a usurer in "peeces" beat together with gold "to make a most cordiall chullice for the devill" (24). Hinting that usurers, rather than he himself, are the true enemies of the state, fit for Giovanni's rebukes, he also creates the imagery of a blackmass's sacrament, and seems to characterize his own spiritual status thereby. He is more shaken by Giovanni's sending a courtier to signal his exile from the court. Giovanni is using distance as a weapon, and disconcerts him by employing one of his own species against him. The courtier, however, has his master's own curtness, and answers only "Very good: you are merry" (40) to Flamineo's long protest. It seems that the Prince's mood casts an aura over the entire environment of the court, and even courtiers cease to be peacocks. Flamineo is immune to this influence, and continues his protestation, likening himself to a naked woman committed to Castle Angelo (for which one might read the Tower of London). Such a parallel refers once again to the expulsion from Paradise, at the same time indicating how ultimately unregenerate Flamineo is, in being able, without shame, to liken himself to an image of total vulnerability. Perhaps this comparison should communicate an as yet unmanifested sense of vulnerability in him.

Following the courtier, the disguised Francisco enters with news of Cornelia's "distraction." His description of the doleful "winding of <u>Marcello's</u> coarse" (49) has a "solemne" tone beyond satire. Whereas Francisco is blinded by his tears, Flamineo "will see them" (58). This resolve allows Webster to present his tableau of grief on the inner stage without spatial incongruity, but might also indicate that Flamineo is attracted to any "extreamity." He wants to experience fully the history of his own act. Although, using faithlessly Brachiano's phrase, he would discover "Their superstitious howling," the urge to do so is to "look death in the face"--to test his ability <u>not</u> to feel the need to be penitent or to acknowledge an order beyond his own will.

The position of the five ladies Flamineo sees winding the corpse could mirror that of the Marys with the body of the deposed Christ. Cornelia's speeches and song, however, contain nature-imagery directly indebted to distracted Ophelia. This scene is of "the eldest child of sin," or grief incarnate, as Christ's death might be considered in Christian history. Cornelia's own identity here is expanded, as though it is meant to embrace a great extent of history. She is "growne a very old woman in two howers" (48) according to Francisco, but also "her grief / Hath turn'd her child againe" (70). Cornelia's distracted vision, as a counterpart to dying Brachiano's, also allows her to see essential truth beyond appearances, but her vision is more encompassing. As both old and young, she is expanded beyond individuality into an ur-maternality. Encompassing her Christian reference is her pagan connection with the earth and the life that springs from it. Webster allows her to identify Flamineo, as Brachiano does in his mad scene, with evil, in ironic ways. She mistakes him for the "grave-maker" (76), which of course he is, sees his hand sinfully "speckled," and calls for cowslip water as good for the memory--with the same emphasis as Giovanni on his remembering his sins. In more universal terms she gives folk-reference for death associated with natural magic (77-84), and her famous song, "Call for the Robin-Red-brest and the wren--" (89-98) limns a pagan burial of dead, like that in <u>Cymbeline</u>, ministered by the creatures of nature, who will both bury and memorialize the dead. The literal source of her song, as Cornelia "explains" (99-100), is that Marcello has been denied a Christian burial because he died in a quarrel, not in a state of penance or with godly mind. This is the state in which Lodovico sought to kill Brachiano, but it is not clear whether Brachiano retained the sanction of the church. We cannot take Cornelia's song as a "pure lyric" alone, since it is so tied to the play's dramatic circumstances. It may be considered a reformer's statement about religion. In a world where virtuous Marcello is denied salvation through a technicality of ecclesiastical law, and the vicious are embraced or tolerated by the church, and even govern it, a pagan burial is more sacramentally significant than a Christian one would be. It calls together a harmony of creation, and is free from the corruption of "gay tombes" (as it were, "whited sepulchres").

Cornelia's song alludes to the condition of Eteocles and Polynices again, as fratricidal brothers, and the question of their burial. Cornelia cannot help bringing awareness of the fatality of this ancient house as a precedent for her own, and the similar visitations of an original sin on succeeding generations. In Cornelia's imagination, though, the sins of the house, almost predestined, work together with freely performed acts of sin in the immediate environment. The "wolfe" of her song, who might disinter a buried Marcello, though "foe to men"

(97) is <u>within</u> every man. Cornelia's final threat to the universe, which is also a complaint, is that "This poore men get; and great men get no more" (105). This recalls Flamineo's discussion with the disguised Francisco--all are of the same clay, wherever they are set in the wall (V.i.105-110). Cornelia's restatement of this formulation reinforces and gives the lie to it at the same time. Francisco, dissimulating, expresses it in terms of relative poorness and greatness in the world of the living. Cornelia's vision of death as an equalizer rebukes the premises of life through which Francisco can feel free to make his own statement, in which he does not believe, so glibly.

Flamineo's reflection on this mad-scene has been sentimentalized by critics:

> I have a strange thing in mee, to th'which
> I cannot give a name, without it bee
> Compassion-- (107-9)

That compassion is the author's word, and may epitomize the moral viewpoint from which he wishes all the action to be seen, is true. But Flamineo's compassion is the subject of Flamineo's concern. He is not responding to his mother's situation as "real," but is observing his own reaction to it, and as a commentator on his reaction, naming it "compassion." His succeeding words of seeming confession, "I have liv'd / Riotously ill, like some that live at court" (112-113),[12] follow a resolution to find out what his sister, as Brachiano's heir, will give him for his service. His "confession" is calculated. That he has smiled despite the "mase of conscience in my brest" (114) in context of his quest for reward implies that he deserves greater reward for having sustained his smile and overcome the disruptive conscience.

I would not contend that Flamineo's sudden moral insight here is meant to be seen as pure hypocrisy. But certainly there is not the slightest "regeneration" involved, and it is more in the nature of a neutral phenomenon which he observes in himself through a perspective glass. The telling commonplace with which he sums up this momentary insight--"Wee thinke caged birds sing, when indeed they crie," 117--obviously refers back to the figure (I.ii.41 ff.) of caged and free birds which initiated the theme of his solipsism. Here it can, presumably, describe Flamineo himself as hypocritically smiling, "caged" within the politic identity he has created for himself, but actually crying with frustrated compassion. The subjection, vulnerability, hidden and misunderstood grief, that Flamineo attributes metaphorically to himself serve to establish the image of one forced to perform acts that he inwardly rejects. The strategy of this monologue seems preparative to the similar strategy of action whereby Flamineo feigns submission to his sister and to Zanche, a submission going to the extremity of suicide, in order to get outside the cage (room) in which they are all trapped. It is

difficult to accept that any use of penitential language by
Flamineo can be sincere, in view of his addiction to the abuse
of language. It is notable however that Brachiano's ghost
appears to Flamineo at this moment of seeming vulnerability to
spiritual influences, as Isabella appeared to Francisco at a
moment of seeming sincere grief. Flamineo had asserted that
he would speak to the dead Brachiano if prayers or oaths could
make it possible, and maybe his pose of contrition is as close
to prayer as he can get.

Brachiano's ghost has a different aspect to Flamineo than
Isabella's presented to Francisco. It is richer in iconography,
yet for this very reason seems to have less of the physical
force of an actual presence. Flamineo's Brachiano, as ghost,
communicates himself as Flamineo's idea of what a ghost should
look like: constructed out of his own brain, and not "given"
to him through the grace or wrath of a higher power. In fact,
Flamineo exclaims "What a mockerie hath death made of thee"
(120), suggesting that he can envisage death only in his own
image as a satirist of life. The stage directions indicate a
Brachiano who is garbed in both military and religious fashion,
with "leather Cassock & breeches, bootes," but also "a coule."
He wears the garb of his persecutors, the "Capuchins," as well as
his own self-imaged garb. He also bears a "pot of lilly-flowers
with a scull in it"--which can certainly be a memento mori emblem combining the imagery of resurrection and of mortality.[13]
But the skull and the lillies recreate a repeated verbal motif
of Flamineo--new life growing from a graveyard, turves to feed
larks (as in IV.ii.67). In both Brachiano's garb and his burden,
death contradicts life, and the philosophical cul de sac of
Flamineo's own thoughts, life having "no purpose" (128), is
mirrored. While the reality of Brachiano's ghost, as Webster's
own audience may have felt it, will probably always be problematic, it does seem that the ghost provides a satire of
Flamineo's own temperament by presenting him with a mirror of
his own mind coming from beyond death, but by denying him any
breakthrough awareness that either doom or release, or anything
else, awaits him.

Flamineo, examining the ghost, is also less troubled than
Francisco seems to be by his ghost. I would not agree that,
viewing the ghost, "Flamineo's poetry rises in tension as he
mistakenly believes he has plunged deeper toward self-under-
standing."[14] He asks appropriate existential questions of his
visitant, but does not wait on the answers, and his questions
are all couched in a manner that suggests he has already
concluded that conditions after death are (see III.ii.331-4)
the same as, or a mirror of, mortal life. ". . . What religions
best / For a man to die in?" (122-3) reduces religion to a
secular choice of death-garments. He also speculates that the
silent ghost may be, like great men living, a shadow walking up
and down "to no purpose." Flamineo's satire of the insubstantiality of wordly great men, such as those he himself has served
in search of substantial reward. which could be used to convey a
Christian skepticism toward the World, describes them as mirrors

of an equally insubstantial world of the Spirit. Flamineo
rejects both this world and the next, and goes "beyond melan-
cholie." To be beyond melancholy is to be beyond worldly and
spiritual despair at one's condition, and therefore beyond the
need of spiritual or material regeneration. Hence, Flamineo,
as "alone in the void," resolves, "I doe dare my fate / To doe
its worst" (136-7). Any monitory effects of Brachiano's ghost
have been totally lost on him, and he reaffirms his belief in a
blind fatality. His conclusion reduces the "horrours" the
audience has witnessed, which he himself has been a prime mover
of, to events impinging on his own fate alone, not involving any
of the other actual participants:

> . . . the disgrace
> The Prince threw on mee; next the pitious sight
> Of my dead brother; and my mothers dotage;
> And last this terrible vision. All these
> Shall with Vittoria's bountie turn to good,
> Or I will drowne this weapon in her blood.   (140-44)[15]

For Flamineo, a gift of money to him can be a good redeeming all
the suffering he has imposed on others. "His only religion is
himself." To a Christian observer, this is a diabolical over-
turning of morality. The rhyming of "good" and "blood" embodies
this: The alternatives Flamineo provides himself as a response
to "horror" have no moral content whatever; both his response to
horror and his threat at denial of bounty are themselves horrors.

V.v

This very short interlude is nonetheless of intense significance. It conveys the ironic sense of service to the state of
Francisco's and Monticelso's black book. Lodovico, as effectu-
ator of Francisco's politic will to dispose of the Corombona
family, is solicitous of Francisco's "good name," pleading with
him to "engage himself" no further in the performing of the
murder. Francisco's blackness of character is completely
revealed here, even more strongly as contrast to his stoic and
egalitarian pose when he was Mulinassar earlier. The full
equivalence of Lodovico and Flamineo as absolute servants of
Francisco and Brachiano respectively becomes clear as well.
Lodovico, rewarded by his master, acts Francisco's will with
suicidal single-mindedness. Flamineo, unrewarded, turns his
released will against his own blood for the second time, seeking
to murder Vittoria under the disguise of a politic suicide.
Lodovico, with the ethics and honor of a mortally ill man of
faith, and certainly in parody thereof, pays all his debts (3-4),
satisfies his creditors, and vows "To quite all in this bold
assemblie / To the meanest follower" (6-7). All these phrases
have religious connotations, suggestive of the spiritual casting
up of accounts and balancing of books demanded of the pious
Protestant. In contrast to Lodovico's mock-piety, the mock-
suicidal Flamineo invents a false vow to his master, and uses

it as a form of sadistic punishment of his sister for not paying what he considers are her debts to him.

Lodovico's act, assuming of course that he is a paid hireling, has that perverse absolutism notable in him from the first scene, where he "would account them nobly merciful / Would they dispatch me quicklie." He values no lives, including his own. Therefore he is willing to give his life for another, as long as this gift has some material compensation. Urging Francisco to leave the city (8), under the threat of forswearing of the murder, he does not appear concerned at all for Francisco's life and reputation. Rather, there is a sense of preserving aesthetic order and decorum, through the preservation of the roles of master and servant. Lodovico wants to maintain the integrity and personal direction of these murders, which he was unable to do in the flawed murder of Brachiano. At the end, Lodovico will have been fulfilled, in that he created a "masterpiece" before he died, but disappointed that he was only wounded, not killed, in its creation.

That Francisco has a related, but less totally amoral, view of Lodovico's work as art is clear from his final words in the play:

> If thou do'st perish in this glorious act,
> I'll reare unto thy memorie that fame
> Shall in the ashes keepe alive thy name. (9-10)

Appropriately to his station, Francisco uses the mannered, ornate rhetoric of traditional commendation, appealing to the highest attribute of both princes and artists (as he did at the end of V.iv), _fame_. The inappropriateness of "glorious act" to describe the bloodbath seals our perception of Francisco as an absolutely corrupt prince. There is a calculated ambiguity in Francisco's final line, though. Although the implication is monumental, Lodovico's name living _in_ ashes could also tell the audience that this black medium is the realm where his name belongs--whether ashes suggest death, diabolism, or destruction.

Hortensio, who overhears this exchange, resolving to raise a force in anticipation of a "blacke deed," allows the audience to anticipate with tension a discovery of the crime, and a presumed retribution. Hortensio's ear is the flaw in the perfect work of art. His allusion to "strong Court factions," bathetic after "glorious act," reduces Lodovico's resolve and Francisco's praise to the actual sordid level of politics, where they really live. His picture of factions as unrestrained horses that break their riders' necks can be associated with other real and metaphoric horses in the play, from the vaulting horse to Flamineo's caution in V.iv. 13-18. Again it evokes court corruptions of traditional knightly martial valor.

Chapter IX

Thomas Adams's White Devil

Perhaps because its specific debts to Thomas Adams's sermon "The Gallant's Burden" have been so clearly noted, the thematic connection between Webster's play and Adams's sermon of the same name have been neglected.[1] That Adams and Webster have not been discussed together in depth is surprising, since Webster speaks with the tongue of the popular preacher in his major plays: the vices he presents are the social vices--from adultery to drunkenness--which contemporary Puritan-leaning sermonizers focused on, and even when they are portrayed as endemic and beyond correction, Webster's perspective on them is that of the enlightened exposer.

Also, popular preachers--particularly Adams, in many metaphors--acknowledged the affinity of their prophetic mode and that of contemporary drama. The year before The White Devil was produced, Robert Milles, in a Paul's Cross sermon, remarked that "Playes are growne now adaies into such high request . . . as that some prophane persons affirme, they can learne as much both for example and edifying at a Play, as at a Sermon."[2] Adams's "The White Devil" is itself a Paul's Cross sermon, delivered on March 7, 1613 (n.s.), about four months after Webster's play was first performed.[3] In harmony with Webster's own joy in harmonizing contraries, Adams wrote a subsequent sermon "The Black Devil" (or "Saint"), in whose epistle he acknowledges that "perhaps thou wilt judge it done for opposition's sake, the Black Devil to the white" (II, xli).[4]

Adams has an attitude remarkably similar to Webster's, regarding his "auditory." To the 1615 edition of "The White Devil" he appends a note to his "Friend Th. A." (who is clearly himself, since it concludes "Yours inseparably, Thomas Adams"): "I have certainty to find now . . . at the least good words, kind looks, and a loving acceptance, which I have not often found." His epistle to his dedicatee, Sir Thomas Cheeke, and to the Reader, also express an "arrogant humility." Like Webster, Adams presents himself as not appreciated, and presents an apologia in the form of an answer to detractors. Webster's critics apparently dislike his play's aesthetics and his slowness in writing; Adams's suggest that he himself is considered "too merry in describing some vice," and "too satirically bitter" (III, xxix). These criticisms could as well have been made of Webster, on the ground that there is no decorous balance between his depiction of vice and his judgement of it (in fact, the English ambassador at Vittoria's trial calls Monticelso's sermonizing against Vittoria "too bitter").

A second level of criticism Adams refutes also relates him to Webster. His critics wish he had not condemned church-thieves, "because it is not yet generally granted that impropriations of tithes are appropriations of wrongs," and that he had not criticized enclosers, because they are generally "great men." "Others affirm, that I have made the gate of heaven too narrow, and they hope to find it wider" (xxxix-xl)--though it is the lack of "grace" that makes us too gross and unfit to enter the gate, wide though it be. In effect, Adams is being accused of excessive "Puritanism." He is too much of a precisian on matters of salvation, and too much of a politician in applying moral law to matters of custom. Tithing and enclosures were major objects of contemporary opposition attacks on established church and secular authority. It is to be noted that, as well as "social vices," abuses of power by "great men," religious and secular authorities, are precisely the objects of Webster's condemnation in his own White Devil. If such rebukes were made of him, he might answer, with Adams, that if the "great" are "abusers," "therefore the greater their sins, and deserving the greater taxation." Of course, Webster has the liberty of attributing anti-establishment commentary to vicious characters, and exculpating himself, as he often does. On the subject of enclosures, it is Lodovico who moralizes "Great men sell sheep thus, to be cut in peeces, / When first they have shorne them bare and sold their fleeces" (I.i.61-62).

Both Webster and Adams hold a moral measure against "customary" behavior. It must be recognized that such a moral measure *can* be simply a matter of conventional exhortative rhetoric, as well as a direct and "novel" attack on established order. The detraction Adams acknowledges suggests that his sermon was seen more as the latter than the former. We should recognize that seventeenth-century political or social criticism is often couched, and not just in self-defense, in moral terms; this does not in itself render it innocuous. For example, replying to a message from the House of Commons (1610) concerning wardship, subsidy, and other prickly issues involving the royal prerogative, James I felt obliged to defend himself in terms of his "most excellent virtues," prior to any political discussion. James disowns, in fact, in his declaration, the vices Webster specifically likes to embody in Great Men: ". . . he is fre from banqueting and surfeytinge; . . . from the sinne of the fleshe, to which princes are usually most prone; . . . from extorcion and covetousnes . . ."[5] As moral purity intrinsically conveys political purity, so moral flaws can be used to "code" more dangerous political disagreement.

A final objection to his sermon which Adams counters concerns the "white devil" itself. "Some have the title sticking in their stomachs; as if Christ himself had not called Judas a devil, and likened an hypocrite to a whited sepulchre;

as if Luther did not give Judas this very attribute, and other fathers of the church from whom Luther derives it" (p. xi). Thus the epithet is not so radically paradoxical as to demonstrate disrespect to God or Scripture; rather, it is justified by the deepest tradition, in a direct line from God to Luther (which is a significant lineage as far as Adams's own orientation is concerned). This justification suggests strongly the context in which Webster's play should be read. Despite "white devil"'s identity as a commonplace, it has living ties with Reformist tradition and with the second Fall which redeemed the first one.

The basic type of the white devil in Adams's sermon is Judas, but Judas existing in the grip of a "secret fatalism." "He who was a devil in the knowledge of Christ seemed an angel, in the deceived judgement of his fellow apostles" (p. 221). Judas is the ultimate hypocrite not only because of his "show of sanctimony," but because only he. and the victim of his hypocrisy, have the awareness of his doubleness. In this dark sense, Judas is Christ's "brother" as Flamineo is Marcello's. As a devil, "black within and full of rancour, but white without, and skinned over with hypocrisy" (p. 221), Judas is necessary to the fulfillment of a fortunate sacrifice.

In Webster's play, where Judas is called upon both implicitly and directly (e.g., CORNELIA: "Bee thy act Judas-like, betray in kissing," I. ii. 291) as the type of hypocrisy,[6] the collective personae, like Adams's apostles, are "decev'd" in the moral judgement of each other, and are at the same time types of Judas in their acts of deception. Even the most virtuous are to a degree "infected" (p. 222) by such hypocrisy. Isabella, who receives the kiss of death from her husband's pictured face, angelically assumes the will to divorce him. Cornelia betrays the truth (vainly) in order to portray her hypocritical son as innocent. Giovanni himself, seen always as free of doubleness, becomes a potential hypocrite of circumstance:

> GIO: You bloudy villaines,
> By what authority have you committed
> This Massakre? LOD: By thine. GIO: Mine? LOD: Yes, thy unkle,
> Which is part of thee, enjoyn'd us to't . . .
> (V.vi.283-87)

Carrying it to a profane extreme, we might say that Christ's sacrifice was performed by his own authority, since his disciples, including Judas are spiritually (not by "blood" in Lodovico's sense) a "part of him." Without imputing such a Marlovian idea directly to Webster or Adams, one can see that they share nonetheless a sense that, as Adams says, "no society hath the privilege to be free from a Judas" (p. 223). The condition of hypocrisy is dominant even among hypocrisy's victims. Adams can conclude from this pessimistic postulate that "there is little difference between permission and commission, between the toleration and the perpetration of the sin: he is an abettor of the evil that may and will not better the evil" (p. 225). There is then a queer twist to Adams's fatalistic view of hypocrisy and evil in general: precisely because everyone who tolerates it is guilty of it, everyone has, in his/her own interest of salvation, the active necessity of opposing it.

Many contemporary Italianate dramas, as well as Webster's, would not measure up to Adams's standard of obligation to "example and edifying." Hypocrisy is an essential element in most dramatic action against hypocrisy: consider the extremes of the Duke in _Measure for Measure_ and Vindice in _The Revenger's Tragedy_. When Francisco is moved to take action against his "honourable brother" (II.i.228) Brachiano, and his company, he progresses from one act of seeming-innocent deception to another, from the honeyed gall of the love letter to Vittoria to the ultimate masquerade of blackness as a Moor. In fact, Monticelso, who does appear as an exhorter against treachery when last encountered in the play, offers early on a sacrifice of innocence as a viable price for the expulsion of vice: "For my revenge I'd stake a brother's life, / That being wrong'd dare not avenge himself" (II.i.388-89). This offer is almost an emblem of the condition of entrapment into hypocrisy: the life of the wronged is offered as a sacrifice to revenge the wrong. Hypocrisy is so slippery because, as suggested before, even Christ Himself can be seen as employing it to a pious end in not revealing to his disciples the imminence of his own betrayal, and the name of his betrayer. And, like Monticelso's "brother," he does stake his own life to expel the sins of the world.

The similarities between Adams's sermon and Webster's play lead one to the assertion that Webster's title is not meant to epithetize Vittoria, or any other specific devil in his play, but, as in Adams's usage, to personify the quality of hypocrisy as an immanent presence in every member of the "societie" of his play (and presumably of his "auditory" as well). Thus, when any of Webster's characters performs an act of deception, the auditory can "see" the White Devil working "in" him/her. The morality mode is thus to a degree signalled by Webster's title, as it is a constant directing undercurrent in Adams's sermons. Not that specific characters personify--even indirectly--specific moral qualities, but ethical qualities as "presences" act their own "moral masque," driving the play's personages. "Needs must he go whom the devil drives" (p. 252), and the audience is asked to experience the appointed rounds of Lust, Pride, Hypocrisy, and their comrades, in Webster's play, as much as it is asked to contemplate an amoral world of chaos and anguish.

To the fatalism that the foregoing discussion points must be added a contrary vision of hypocrisy, which might be initiated in Adams's words: "Many Parliament-Protestants go but a statute pace, yet look to come to heaven; but, without more haste, it is like to be when the Pharisees come out of hell" (p. 252). Is Adams here saying that the reforms proposed by the Parliamentary "opposition" are ineffectual--if not diabolical--because they arrogate to a secular means what can only be accomplished spiritually by each individual? Or, in the manner of political statement couched in moral terms, is he saying that such reforms are not radical enough, and that both church and state must be reformed, or else society will run with Judas downhill to hell? Here Adams wears both a bare head and a mitre. I would say that his query is studiedly provocative and ambiguous. He will not take a particular political or religious sectarian position but will dangerously inject the issue of socio-political action into a moral harangue. Adams's vision of Judas earlier in the sermon has been that if he can be escaped at all, it can only be by the self ministering to the self, and disowning its own hypocrisies. But Adams plays against this view using a very traditional theme in a new way, "the power and force of example" particularly the example of the Great. This is a normative commonplace in The White Devil:

> The lives of Princes should like dyals move,
> Whose regular example is so strong,
> They make the times by them go right and wrong
> (I.ii.279-81)

and

> It is a more direct and even way
> To train to vertue those of Princely bloud
> By examples than by precepts . . . (II.i.105-07)

Webster's plot of unfolding dissimulations demonstrates the truth of this maxim in a black mode: example of vice in the great breeds vice in underlings. As Adams says, "It is safe sinning after such authors" (p. 223).

Adams's attack on vicious example expands a specific observation of Judas's hypocrisy in his text (John, xii). Judas condemns Mary Magdalen's anointment of Jesus with rare (and expensive) oil, while the poor go starving; he does so to whiten his blackness with the skin of Charity. But "Judas cares not for the poor" (p. 232). The example of his hypocritical concern for the poor is taken up, Adams imagines, by all present at the gathering, and the poor are toasted by all. Those who follow Judas's example, presumably, are reinforcing his own design of turning Christ's own teachings against him, even if they themselves have no subversive intent. But Adams's specific point about the example of the great is not this one of inevitable betrayal; rather, it is the possibility of consciously choosing not to follow a vicious example. To rebel against precedent ("He that is greatest in his government is yet greater in his precedent," p. 223) requires a higher precedent that the highest offered by the World. This may be why Adams is skeptical of Parliamentary reform by statute, even though he may sympathize with its goals. The true imitator of Christ might be asked to rebel against the highest precedent the World offers; such a faithful rebellion could be most dangerously revolutionary. There would certainly be the opposite of fatalism in such a following of a divine example.

"If the master drink ad plenitudinem, to fulness, the servant will ad ebrietatem, to madness; the imitation of good comes, for the most part, short of the pattern, but the imitation of ill exceeds the example" (p. 223). The best exemplar of Adams's "imitation of ill" is this formulation, in The White Devil, is of course Flamineo. This role of servant (and, pointedly, the devil's secretary), he himself emphasizes satirically enough to imply that he is the true master of ill, and his imitation of Brachiano does exceed the example enough to become instigation (as in his pandaric scenes, I.ii and IV.ii). As Vittoria says in the latter case, when Flamineo asks "Am I the author of your sinne?" "Hee's a base theif that a theif lets in" (IV.ii.139-40). The most striking connection in Webster's play between hypocrisy and the corruptive example of the great as Adams connects them is in Lodovico's response to the new Pope and his brother in IV.iii. Adams is, of course, flamingly anti-Catholic: "Let Rome have the praise without our envy or rivalry: Peccatis Roma patrocinium est. Sodomy is licenced, sins to come pardoned, drunkenness defended, the stews maintained, perjury commended, treason commanded" (p. 225). Webster's Papal election (with Lodovico, the poisoner, as food tester) is inherently corrupt in the minds of a Red Bull (or a Paul's Cross) audience. However, the new Pope's attitude towards a subverted Lodovico is, despite this prejudice, a strong contrast to his subversive secular "brother." Is Monticelso, under his Papal hat, being the whitest of devils in excommunicating Vittoria and Brachiano, and exhorting Lodovico to penance? Is Lodovico, as a penitent sinner (IV.iii.111) imitating this example of spiritual hypocrisy? Or does Monticelso represent a true rebellion against the Papal patrimony of sin? Are the Pope's paired legal (the excommunication) and spiritual (the exhortation) initiatives meant to suggest the potential in him of reform, by way of virtuous example?

The Pope's initial exchange with Lodovico involves this paradox. His query as to why Francisco worked so hard for Lodovico's pardon implies by tone that the pardon was an act of hypocrisy. Lodovico's riddling answer puts the parton in the context of Adams's Judas: charity to the poor is used to whiten the sepulchre of self-interest.

> Italian beggars will resolve you that
> Who, begging of an almes, bid those they beg of
> Doe good for their own sakes . . . (IV.iii.85-87)

Lodovico twists the idea, as found in Adams's sermon, though. Here it is the poor themselves who cloak their covetousness in an appeal to their donors' own covetous desire to appear charitable. The application of Lodovico's figure is that his role as grateful recipient of grace is as hypocritical as the "free gift" of pardon that he has been given. Adams proclaims "A great man's warrant is like a charm or spell, to keep quick and stirring spirits within the circle of confined mischief" (p. 223), and this simile echoes the Pope's own suspicious response to Lodovico: "Come, what devill was that / That you were raising" (IV.iii.91-92). But the suspicion of hypocrisy, to the alert auditory, might fly back on the great Pope, who, as a Cardinal earlier, had broached as news to his brother, and as a beneficial possibility, Lodovico's return from the sea and letters of appeal for this very pardon (II.i.376-80).

Thus Lodovico's seeming conquest of his hypocrisy, in confessing his revenge plot, as well as his momentary resolve to relinquish it as "damnable," can be seen as hypocritical, as much as the Pope's sermon to him on penitence (V.iii.119-30). The fatalism of this sermon suggests its hypocrisy: Monticelso sees Lodovico as inherently incorrigible; instruction cannot pierce him deeply (1. 126). Lodovico's "white" fear of damnation, confirming this fatalism, soon becomes "black" disappointment of expectation for the Pope's "suffrage." Lodovico's situation thus shares qualities of both Adams's pessimistic and his optimistic views of the "imitation of ill."

The hypocrisy of Francisco in this scene is not as ambiguous here as the Pope's is, but is a good example of the power of the Great as analyzed by Adams. His bribery of Lodovico with coin sent him under the name of the Pope "confirms" Lodovico's view view of the Pope as a Judas, and confirms even more strongly the audience's view of Francisco as a Judas. In effect, the great nobleman's hypocrisy, and the great prelate's feigned hypocrisy (feigned, hypocritically, by the nobleman) lay upon Lodovico a weight of example of ill against which he has no motivation to rebel--even if his momentary desire to reform *can* be perceived as "sincere." Adams's metaphors describe Lodovico's situation, and that of the whole play, well: "Thus spreads example, like a stone thrown into a pond, that makes circle beget circle, till it spread to the banks. Judas's train soon took fire in the suspectless disciples; and Satan's infections shoot through some great star the influence of damnation into the ear of the commonality" (p. 223).

This vision is also presented in Webster's scene when greatness and hypocrisy that Adams does. He compares the great to brides who feign modesty at weddings, while their thoughts are running lasciviously on the wedding-night's sport (IV.iii. 146-50). "Now to th'act of blood," he declares, without concealment. The white devil in Lodovico is perfectly manifested by his verbal satire of the very hypocrisy that is his main mode of action, as Judas, in Adams's text, speaks against hypocrisy in Christ, while hypocritically plotting against Him.

So much of the texture of life and of human interactions in it is irrecoverable from the time of Webster and Adams, as from any distant period, that the actual commerce between them, and the possible direct inter-influences of their diabolical works, cannot be assumed. Certainly the above discussion is not meant to imply such a connection; however, it can be employed to suggest the currency of Judas as a figure of social sins, and to suggest the closeness of both Webster and Adams to direct political criticism of the Jacobean state and the Anglican church.

Chapter X

Fifth Movement: "Cease to Dye by Dying."

V.vi

The final scene of <u>The White Devil</u> is much more climactic than criticism of the play's aesthetic has often recognized. Representative of this criticism is Roma Gill, who sees the concluding scene fulfilling the "botched revenge play aspect" of the play, in that the preceding revenges have not reestablished a moral order.[1] Jacqueline Pearson's sense of a purposeful "ironic undermining of tragedy"[2] seems more consistent with Webster's directed ambiguity. While it may be too nicely schematic to declare that the play presents "a series of anti-tragedies: ironically inverted or incomplete versions of the tragic experience," which culminate in Flamineo's parody of tragedy,[3] Webster does move in a different direction than do some of his contemporaries. In Shakespeare the ultimate moment in the life of the tragic protagonist is usually the ultimate moment of the play itself. Webster is more ironic in his attitude to his protagonists, all of whom lack saving virtues mingled with their vices; this may be one reason why his original auditory lacked understanding. In the fallen world, of white devils, the agents and intelligencers of the great have a more crucial role in the fates of individuals and states than do their masters, because it is their non-moral stance that allows the great to sanction their absolute freedom of action. <u>King Lear</u>, with Lear in the background and Edmund in the foreground, approximates Webster's emphasis. Flamineo and Lodovico, or even Bosola, are servants, and tragic circumstance does not involve a fatality of wrong choice of their masters as much as their own willingness or unwillingness to be the agents of their masters' predetermined choices.

As well, Webster places women in the central positions that many of his contemporaries reserved for men, with their women as choric sufferers. Women are granted strong wills by Webster, and this weakens his potential to create traditional homocentric tragedy, but this does not mean he evasion of tragedy implies a contemporary idea of "liberation." On the contrary, it is precisely because women are more subject to, and not driven to dominate, circumstance, that Webster sees them as more significant. Vittoria, Lodovico, Flamineo, and Zanche--who dominate this final scene--all are vulnerable and incomplete. The condition of a "fall" does not apply strongly to them, because they have begun fallen, morally and socially, and the course of any "rise" they have accomplished is foredoomed. Even the Duchess of Malfi is initially in jeopardy in her rule, isolated and beset, before her alliance with Antonio. The significance of these characters is that despite their status, they are engaged with the deepest questions of life and death, while the Cardinals and Dukes, manipulators of others, are passive and above the fray. Or, like Brachiano, they fall without experiencing their own fall in a tragic manner. Thus, despite his Italianate atmospheres, we might consider Webster even more radically a "bourgeois tragedian" than the Middletonians are. In a context of aristocratic hierarchy, he demands the deepest attention be given to those most out of place in this hierarchy, and least definable in terms of it.

Initially, in this scene, Flamineo accosts Vittoria "with a book in her hand," as "at your prayers."[4] With presumed scornfulness he orders her to "Give o'er," and attend to his "wordly business." The opposition between wordly and spiritual affairs appears surprising, as dividing this brother and sister, and particularly as coming from the misogynic politician who discounts female intelligence. If we imagine that Flamineo's real aim and desire is to shed Vittoria's blood, then his dissuasion of her from prayer may be compared with Lodovico's desire to kill Brachiano in an impious situation, so that salvation will be denied him (V.i.67-72). But Flamineo is also playing the role of his dead master in his attacks on Isabella for pretending an excessive piety merely to mask an excessive profligacy.

Flamineo may be playing the advisor to his sister, but the "Reward" she decides to give him for his "long service" mocks this pretence. Her "conveyance," which satirizes the situation of a bargain with the devil, makes Vittoria the ironic moralist and advisor regarding her brother's actions: "I give that portion to thee, and no other / Which <u>Caine</u> gron'd under having slaine his brother" (14-15). Vittoria "plays God" in rewarding him with the reward of his prototype, banishment. Although her book can be considered a Bible or an account book, or simply emblematic of the metaphoric sense of account-taking, its ambiguity is essential at this point. We must not know clearly at this moment whether Vittoria is actually transformed by an awareness of sin or whether she is pretending to piety, having taken a lesson from the Cardinal, in order to counterattack her brother. However, her statement "You are a villaine" (17)-- similar to those of Brachiano to Flamineo in IV.ii at another high moment of dissension--seems so direct as to be meant to be taken as sincere. If so, it amounts to a denial of Flamineo's brotherhood, insofar as that blood tie implies that she owes him anything.

Vittoria's words come across as unexpected to Flamineo, and seem to have the same message of willed family disruption as his intial pandaric activity, on her behalf, did. To make such an absolute moral judgement without irony, as Vittoria has just done, and as Giovanni does of Flamineo in V.iv, is to proclaim emancipation from the power of the devil or the devil's earthly representatives. To imitate God in this manner is not presumptuous, because it acknowledges God's laws as the first cause of wordly action. Vittoria's two judgements of her brother, soteriological and ethical, also manifest the power of rhetoric, discussed throughout the play. The elegance of the banishing couplet, and the harsh abruptness of "villaine," mirror the two realms of life in which each punishment is effectual. Since Flamineo at his most hypocritical uses the highest style, Vittoria's couplet can be seen as a parody of his own hypocrisy, in this case because the elevation of her speech <u>does</u> harmonize with the truth-value of her message. But she, one individual, is perfectly capable of both judgements, since she is making different implications with each. It is anachronistic to criticize such inconsistencies of language in terms of "credibility."

Flamineo, accusing Vittoria of having a Devil in her (19), is self-reflectively ironic: he contains the devil. To Flamineo, the diabolical is that which counters his own will. Using references to conjuration again, as Isabella initially did in trying to redirect a perverse will--Flamineo exits to seek "two case of Jewels," which he reveals as "two case of pistols" (s.d.). Here, as in Brachiano's wooing scene and later, jewels are given sexual connotations. Here, further, the association of jewelry with Vittoria's own treacherous personality is played on: the last jewel one may wear is death. Flamineo's pistols initiate a strange <u>en famille</u> sequence of deceptions, culminating in the greatest of all deceptions, the counterfeiting of the final jewel death. The death-tricks that Vittoria and Flamineo play on each other--Vittoria and Zanche getting Flamineo to "shoot" himself first, Flamineo feigning death from blank cartridges--epitomize and parody the deceptions of the preceding actions. The action here is skillfully balanced between tragedy and burlesque. The mutual deceptions have the quality of "game," or jest, yet they are at the same time in deadly earnest. Tricking Flamineo into shooting himself first is for Vittoria and Zanche, until they are disillusioned, as much an earnest fratricidal act as was the murder of Marcello, Marcello, which Vittoria has so condemned. On the other hand, the act balances unresolvedly between murder and self-murder, the latter being a self-damning act of the perpetrator. Since, however, Flamineo "knows" all the time that his guns contain no bullets, one could see him as more merciful than the ladies, and almost take seriously within its limits his argument that he was, in the Griselda context, testing their loyalty. The entry of Lodovico and cohorts, with their direct and murderous intent, again reduces the previous death-games to the level of "play." The total vulnerability, at the end, of the three who moments before had been seen as exchanging power over each other seems, awkwardly, to discredit all the tumultuous emotions generated by their conflict.

Initially, Vittoria's protest on seeing her brother's pistols is loaded with irony: "Is not all mine, yours? have I any children?" (31). This defensive piety directly contradicts her previous bequest of damnation, unless it is read to suggest that she is willing to share Flamineo's banishment. Flamineo, aware of hypocrisy in this contradiction, counters by contradicting his own first words to Vittoria in the scene: "Pray thee good woman doe not trouble mee / With this vaine wordly businesse; say your prayers . . ." (32-33). His invented vow to Brachiano that they not outlive him (34-35) is of a piece with other violated sacred bonds--e.g., Brachiano's marriage. This false contract is an ultimate pretence, since Flamineo pretends that he attributes to it wordly motives: Brachiano's jealousy of Vittoria's sexual future, and his own fear for survival after Brachiano's death. His invented cynicism, combined with idealism, apparently persuades Vittoria, despite her brother's reputation for dissimulation. To the audience, however, it can appear as a grotesque jesting with the ideals of stoicism, which has been a constant ideological antagonist of Flamineo's throughout the play:

> Foole that thou art to thinke that Polititians
> Do use to kill the effects of injuries
> And let the cause live: shall we groane in irons,
> Or be a shamefull and a waighty burthen
> To a publicke scaffold? This is my resolve--
> I would not live at any mans entreaty
> Nor dye at any's bidding. (44-49)

Some of the above sounds strangely like Lodovico's scornful rejection of servile life in I.i. Its major import seems to be to argue that the stoic view of life is not alien to the politician's ethic. Flamineo anticipates that the politicians who arranged Brachiano's murder will not hesitate to attack him and his sister, as the first cause of injuries done them, and that it is more politic for brother and sister to anticipate this revenge, and to avoid undergoing inevitable suffering, by committing suicide immediately. The broadest dramatic irony of this speech is that this whole argument is purely suasive, to fortify the political deception of Vittoria, and evidently is not considered valid by Flamineo himself. His "My life hath done service to other men, / My death shall serve mine owne turne" (51-2) is similarly disingenous, since all of Flamineo's service to other men has been ultimately to serve his own turn. As in his argument with Brachiano at the House of Convertites, Flamineo sees service as an instrument to escape service, not as a permanent condition of life. Perhaps Francisco's own hypocritically stoic argument that no one is ultimately another human's servant (V.i) is relevant here. No wordly discussions of service--self-service or other--recognize the ultimate servitude of humanity to God, and their conclusions are therefore self-deceptive.

Flamineo vows that he will die "With as much pleasure / As e'er my father gat me" (54-5). If the "father" here is in no way to be perceived as the Father in Heaven blasphemed, Flamineo's cheerful remark is still an utter blasphemy against divine creation. More directly than in earlier utterances, he gives death the attributes of life and generative sexuality, in so doing denying nature and the grace that gives nature meaning. The Freudian imagination can revel in such a direct identification of eroticism and death, and see, thereby, more than a motivation of reward in Flamineo's pandarism: Flamineo, as pandar, is in his own mind a deaths-man, and black Zanche the only one he <u>could</u> love for himself. More relevantly, Flamineo's statement is, as Vittoria recognizes, that of an "Atheist" (57). It at one and the same time separates physical pleasure from its spiritual justification, and suggests that his own (or anyone's) creation serves no purpose but the pleasure of the creator. Another quality of this expression is that it is self-destructive beyond Flamineo's immediate intent of suicide. With the memory of the broken cross at Cornelia's breast, which is a denial of the mother's physical and spiritual parenthood, it completes a vision of Flamineo as one who has no sense of his own value and, in modern terms, "identity." He has absolutely denied his birthright. Though his suicide is a deception, he has already committed suicide in the spiritual (or, in modern secular conception, psychological) sense, and has settled into an inner cave of Despair.

The above considerations of a single phrase are justified in view of Vittoria's responsive "sermon against despair" (57-63). This sermon seems less burdened with self-contradiction than previous ones in the play, since Vittoria has clearly perceived what the audience probably does, that despite Flamineo's protestations his acts of cruelty are motivated by inward pain and suffering. The "cursed Devill" candies most sins (that is, whitens them), but despair is left bitter as gall: "yet we carouse it off" (62). Flamineo's mania of words and action is a self-candying "carousal." Vittoria's sermon is pronounced at a white heat of desperation, and is itself a candied attempt to gain time against imagined murder (as in her aside to Zanche, "Cry out for helpe!", 62). So Vittoria's words bring up, but do not resolve, the theological question of how a sinner such as Flamineo can be the servant of the devil and also the victim of non-spiritual disturbances within him/herself. Vittoria does provide a brilliant cautionary image of Despair which

> Makes us forsake that which was made for Man,
> The world, to sinke to that was made for devils,
> Eternall darkenesse . . . (63-65)

This image of suicide as a choice of darkness over the world is carefully distanced from being doctrinally Christian. Vittoria's "world" does not have the religious connotations it had earlier. Darkness is "made for devils," but not literally hell, and "world," the antagonist of "heaven" in this play, takes the place that "heaven" would in an orthodox sermon. Vittoria might well be describing the darkness of the human heart, or a dark nothingness after death, such as she sees at the point of her own death later. It is true that immediately after this (67-68), she calls up a literal apocalypse, sermon-style, where those who have sinned in life will rise from the grave "shrieking."

Flamineo's response could coincide with that of a literary audience: Vittoria is indulging in effeminate "pulpit oratory"-- all words and no "sound Doctrine." Calling her words "grammaticall laments," he recalls the logorrheic lawyer at Vittoria's arraignment, whom Vittoria ridiculed for the same reasons. By so speaking, Flamineo reduces her sermon to "words" in order to preserve his own invulnerability to it. But Vittoria's response is to take Zanche's advice and use words treacherously against the one to whom she is preaching virtue: "Seeme to consent, onley perswade him teech / The way to death; let him dye first" (74-75). "This glorious white devil is rescued from her weakness only by the strength of the black devil."[5] Zanche is alluding to the popular subject of many writers such as Christopher Sutton and Thomas Fuller--the preparations for a holy death. The worst such preparation in a religious context is preparation for suicide. Vittoria, however, immediately pretends to take on the role of convert to, and proselyte of, the "sound Doctrine" of self-murder, and seconds Flamineo strophically, as is done in earlier scenes of false harmony.

In this debate over suicide, Vittoria argues that "To kill one's selfe is meate" (77), and we must quickly swallow, rather than chewing. The "trebble torments" usually ascribed to hell she ascribes to the physical condition of one fearful of suicide. Flamineo seconds her with a statement of sound Christian doctrine, terribly perverted as a defense of suicide:

> . . . I have held it,
> A wretched and most miserable life,
> Which is not able to dye (80-83)

Vittoria, "resolved," contrasts her prior "sacrifice" at the "flaming Altar of my heart" for Brachiano to this final sacrifice of "heart and all." The sonnetteered Altar is itself profane; the idea of suicide as sacrifice is more so, as it resonates with the rival sacrifices of Cain and Abel. Here we have the sacrificing of others' lives for material ends to the utter confounding of the redemptive sacrifice of Christ. All the <u>double entendres</u> of these speeches are themselves confounded by the arrival of Lodovico and other murderers. Then we realize that while this trio have been playing treacherous games with death, they have been preparing themselves, unknowingly, for real death at Lodovico's hands. The partial stoicism they manifest at their actual deaths may owe something to their habituation to death induced by this preliminary jesting with it.

Zanche, in subsequent lines (88-100), leads the action, proposing, and having accepted, Flamineo's dying first. In response, Flamineo demands a vow that the women will not outlive him, which they accept, with a remarkable cleverness of ridicule, "most religiously" (100). Possibly Webster errs in not having the women show suspicion of the sincerity in Flamineo's acceptance of death, particularly at this point. Of course, their credulity gives them an aura of innocence which separates them morally from Flamineo. But the implied staging of this scene denies that innocence, since we know from Flamineo's instructions (97-98) that they hold the guns and shoot him, in the clear posture of executioners.

Flamineo's last words are overtly satiric of dying speeches, similar to the one he will shortly deliver in earnest, not in jest. The contrast between his mock death-speech (101-119) and the probable postures of Vittoria and Zanche, is calculated to evoke incongruous emotions in the viewer. The text reveals nothing about the staging, but if they are to shoot him on his signal at the end of his speech, having stood at arms waiting for him to finish speaking, the satire would be pronounced. Flamineo's speech is allusive. His lament at the inadequacy of physic to sustain life (101-3) parodies Brachiano's in V.iii.21-23 at a similar inadequacy in hangmen. His "Whither shall I go now?" (108), followed by a Lucianic inventory of the regal dead performing lower-class trades in purgatory, prefigures the much more serious "whithers" at the play's end. The "low comedy" of these Lucianic speculations on mortality is immediately followed by lofty Parmenidean or Heraclitean reflections: "Whether I resolve to Fire, Earth, water, Aire, / Or all the Elements by scruples; I know not . . ." (114-5), and these potentially meaningful reflections are further bathetically demolished: ". . . Nor greatly care . . ." Finally, Flamineo's death-speech is resolved in a defense of violent death: "For from our selves it steales our selves so fast / The paine once apprehended is quite past" (118-9). This is precisely the real death he will soon suffer.

All these versions of death, satiric in themselves, are non-Christian. Violent and unprepared death is most dangerous for a Christian, as it is for a Stoic, and perhaps even for one who, as Flamineo at time does, evokes a sexually pleasurable death. Actually, Flamineo gets exquisite pleasure, as Volpone does, from experiencing the vindictive pleasure of those who imagine that he is dead. This pleasure is involved with an ironically presented icon. According to the stage directions, having shot Flamineo the women "run to him & tread upon him," meanwhile epithetizing him, presumed dying, as a devil, doomed to hell--the same treatment Brachiano receives. Visually this trampling can appeal to popular iconography of the devil being trampled by the just, and it is ritually complementary to the litanic Capuchins trampling dying Brachiano with their words and consigning him to hell. But here, more blatantly than before, the ritual is undercut by the audience's awareness that the just tramplers are murderers and that the trampled devil is not injured at all. Where Brachiano's death-scene is filled with actual suffering, with cruelty and sadism, this one is more the corruption of the corruption of a sacramental ritual, where no experience of triumphant virtue or vice exists; all is deception.

The self-righteousness of Vittoria and Zanche is complemented by the self-parody of Flamineo: "O the waies darke and horrid! I cannot see, / Shall I have no company?" (139-40). In this simulated death-agony, parodying Brachiano's,[6] Flamineo plays Everyman. With "My liver's purboil'd like scotch hollybread" (144), he burlesques the presence of the actual pains of hell. His last act of mockery of a Christian death--the death of an unbeliever as seen by Christians--is to rise again from the dead with the word "Devils" (149) on his lips. Flamineo, risen, in turn takes the language of offended righteousness, calling his deception a proof of "kindnesse," and resolving to punish "ingratitude."

At this point one might note the fulfillment of The White Devil's obsession with the power and corruptibility of language--a theme that Flamineo himself, the wordsmith, has noted (69-74). "Kindness," "ingratitude," and other moral-connotative words, have been applied to so many inapposite situations that they have been deprived of functional meanings, just as morality itself has. They justify the wills of their speakers. Webster may have in mind the archetype of Babel; in the fallen world, words are denatured, become tools, as hirelings like Lodovico are, rather than images of ideal meanings in some unchangeable realm. Corrupt words, like corrupt individuals, infect the healthy ones through imitations. This may be one reason why Giovanni speaks very little; he keeps his words in quarantine.

Flamineo's words are the most infected and the most corrupt. In this last instance he turns to a slightly irrelevant mysogynic diatribe against "howling wives" (157), who dispose of husbands to acquire new ones. It is striking that with Brachiano as his "precedent" (162), Flamineo's wrath is directed against wives rather than against sisters. Certainly he imagines marriage as a purely sexual relationship: "we lay our soules to pawne to the Devill for a little pleasure, and a woman makes the bill of sale" (162-3). Is there covert guilt or revulsion at the pleasure of sexuality here, or is this rant carried on precisely for its inapplicability--another discrediting of language? Certainly when Flamineo shows his remaining two pistols to Vittoria and Zanche, with the words "Here are two other Instruments" (167), the sexual references of the noun seem undeniable. Flamineo's "sexual" relationship with these women will be perfectly consistently with his doctrine, the killing of them.

"Instruments" also has an unconsciously ironic application, as referring to Lodovico and Gasparo, who enter more or less simultaneously with Flamineo's utterance, presumably ("Churchmen turn'd revellers!" 172), in the monkish guise they wore when killing Brachiano. They cut the thread of Flamineo's own murderous intent, but as harmoniously as though they were part of a scripted, pre-rehearsed sequence of action. Lodovico's punning "We have brought you a Maske" (170) fits into this pattern of intentionality as does Flamineo's seemingly unperturbed observation, "A matachine it seemes;" to Flamineo this antimasque is in symmetry with the previous masque of death. Lodovico's entry is in accord with the conventional "surprise" entry of disguised revellers, such as is dramatized in Shakespeare's <u>Henry</u> <u>VIII</u>, I.iv. Flamineo defines their entry as an antimasque not just because of the masquers' outlandish guise, but because their earnestness distorts and darkens the jesting tragedy he has just been acting. Lodovico's antimasque is thus not an intrusion of chaos <u>preceding</u> a cathartic return to order; perceived at this moment, it is a vehicle for the restoration of order, evil though it be. To the community of Flamineo and the two women it is a final chaos. As masquers the murderers also dramatize a metaphor for the deception which has governed the entire play.

The masquers immediately unmask themselves, reveal their true identities, and prepare to bring their play within a play to its climax. Gasparo's cry of "<u>Isabella</u>, <u>Isabella</u>!" just before unmasking constitutes the entire <u>verbal</u> content of their masque. It is a <u>memento</u> <u>mori</u>. It parodies Brachiano's cry for Vittoria at the point of his death, and recalls the masque-like dumb show wherein Isabella was murdered silently invoking Brachiano's name; it announces therefore the justification for these new killings.

It is totally in character for Flamineo to name, but be immune to, this justification of, the masque in which he is mousetrapped. His response is ethically and aesthetically inappropriate. He protests "You shall not take Justice from forth my hands, / O let me kill her Vittoria " (176-77), unaware that Justice has fled to the heavens long ago, that its nearest approximation right now is in the hands of the killers of himself. Similarly he delivers two false and fatalistic sententiae: "Man may his Fate foresee, but not prevent," and "'Tis better to be fortunate than wise" (181,3). These pagan sentiments are not morals derived from, but causes of, Flamineo's present condition. They posit a non-Christian universe again, and a Christian viewer would be drawn to feel that Flamineo's death is a warning to be virtuous and avoid such a fate, to be wise and avoid subjection to a fatalistic world view.

The joined pleas for life of Vittoria and Flamineo mock the conditions they imposed on each other shortly before. In this case, Vittoria and Flamineo have no resources except words, and words have no substance in the presence of Lodovico. He represents insensitivity to the content of words, an insensitivity akin to their own. "Pitty" and "hope" are named as deceptive by Gasparo (187), and Flamineo fails to evoke shame in Lodovico by likening him to the "base hangman" who kills the defenseless. Lodovico's answer is to recall Flamineo's blow to him in III.iii ("Sirha you once did strike mee, Ile strike you / Into the Center" (191-2), just as Brachiano remembered and revenged Flamineo's defiance of him. Flamineo associates his death with birth, as he did in lines 54-55, but with a different attitude: "Wouldst have me dye, as I was borne, in whining?" (196). Lodovico's "The famine of our vengeance . . ." (202) also links to Vittoria's imagery of suicide as meat (76).

The revengers are almost the realization of a represented desire for oblivion felt by brother and sister. But the murderers' desire to carry on a colloquy with their victims gives the victims time to adjust, at least partially, their own reality to this open and unmasked death. Thus, Flamineo, queried, thinks on "nothing," remembers "nothing." "Nothing" is unregenerate content for one's last thoughts, but it is more acceptable than Flamineo's customary thoughts. Flamineo actually avoids thought at this moment; an actual memory, such as has been urged on him by Giovanni and by Vittoria, might weaken his resolve to an amoral invulnerability. "There's nothing of so infinit vexation / As mans owne thoughts" (206-7), is, unlike his last sententious pronouncements, absolutely true, though the vexation would better bear another name he uses earlier, "mase of conscience."

Vittoria's response to the presence of death also has some flavor of moral regeneration. She seeks, without hope, to flatter her "Deathsman" Lodovico, although in a way that may provide a clue as to how he would have appeared to Webster's first audience: "Thou hast too good a face to be a hangman" (212). But then she collaborates in his sense of assassination as a work of art (we note in I.i.53-55, Lodovico has "seen some" condemned who give pleasant looks and grow familiar with the hangman). Vittoria demands that his execution of her be in "right forme," and insists on preceding her servant in death, as fitting her station. Where Lodovico thinks fear should "dissolve" her, she tacitly rebukes his definition of femininity: "I am too true a woman: / Conceit can never kill me" (224-25). Similarly Zanche is proud that "Death cannot alter my complexion," and that she will never look pale (with fear).

The tone of all of this defiance bespeaks "nobility," and the sort of commendable stoicism that has been deprecated by politicians in this play. But from a Christian perspective Vittoria's aesthetics of death are equivalent to Flamineo's "nothing." By affirming <u>social</u> order, by dismissing "conceit," Vittoria is denying meaningfulness in her death, not contemplating any principle beyond death in the light of which her death can take on any sense of value, and be considered either reward or punishment. She and Flamineo go to their executions at Lodovico's hands the way Lodovico, the exile from grace, has imagined himself going in the first scene. Certainly, though, Vittoria's character is not "flattened" in this reduction. She ironizes over manliness in exhorting Lodovico to "murder some sucking Infant" (234), and nursing receives its final reference as a condition of innocence. She also acknowledges sin: "my greatest sinne lay in my blood. / Now my blood paies for't" (240-41). This is a Christ-suggestive acknowledgement of Justice, but Vittoria is ambiguous. Her sin may have been in her blood--her heritage--, or in her blood--her passion--and in either case Lodovico places it beyond her power and responsibility to alter or recant. The view that "the courage and spirit with which Vittoria and her brother die is exceptional, and constitutes something wholly admirable in a whole of treachery and baseness"[7] seems difficult to sustain in the presence of these ambiguities.

Similarly, Webster gives Flamineo curiosity over the make of his death-blade, as an expression of his contempt for death, and perhaps as a glance back at his murder of Marcello with Marcello's own sword, given him to measure its length. But his "Search my wound deeper" (239) is an urge to experience as deeply as possible the experience of dying, in the erotic mode he has given it before. There is a total exclusion even of satiric speculations on the meaning of death, such as he gave forth at his mock-death before (101 ff.). Flamineo, in yielding to the blade, might be considered to have become "womanish," as Vittoria, going to meet it, has becomes "mannish," and Flamineo seems to perceive, as well as welcoming with new love (242) this interpenetration of identities. But this restored "love" for the sister is not redemptive, as it has often been interpreted. It is based on an inversion of natures, and in his praise of Vittoria's courage Flamineo is still the politician. Many women famous for masculine virtue have actually been secretly vicious, he moralizes, and it is unfortunate that Vittoria's reputation could not profit from this happy silence. "Shee hath no faults, who hath the art to hide them" (247) in his sentence, which is a defense of the politician's art.

Flamineo's praise of his sister is actually politically-candied blame, a turning of the verbal knife in the wound for her failure to dissimulate her vices. Even his response to her stylized yet justly famous image of her own death's consequence, "My soule, like to a ship in a blacke storme, / Is driven I know not whither" (248-49), he dismisses by extending her metaphor almost into comedy. His first response, "Then cast ancor" (249) is a bathetic joke, and he continues sententiously referring to her image in a mockingly concrete way. His actual philosophy in response to her wonderment about the fate of her soul, precisely what one should focus on among Last Things, is to deny the meaningfulness of all spiritual consciousness of death:

>   . . . I doe not looke
>   Who went before, nor who shall follow mee;
>   Noe, at myselfe I will begin and end. (256-8)

The literal self-centeredness of this creed is where Flamineo did begin; he has not changed. Therefore, his words would prophesy for a Christian audience that he is beyond salvation or any life beyond his "end." "While we looke up to heaven wee confound / Knowledge with knowledge" (259-60). Flamineo wagers his life on the materialistic knowledge expressed in the commonplaces which he has uttered throughout the play. Divine "knowledge" would but create ignorance by uprooting the cynical certainties in which he so strongly believes, without replacing them with anything more tangible. The above expression, though, could also be directed to bringing up the ultimate sense of vulnerability and dispossession that Flamineo has betrayed intermittently, particularly when his parentage is evoked. The consuming "my selfe" is worshipped because it is not subject to other forces, and it is not subject because it has no "content"--no values, affinities, dislikes, which can subject it to a surrounding of emotion, ideology, spirit, or anything else.

Vittoria's dying couplet, "O happy they that never saw the Court, / Nor ever knew great Man but by report" (261-2) is sometimes seen as articulating epigrammatically a basic social theme of the play, or else as a final evasion by her of responsibility for her own actions.[10] Its woodenness seems to cast it in doubt. Applied to the whole play, it might seem to suggest the latter.

At the point of death, revived like a taper, Flamineo is unchanged enough to utter one of his secular parables, applied to "all that belong to Great men," but relevant to general humanity: ". . . to be like the Lyons i'th Tower on Candlemas day, to mourne if the Sunne shine, for feare of the pittiful remainder of winter to come" (266-8). This is a naturalistic argument against faith. Candlemas day celebrates the purification of the Virgin (antitype of Vittoria), and its candle-lighting ritual remembers Christ's light in the world. The hope represented by sun (Son) and the possible restoration to purity of a fallen world in exile (or imprisonment, as the Tower suggests) is denied by Flamineo, a false flame himself, as deception; the inevitable conclusion is winter and darkness. Flamineo describes his own life as being a place of ultimate lightless and lifeless confinement: "My life was a black charnell" (270); it was not even a whited sepulchre.[11] This is a description, though, not a confession. Flamineo apostrophizes his killer (and, presumably, Vittoria and Zanche as well) as "glorious villaines" (272), and invokes, not Christian passing bells, but pagan thunder, as signal of his departure from life. He is at the end proud of his life, and feels that he is, in dying, entombed with a community of like spirits, both the killers and the killed.

The implicit staging emphasizes this impenitence. At the last word and death of Flamineo, the English Ambassador (in whom, as at the arraignment, the audience may be expected to see itself), enters, crying "breake ope the doores" (277). The room as charnel is a tomb broken open to the English light of day. The English ambassador plays a role analogous to that of the priest who may, symbolically or literally, open the sepulchred church's doors on Easter morning. Lodovico, as one of the devils uncovered by this light, seems to refer both to the living and the dead when he queries "are wee betraid?" (278). Betrayal is ironic here, in the continuing Christian context, because he himself is of the tribe of the betrayers of Christ. Lodovico, who has to a great extent appeared as the opposite of Flamineo in nature, though not in morals, responds to Giovanni's query that it was by his own authority that this "Massakre" was committed, because his uncle Francisco "is a part of thee" (287). This is a very Flaminesque subterfuge, to attribute blackness to the white by association, to implicate the virtuous in the actions of the vicious. But Lodovico is partly accurate, not only in terms of blood-ties, but almost prophetically in suggesting that Giovanni is so much the creature of his political environment that he will not be able to sustain Christian virtue within it. Obviously, his argument is more pro forma than effectual. Condemned to prison and torture, he echoes Flamineo's proclamation of existential pride "That I can call this act mine owne" (197). Lodovico, by his own standards, has been actor in a tragicomedy, not a tragedy, his banishment and subjection redeemed by the completion of a triumphant self-controlled masterwork. At the same time his prized autonomy can be seen as defensive against the deepest fears of not being a free agent. We can hardly agree with Roma Gill that the stoic dignity of Vittoria's end "takes away any least shred of honour" Lodovico might have.[12] His defiance may be amoral, but it contains as much "dignity" as any defiance could have. His boast "I limb'd this night-peece and it was my best" (299) does possess dignity, but it indicts the misuse of art, or any human activity, whose goal is but to demonstrate its own autonomy.[13]

Webster's play, a night piece that he presumably hopes is his best, is the equal and opposite of Lodovico's play. Webster's play can have meaning only if the viewer approaches it from a viewpoint defined by its direct opposition to Lodovico's—the assumption of spiritual power in the universe, to which human will is automatically subject. In this view, Lodovico's best becomes the worst of all. A politic viewer will see as white actions which the Christian viewer sees as black, and would agree with Lodovico's judgement of his own act. Giovanni's monitory sentence, which concludes the play, "Let guilty men remember their black deedes, / Do leane on crutches, made of slender reedes" (302-3), may harmonize with the Christian viewer's response and reflect confidence in Giovanni as redeemer of the whole state.[14] But as befits Webster's moral paradoxes, the Christian may also find that the sentence does not accurately describe the power of light in this dark world.[15] The guilty, like the halt, and lame, the humble, may, after all, inherit the earth.

Chapter XI

The White Devil and Biathanatos

John Donne's Biathanatos was written around 1608-09, at a low point in his material and spiritual fortunes.[1] Although it was not printed until 1646, it, like much of his other early writing, was available in multiple manuscript copies. In fact, as early as 1610, Donne sent a copy to Lord Herbert of Cherbury, with a mocking declaration of its worth: "It shall not therefore kill it self; that is, not bury it self; for if it should do so, those reasons, by which that act should be defended or excused, were also lost with it."[2] Even later, partially disowning it as the work of "Jack Donne," rather than "Dr. Donne," he sent another copy to Sir Robert Ker (1619), with the request, "publish it not, but yet burn it not . . ."[3] Thus, while there is, and can be, no direct evidence that John Webster did or did not read Biathanatos in manuscript, there can be some certainty of the access of individuals in intellectual circles to it, and thereby of the currency of ideas on suicide in the air of The White Devil's time. Since both works so paradoxically meddle with an often taboo subject, and at such a close proximity in time to each other, it may be instructive to examine their treatments of suicide in each other's light.

Donne's Biathanatos defends the thesis that "Selfe-homicide is not so Naturally Sinne, that it may never be otherwise." It is paradoxical for the "thesis" to be made a "paradox," since this is what a thesis, particularly a Christian thesis in the ethical realm, sui generis is not. But Donne's thesis can be construed as a paradox under the assumption that it is defined by its opposition to any conception of Truth that is not paradoxical. So, in the expansion of the thesis, the more binding the defender's logic, the more the reader might be persuaded that he errs.

The paradox of Biathanatos is analogous to Flamineo's defense of his own suicide. Although Flamineo does not use Donne's own patristic resources, but rather the language of secular moral philosophy, his verbal defense and exaltation of death become increasingly compelling, as Donne's do, as he approaches the moment when the act of his death is revealed as a deception. Flamineo does overreach Donne, although Donne does discuss the subject, when his mock-suicide emerges as a spiritually obscene parody of the heretical yet persistent belief that Christ feigned His own crucifixion.

In his initial, and uncharacteristically autobiographical, remarks in <u>Biathanatos</u>, Donne relates, without the guile of Flamineo's autobiography, his own "sickly inclination" to suicide; he attributes it to his Catholic upbringing, his "first breeding and conversation with men of a suppressed and afflicted religion, accustomed to the despite of death, and hungry of an imagin'd Martyrdome."[4] The ironic identification of ardent Catholicism and its glorification of martyrdom with the strongest defense of suicide persists throughout Donne's treatise; it is also eminently, and ironically, present in <u>The White Devil</u>. For although, in Webster's Italy, no one explicitly courts death for spiritual reasons, there are three "martyrs"--Marcello, Cornelia, and Isabella--whose courting of death is almost extreme enough to be named self-homicide.

A basic endeavor of <u>Biathanatos</u> is to discover if a distinction can be made between homicide and self-homicide, and, if so, what one. The act of making the distinction involves demonstrating that, in some cases, the distinction cannot be made. But Donne does not even start with the premise that homicide itself can in all cases be defined as a <u>sin</u>. He insists on evoking the paradoxes of homicide committed to further morally defensible ends: for example, the conscience casts a stronger obligation upon one "than the precept of any Superior" (pp. 142-43), even if it is followed in <u>error</u>. ". . . If one in his conscience thinks that he ought to ly to save an innocent, or that he ought to steal to save a famished man, he is a <u>Homicide</u> if he ly not or steal not" (pp. 142-143). Left to ambiguous implication is whether a homicide committed to prevent another homicide is justified by conscience.

Further, however (p. 165), Donne emphasizes that the Mosaic commandment, "Thou shalt not kill," obedience to which is to "the Honour of God," has a lower moral priority than "Do unto thy neighbor . . .," which is the command of Charity. ("I am as much forbid to kill my neighbor as myself.") The conclusion drawn from this priority is that "If therefore there could bee a Necessity out of charity that I must doe an act of Idolatry, or kill, I were bound to the later" (p. 166). As is his practice in <u>Biathanatos</u> of confronting moral theory and social practice, he supplements the ideological priority of charity as a social ideal with reality: "For though the words be generall, <u>Thou shalt not kill</u>, we may kill beasts; Magistrates may kill men; and a private man in a just warre, may not onely kill, contrary to the sound of this Commandment, but hee may kill his Father, contrary to another" (p. 165).

In light of Donne's move toward a justification of self-homicide by showing that the homicide of others can be justified despite the Commandments, Flamineo's offer of self-homicide may seem perfectly consistent with the homicides he has previously committed, since he is at last doing unto himself what he has done unto others; he is practicing, retroactively, perfect charity. By cheating death and feigning suicide, he confutes

Vittoria's charge that he is "turn'd Atheist," and affirms her own rejection of Biathanatan arguements for suicide. But, in so feigning, <u>bona fide</u> or <u>mala fide</u>, he is, in Donne's terms, ultimately putting the Glory of God (and the Old Law) above the New Law of Charity, which his actual suicide would have obeyed.

Of course, in his self-resurrection, Flamineo also reveals the virtual equivalence of homicide and self-homicide. His plan of suicide is actually meant to provoke the acts of homicide of Vittoria and Zanche. In fact, he might be seen to be provoking them to self-damnation, according to Vittoria's own homily of V.vi.57-65, as Brachiano's murderers sought to assure <u>his</u> damnation during their homicide. The difference between homicide and self-homicide <u>seems</u> in our play to be only the a-ethical consideration of who fires the first shot. Flamineo, arisen, accuses the women of that worst of sins, absence of charity, and in his continuing pretence seems to deny that blurring of distinctions between homicide and self-homicide to which he has just contributed. Zanche, contrarily boasting at his downfall that they will

> . . . drive a stake
> Thorough thy body; for we'le give it out,
> Thou didst this violence upon thy selfe.   (V.vi.146-148)

seems to attach damnation, or popular beliefs concerning damnation, to self-homicide rather than to the homicide she and Vittoria have just (supposedly) committed.

Of course, the women's professed justification is homicide in self-defense; for to acquiesce in one's own destruction is regarded as self-homicide by "Dessertion" (Donne's term) of the will to resist one's own murder. <u>Biathanatos</u>, however, justifies, by precedent, the principle of non-resistance: ". . . even by a theefe, I may suffer myselfe to be killed, rather than kill him, in that mortal sinne" (p. 125). Here Donne appeals to English law, which punishes one who kills in self-defense with loss of goods, not of life, which is remitted by pardon; he makes this appeal to support the principle that killing in self-defense is sinful, and non-resistance is not. In fact (p. 126) he points to the contradiction between unprovoked suicide and murder in self-defense both being considered sinful. Since Vittoria and Flamineo seem to disagree so clearly on the issue of self-homicide, it is interesting to see them ultimately in accord on affirming such non-resistance when Lodovico and his crew present them with death. Vittoria and Flamineo do accord with the teachings of <u>Biathanatos</u> in this case; Donne permits one, despite non-resistance, to accept "any extrinsique or accessory helpe" (p. 126) without committing sin, if that help, when life is threatened. is offered by circumstance or by Providence; thus Vittoria appeals to the murderers' pity and their sense of sin ("aske forgiveness," l. 214), and Flamineo to bravado: "I'll cut my safety/Through your coates of steele" (ll. 177-78). But, circumstances failing, both quickly turn to acceptance. Although their very acceptance of death is tainted, in Christian terms, with bravado rather than the proper humility of martyrdom, it also goes beyond <u>mere</u> acceptance to conform to Donne's last species of homicide, "an actuall helping and concurrence to it" (p. 134) as committed against oneself. Flamineo's striking expression of this concurrence is "search my wound deeper" (1. 239), whereas Vittoria's has more the blush of spirituality: ". . . my greatest sinne lay in my blood. / Now my blood paies for it" (11. 240-241). Vittoria does seem paradoxically both to affirm and to deny her responsibility for her acts, and therefore as well the justice of her blood being split in expiation of them (as we have seen, her "blood" here can be the heritage over which she has no control).

Thus Flamineo and Vittoria move from the masquerading of death, where they toy paradoxically with the distinctions between homicide and self-homicide, to a final stage, where they are murdered in the condition closest of all to self-murder: concurrence. It is interesting to note that this concurrence in self-homicide is anticipatorily parodied in the murder of Brachiano. Donne makes the distinction between one's own concurrence in one's death, and the acts of strangers and relatives in aiding the death of one whose suffering they pity. He refers, among other examples of mercy-killing or euthanasia, to the Italian Sansovino's false account of English customs wherein relatives pull on the legs of a hanged man to hasten his end. For Donne, the aid of "strangers" is an injury to the doomed, who might be suddenly pardoned, and to Justice, "who hath appointed a painfull death to deterre others" (p. 137). It is almost in the exact terms of this discussion that Gasparo calls for the final solution to the poisoned Brachiano's torments:

> Strangle him in private. What! Will you call him againe
> To live in treble torments? for charitie,
> For Christian charitie, avoid the Chamber.
> (V.iii.172-74)

Such is Webster's beautifully ironic version of the assisted concurrence in homicide. The murderers themselves will "charitably" assist the condemned man's death; the wife and friends of the victim are accused by the murderers of "uncharitably" furthering his torments by calling him to life. We might see Lodovico and his crew as similarly assisting Flamineo and Vittoria actually to consummate the homicides they do not have the will to perform on each other with their own hands.

Both the issue of choice between concurrence and self-defense in homicide, and that of the distinction between homicide and self-homicide, are at the center of <u>The White Devil</u>. To what extent can <u>all</u> the killings in the play actually be considered suicides? To what extent do the victims in some way accede to their own destruction? To what extent can all the deaths in <u>The White Devil</u>, in the justificatory terms in

Biathanatos, be considered the results of virtuous action, in that they work to an ultimate higher collective good, to the fulfilling of the Laws of Nature, Reason, and God?

It is under the rubric of its possible violation of each of the above Laws that Donne discusses self-homicide. Although the Law of God is the highest, Donne repeatedly shows that there is no Scriptural justification for the absolute characterization of self-homicide as a violation of it. In fact, the Laws of Reason--those established by humans to govern human institutions--are repeatedly appealed to by Donne in response to those who would give absolute primacy to the laws of God. If "all authority of Life and Death is from God," "shall we therefore dare to condemn utterly all those states and governments, where Fathers, Husbands, and Masters had jurisdiction over Children, Wives, and servants lives?" (p. 159). In fact, Donne rejects a definition of sin as that which is against divine law, in favor of one deriving from Aquinas, of that which is against the rules of natural reason or eternal law (p. 34), and he asserts that in practice these laws are so intertwined that to separate one from another is "a Chymick Work" (p. 340). His reductive ambiguity tends to leave us with the foundation of Natural Law, "selfe-preservation," as one certain gauge whereby the sinfulness of any act may be judged; and, certainly by slight canting, self-preservation becomes "no other thing than a naturall affection and appetition of good, whether true or seeming" (p. 49).

That this primal principle of self-preservation is not to be construed naturalistically Donne immediately establishes by: "Certainly the desire of Martyrdome, though the body perish, is a <u>Selfe-preservation</u>, because thereby, out of our election our best part is advanc'd" (p. 49). To complete the paradox, then, having spiritualized the concept of self-preservation, Donne can assert that self-homicide, seeming to be the antithesis of self-preservation, can actually be a form of self-preservation if the suicide proposes in the accomplishment of his/her act a "greater good." Self-homicide can thereby fulfill the general law of nature, "which is an affection of good, true, or seeming; . . . if that which I affect by death bee truely a greater good . . ." (p. 50).

Judged by these standards, it is difficult to separate the suicides in <u>The White Devil</u> from the homicides, or to find any homicide, self-homicide, or propensity thereto, in the play, to be sinful. Camillo concurs, through his credulity, in Flamineo's gulling, and, as part of this, in seeking the imagined good of Vittoria's sexual approval, in the military adventures whose preparatory "exercise" costs him his life. He lends himself to self-destructive acts voluntarily, in "appetition of a seeming good," and thereby places Flamineo's killing of him within the confines of Natural Law. The same can be said of Isabella and Marcello. In taking the onus of divorce upon herself, Isabella imitates the condition of martyrdom; she accepts the death of her public self, her reputation. In the terms of <u>Biathanatos</u>, this is not sinful, since her conscience, however errant, led her to the act in good faith. As she offers her virtuous reputation to her husband, its scourger, she offers her lips to her poisonous husband's picture, concurring in his sentence of her, "Deserting" her life in offering it to him. There is a connection of circumstance between Isabella and Cornelia as martyrs, since Cornelia, after Marcello's death, subjects herself to mutilation of mind (and presumably of body, in self-lacerating gestures), and Isabella, assuming the responsibility of divorce, mutilates her spiritual body--in Calvin's figure, quoted by Donne: since God made husband and wife one body, divorce is a mutilation thereof (p. 134).

Donne himself seems ambivalent about whether self-mutilation falls under the category of self-homicide for a greater good. Certainly Cornelia, though she might seem to merit the label of "martyr" in common social parlance, has a more complex homicidal identity than this, or than that of self-mutilator. With her "you shall put us both into one coffin" (V.ii.37) she gestures towards self-homicide from grief and despair. This is the motivation which Vittoria, using traditional doctrine, preaches against in Flamineo, and which Donne uses Scriptural example to deny: "all desperation is not sinnefull" (p. 27). Charging Flamineo and then dropping her knife, Cornelia relinquishes her own act of homicide, and, imitating Isabella, distorts the truth to implicate the innocent; she declares Marcello the aggressor, making his death even closer to self-homicide than it actually was. Certainly, curing Flamineo with "Halfe of thyself lies there" (V.ii.56), she accuses him of self-mutilation, yet her ultimate defense of him seems to affirm what Donne asserts in refuting the connection between self-homicide and despair: that any person, no matter how desperate and faithless, may yet be repentant up to the very last moment of life (pp. 31-32).

Marcello himself seems to offer himself to the sword by refusing to moderate his criticisms of Flamineo's morality, in full knowledge of Flamineo's willingness to kill. We might consider Marcello most clearly offering himself to martyrdom, of all the play's "virtuous" characters, since he involves the emblem of the crucifix over his death-scene, takes on almost a Christlike posture in relation to his mother, and dies with the affirmation of Christian ideals on his lips.

Brachiano is by far the most difficult case to portray as a self-homicide. Yet all the tendencies of his romantic adventurism are to put him in obvious self-jeopardy. By taking Vittoria from her house of refuge, and himself from Rome, he exposes himself to willing vengeance. His assumption of invulnerability leads him to host and court his killers. As Francisco exclaims when Brachiano calls for his beaver, "Hee cals for his destruction" (V.ii.79). It is his murderers' fervent desire that his "perpetual damnation" be achieved, so that the condition of martyrdom cannot be attached to him, by the judges of this world or the next; his acceptance of death, without any last minute calls for retaliation against his murderers, contradicting their intent, does create such a condition. He has been a murderer for a seeming good--the love of Vittoria; while this does not justify his actions, in terms of any law, it makes his acquiescence in his own death seem more justifiable, in that he is dying "for" her, with her name ambiguously on his lips.

I am suggesting that the chain of homicides in The White Devil can be seen as in essence self-homicides, the victims co-participants with the assailants in their achievement. The final scene, where homicide and self-homicide mirror each other, ironically declares the impossibility of passing negative moral judgement on either of them. To the degree that these crimes can be considered self-homicide, and therefore, by the criteria of Donne's discussion in Biathanatos, not sinful, they all occur to effect a "greater good"--the restoration of civic order and virtue.

Donne is very clear that Death, in itself, "is an act of Gods justice, and when he is pleased to inflict it, he may chuse his Officer, and constitute my selfe as well as any other" (p. 103). Not only this, but (following Bellarmine), God may "work evill in us" by disposing us "rather to this then to that evil, and He may conversely direct our evil act to His ultimate good." ". . . There is no externall act naturally evill; . . . circumstances condition them and give them their nature" (pp. 172-173). Those who kill others, and themselves, in The White Devil, by this standard, can be seen as evildoers only if circumstances define their acts as evil. In The White Devil circumstances define a course of divinely-directed evils, resulting in the elimination or disempowering of evildoers and the ultimate civil triumph of the virtuous Giovanni, who alone is implicated in no acts of homicide or self-homicide. Perhaps beyond control of their consciousness, those who die in The White Devil--including those we might say "deserve to die"--give their bodies for the Good of others. ". . . We are all shepherds of one another, and owe one another this dutie, of giving our temporall lives, for another's spirituall advantage; yes, for his temporall" (p. 187).

Notes

Chapter I

[1] Elizabeth M. Brennan, "An Understanding Auditory: An Audience for John Webster," in _John Webster_, ed. Brian Morris (London: Benn, 1970), p. 11.

[2] Lee Bliss, _The World's Perspective: John Webster and the Jacobean Drama_ (New Brunswick, N. J.: Rutgers Univ. Press, 1983), p. 199.

[3] Brennan, p. 14.

[4] Inga-Stina Ekeblad, "Webster's Constructional Rhythm," _ELH_, 24 (1957), p. 169.

[5] Anders Dallby, _The Anatomy of Evil: A Study of John Webster's The White Devil_ (Lund, Sweden: Gleerup, 1974), p. 25. See also pp. 35-37.

[6] Paula S. Berggren, "Spatial Imagery in Webster's Tragedies," _SEL_, 20 (1980), p. 288.

[7] Coburn Freer, _The Poetics of Jacobean Drama_ (Baltimore: The Johns Hopkins University Press, 1981), p. 19.

Chapter II

[1] The Quarto makes the first word a question, but John Russell Brown in his Revels edition (London, 1960), states that "?" often stood for "!" in contemporary typography.

[2] "Some form of Lodovico's "Banisht!" was from earliest medieval times the sign of Satan's arrival in hell," Peter B. Murray, _A Study of John Webster_ (The Hague: Mouton 1969), p. 108; see Murray's discussion of banishment in the play, pp. 100-112.

[3] Norma Kroll, "The Democratean Universe in Webster's _White Devil_," _Comparative Drama_, 7 (1973), p. 3.

[4] Kroll, p. 3.

[5] Murray, p. 48. See his detailed discussion of the connection between World, Fortune, and Whore, pp. 57 ff.

[6] Vittoria also shares with her deaths-man the taste for prodigall feastes, according to her accusers; see III.ii.75-80.

[7] Susan H. McLeod, *Dramatic Imagery in the Plays of John Webster* (Salzburg, Austria: Institut for Englische Sprache und Literatur, 1977), p. 32.

[8] "These allusions to religious precepts create dramatic tension by establishing the possibility for men to avoid what is clearly for Webster the ultimate tragedy, spiritual damnation," William W. G. Dwyer, *A Study of John Webster's Use of Renaissance Natural and Moral Philosophy* (Salzburg, Austria: Institut fur Englische Sprache und Literatur, 1976), p. 26. But is Webster not as sympathetic to wordly suffering and abuse as he is to spiritual?

[9] S. W. Sullivan, "The Tendency to Rationalize in *The White Devil* and *The Duchess of Malfi*," *Yearbook of English Studies*, 4 (1974), 77-84. Sullivan finds this evasion everywhere, even in Francisco, who evades acknowledging his evil through appeals to "a pleasing concept of honor and nobility" (p. 78). It would take more than assertion to prove that Francisco's revenge "is" an evasion rather than something he actually believes is morally justified, whatever we might hypothesize about its appearance to his audience. There is much verbal *evidence*, discussed later, that Francisco is a politic exploiter of the language of "nobility."

[10] Here, and subsequently, Webster's homiletic "borrowings" from traditional literature *must* be seen in their dramatic context, and that context shows that they interact problematically with "reality," questioning, even if not discrediting, the tradition from which they are drawn. They are active propositions about the real world placed in question. How can it be said that "Webster has no interest in philosophical issues or metaphysical ideas," as Robert Ornstein does in his *Moral Vision of Jacobean Tragedy* (Madison, Wis.: University of Wisconsin Press, 1960), p. 134.

[11] This aesthetic concern culminates in his characterization of the final murders in V.vi, as his masterpiece of limning.

[12] In contrast, E. B. Benjamin feels that "as we come to know Lodovico, we feel that he is not wholly bad." E. B. Benjamin, "Patterns of Morality in *The White Devil*," *English Studies*, 46 (1965), p. 2.

[13] Robert P. Griffin, *John Webster: Politics and Tragedy* (Salzburg, Austria: Institut fur Englische Sprache und Literatur, 1972), p. 68.

[14] See Bob Hodge, "Mine Eyes Dazzle: False Consciousness in Webster's Plays," in *Literature, Language, and Society in England, 1580-1680*, ed. David Afers, et. al. (Dublin: Gill and McMillan, 1981), pp. 102-106.

Gunnar Boklund, *The Sources of The White Devil* (Cambridge, Mass.: Harvard University Press, 1957), p. 162.

[16] James T. Henke, "John Webster's Motif of 'Consuming:' An Approach to the Dramatic Unity and Tragic Vision of *The White Devil* and *The Duchess of Malfi*," *Neuphilologische Mitteilungen*, 76 (1975), p. 630. R. W. Dent shows in his *John Webster's Borrowing* (Berkeley: University of California Press, 1960), pp. 78-80 how much of Flamineo's satire in these passages is borrowed from Montaigne. ". . . the whole Bracciano-Vittoria affair plays allusively against *Antony and Cleopatra's* titanic passion" (Bliss, p. 102).

[17] Roger Stilling, *Love and Death in Renaissance Tragedy* (Baton Rouge: Louisiana State Univ. Press, 1976), p. 230.

[18] The same *discordia concors* that we find between Lodovico and Flamineo in III.iii.

[19] Robert F. Whitman, "The Moral Paradox of Webster's Tragedy," *PMLA*, 90 (1975), p. 898.

[20] "Perspective glasses" provided the sense of dangerous visual deception; the viewer had constantly to review and reinterpret their pictures to move towards the truth. Flamineo's vision characterizes a way of viewing the whole play, and a way of viewing the world, by means of the play. See M. L. Bradbrook's discussion of this in her John Webster, *Citizen and Dramatist* (New York: Columbia University Press, 1980), p. 126. For more views of visual deception in 17th century literature (with no mention of Webster), see Ernest W. Gilman, *The Curious Perspective: Literary and Pictorial Wit in the Seventeenth Century* (New Haven: Yale Univ. Press 1978). The "perspective" approach has also been considered an aesthetic flaw, as in this scene, with Flamineo's and Cornelia's views of the love-scene in conflict: ". . . there will be nothing but 'laterall views' presented to us . . . nothing will emerge from the confusion, leaving us all in a mist," Inga-Stina Ewbank, "Webster's Realism, or, 'A Cunning Piece Wrought Perspective.'" in *John Webster*, ed. Brian Morris (London: Ernest Benn, 1970), p. 168.

[21] "Opening your case hard" alludes to the tapping of a wine cask: Floyd L. Goodwyn, Jr., *Image Pattern and Moral Vision in John Webster* (Salzburg, Austria: Institut for Englische Sprache und Literatur, 1977), p. 18. This is a sexually suggestive reference, and ties in with other evocations of wine as a source of self-abandon.

[22] Although in III.ii.148, Vittoria sees them as unbreakable.

[23] That Zanche "brings it out" suggests that the tryst has not been taking place on the intimate inner stage, but in a centerstage "garden." See Brown, p. 23.

[24] As noticed by Jacqueline Pearson, *Tragedy and Tragicomedy in the Plays of John Webster* (Totowa, N. J.: Barnes and Noble, 1980), p. 59.

[25] Kroll, p. 6.

[26] Muriel West, *The Devil and John Webster* (Salzburg, Austria: Institut fur Englische Sprache und Literatur, 1974), p. 159.

[27] Kroll, p. 7.

[28] West, p. 163.

[29] Bradbrook, p. 123.

[30] See Brown, p. 25.

[31] Brown, p. li.

[32] Lucas's edition, p. 113.

[33] Holy Sonnet IX: "If poisonous minerals, and if that tree."

[34] B. J. Layman, "The Equilibrium of Opposites in *The White Devil*: A Reinterpretation," *PLMA*, 74 (1959), p. 338.

[35] Vittoria kneeling to Cornelia's reproaches parodies "the dutiful child claiming a parent's blessing," D. C. Gunby, *Webster: The White Devil* (London: Edward Arnold, 1971), p. 26.

[36] Throughout the play, the kiss is a major example of the "figure in action" defined by Hereward T. Price in an influential article, "The Function of Imagery in Webster," *PLMA*, 70 (1955), pp. 717-739. See a discussion of the staging of the figure here in Peter Thomson, "Webster and the Actor," in *John Webster*, ed. Morris (op. cit.), pp. 39-40.

[37] Roma Gill, "'Quaintly Done': A Reading of 'The White Devil,'" *Essays and Studies*, 19 (1966), p. 51. See also Paula Berggren, "Womanish Mankind: Four Jacobean Heroines," *International Journal of Women's Studies*, 1 (1978), 394-362. To Berggren, Vittoria is driven to manipulate others because she, as many other contemporary women, has been denied the "right to act honestly and openly" (p. 352). It is revealing to see her as "family ridden" (p. 352) and under great pressure as bait to Webster's original audience would not have been emancipated enough to empathize with such a condition.

[38] W. G. Dwyer, *A* *Study* *of* *John* *Webster's* *Use* *of* *Renaissance* *Natural* *and* *Moral* *Philosophy* (Salzburg, Austria: Institut fur Englische Sprache und Literatur, 197), p. 35.

[39] cf. Donne's Satyre III.

> . . . on a huge hill,
> Cragg'd and steep, Truth stands, and hee that will
> Reach her, about must, and about must goe;
> And what the hills suddennes resists, winne so.

[40] The winding path is an ancient commonplace; Donne directs it toward truth, Flamineo toward falsehood.

[41] In fact, as J. W. Lever says, in *The* *Tragedy* *of* *State* (London: Methuen, 1971), p. 94: "The total effect of this scene is not to focus attention on illicit romance, on Camillo's marital rights, on the cynicism of the go-betweens, or on Cornelia's virtue, but to place all these in the wider context of a society where declassed intellectuals i.e., Flamineo find the only alternative to galleys, or gallows, in serving without scruple the desires of their rulers."

[42] David Gunby sees Webster combining in the major characters, such as Francisco and Brachiano, both individualized and humour/morality derived characteristics. For example, Francisco is "not only an Old Duke, but also phlemagtic in temperament, and a descendent of the morality vice" (Gunby, p. 14). Does analysis in terms of Renaissance psychology contradict individuation of character" Francisco becomes choleric later in the play; in this scene, politic though he be, it is hard to find Iagoesque attributes in him.

[43] The historical Isabella was known for her loose living. She was "a gay, unrepentant adultress, turned by Webster into a faithful, long-suffering wife" (Boklund, pp. 21, 39). Does any of the historical Isabella remain in this scene of assertion?

[44] As articulated to a wide audience in Guevara's *Diall* *of* *Princes*, Elyot's *Governour*, Erasmus's *Education* *of* *a* *Christian* *Prince*, Baldwin's *Treatise* *of* *Morall* *Philosophy*, and other Works; see Dwyer, *passim*, and George Holland, "The Function of the Minor Characters in The White Devil," PQ, 52 (1973), p. 52.

[45] Brown, p. 39, sees Francisco quibbling on "discretion" as "prudence," when Giovanni, two lines above, meant "discernment, good judgement."

[46] Brown, p. 38.

[47] For the Jacobean urge to nostalgic Tudor restoration, see Richard F. Hardin, *Michael* *Drayton* *and* *the* *Passing* *of* *Elizabethan* *England* (Lawrence, Kansas: Univ. of Kansas Press, 1973).

[48] Among other discussions, see Dallby, pp. 114-117 and Ralph Berry, *The Art of John Webster* (Oxford: Clarendon Press, 1972), pp. 83-89.

[49] Freer (p. 140) sees this tirade (ll. 180-91) of Brachiano as a stylized piece, of "lyric integrity," its two sections each concluding with "hieratic" figures ("the great Duke," the "Priest that sung the wedding Mass,") corresponding to Francisco and Monticelso, and both ridiculed.

[50] James R. Hurt, "Inverted Rituals in Webster's *The White Devil*," *JEGP*, 61 (1962), p. 44. It has been shown that this, rather than extreme unction itself, is the ritual parodied by the assassins (see below).

[51] Hurt, pp. 42, 45. The same inversions of ritual occur in *The Duchess of Malfi*. See James C. Calderwood, "*The Duchess of Malfi*: Styles of Ceremony," *Essays in Criticism*, 12 (1962), pp. 133-147.

[52] Irving Ribner sees her as "forced" to appear evil, as other virtuous characters are (e.g., Cornelia forced to lie), and this forced appearance of evil as a deep symptom of corruption. Irving Ribner, "Webster's Italian Tragedies," *Tulane Drama Review*, 5, no. 3 (1961), p. 109. "Isabella is as virtuous as her source--original was dissolute" (Bliss, p. 115).

[53] "When she does put the blame on herself, she does it with such an abandoned hatred towards Vittoria . . . that we may be tempted to think she is indeed that which she seems, 'a foolish, mad, and jealous woman,' perhaps deceiving herself" (Brown, p. lii).

[54] "Unkindness" has its dual senses of a lack of charity and a betrayal of kinship.

[55] Francisco's goal in thus dishonoring a rival Duke at this point could itself be seen, it is true, as not "sincere" but "politic."

[56] Webster fantasizes about the secrecy of the counter-irritant effects of *cantharis*, the Spanish fly. See Brown, p. 47.

[57] "Plenty makes me poor" is an emblem-book commonplace; the throwing of pasquils and satires in at windows was a commonplace of action; a dramatic example is in *Julius Caesar*, II.i.

[58] See Robert B. Bennett, "John Webster's Strange Dedication: An Inquiry into Literary Patronage and Jacobean Court Intrigue," *ELR*, 7 (1977), pp. 352-367.

[59] Dwyer, p. 24.

Chapter III

[1] See Freer, p. 242, note 10, who quotes Thomas Blount's *Nomo-lexicon: A Law Dictionary* (London, 1670), to the effect that an arraignment is "a calling upon the prisoner by name, reading the indictment, demanding his guilt or innocence, then entering a plea; if the plea is guilty, the court gives judgement." Here Vittoria's plea is implicitly not guilty, so the legal process can be considered corrupted in two ways: either her arraignment becomes a corrupted trial, or else she is treated as though she had actually pleaded guilty, and is sentenced prior to a justified trial. Bliss, as an example of many (pp. 112-114) continues to make no distinction between "arraignment" and "trial."

[2] Brian P. Levack, *The Civil Lawyers in England, 1603-1641* (Oxford: Oxford Univ. Press, 1973), p. 104.

[3] Sir Henry Finch, *Law, or a Discourse Thereof* (London, 1627), pp. 81 ff.

[4] See Sir Edward Coke's *Reports*, ed. George Wilson (Dublin, 1793), p. 25.

[5] *The Arraignment of John Selman* . . . (London, 1612), pp. 16-17.

[6] *Selman*, p. 12.

[7] For examples see John H. Langbein, *Prosecuting Crime in the Renaissance: England, Germany, France* (Cambridge, Mass.: Harvard Univ. Press, 1974), pp. 45-55.

[8] For example, *The Arraignment, Judgement, Confession, and Execution of Humphrey Stafford, Gentleman* (London, 1607).

[9] Robert Lacey, *Sir Walter Raleigh* (New York: Atheneum, 1974), p. 296.

[10] Thomas B. Howell, ed., *Cobbett's Complete Collection of State Trials* . . ., II (London: Hansard, 1809), col. 7.

[11] *State Trials*, II, col. 9.

[12] *State Trials*, II, col. 22.

[13] *State Trials*, II, col. 20.

[14] *State Trials*, II, col. 20.

[15] *State Trials*, II, col. 18-19.

Chapter IV

[1] Each (apocryphally defined) "act" is centered upon a ritual or spectacular set-piece: the procession in I.ii, these murders, the arraignment, the Papal election, Brachiano's marriage procession and tournament (Dallby, 36).

[2] "Though Isabella is a symbol of idolatrous Roman Catholicism, she also represents an evil over-emphasis on married devotion."

[3] "The Black Book" in *The Works of Thomas Middleton*, ed. A. H. Bullen (repr. N. Y.: ADS Press, 1964), 8, p. 21.

[4] Marcello, a future victim, is authoritatively described as "vertuous," and his joint arrest with Flamineo following the incident further confuses guilt and innocence.

[5] Lucas, I, 224.

[6] Brown (p. 60) suggests that this "Lawyer" is so ignorant of the law, and so different from the lawyer in III.ii, that the speech preface may be a miswriting of "courtier."

[7] Harry Bruder, "Analogic Form in Webster's *White Devil*, *PAPA*, 5 (1979), p. 45.

[8] Devils are associated with blackbirds; the blackbird's claw is the devil's claw; therefore "no auditor in Webster's day would have needed a definition to understand that the day would have needed a definition to understand that the Spanish Ambassador was a devil" (West, pp. 32-33). But Vittoria does not, contrary to West (p. 31), "become" a blackbird herself in V.vi.184; she uses "blackbird" as a metaphor for any prey.

[9] H. Bruce Franklin, "The Trial Scene of Webster's *The White Devil* Examined in Terms of Renaissance Rhetoric," *SEL*, 1 (1961), p. 36.

[10] Dent, *Borrowing*, pp. 10-11. In contrast, Bliss (p. 112) says, "In demonstrating the corruption of justice by powerful self-interest . . . the trial brilliantly displays the public world to which Flamineo and Vittoria aspire."

[11] Brown, p. 65.

[12] Griffin, p. 85.

[13] Franklin, pp. 37-38.

[14] Gunby, p. 34. He also considers her "ravished justice" exclamation later to be self-serving and hypocritical, since she has actually gotten off easily; it was "a sentence just and merciful."

[15] Dallby (p. 79) notes the pattern of critiques of rhetoric throughout the play--ironic in contrast to the play's dependency on false rhetoric for its linked ironies. As Brachiano says, the devil is a linguist (V.iii.102-5).

[16] R. W. Dent, "The White Devil, or Vittoria Corombona?" Renaissance Drama, 9 (1966), p. 194; Murray, chapter IV.

[17] Dallby, p. 129.

[18] Imagery recalling the condition of defiled garden and fallen Eden is also strongly evoked in I.ii (see McLeod, p. 51); here euphuistic rhetoric is parodied (Franklin, 40).

[19] Franklin, p. 40.

[20] Franklin, p. 41.

[21] Brown, quoting D. P. V. Akrigg in N & Q, cxciii (1948), pp. 427-8, suggests the "estates" reference alludes to Raleigh, who lost Sherborne because a few words were omitted in its deed of trust to his wife. See chapter III.

[22] Franklin, p. 42.

[23] Franklin (pp. 42-43) defines Vittoria's rhetoric as Attic, ". . . of extreme brevity, plain language, lack of rhythm, and an apparent carelessness."

[24] Franklin, p. 44

[25] "Vittoria speaks as if she were the rich source from which man gleans his worth. She speaks as if she holds over man a power with which he cannot deal, as if, through her, his fortunes prosper or fail" (Goodwyn, p. 27).

[26] Murray, pp. 33-37.

[26a] West sees Vittoria as a black and fiery, not a white, devil, for the transparency of crystal (see IV.ii.89) makes it invisible, not white (see West, p. 27).

[27] Often it ends in such formulations as "Vittoria seems to us a splendid creature, though fallen, her dignity greatest when she stands at bay, on trial or facing her murderers," Margot Heinemann, Puritanism and Theatre: Thomas Middleton and Opposition Drama Under the Early Stuarts (Cambridge: Cambridge Univ. Press, 1980), p. 174.

[28] See John F. McElroy, "The White Devil, Women Beware Women, and the Limits of Rationalist Criticism," SEL, 19 (1979), p. 301.

[29] This is James I's motto. "Certain people must have taken this as a joke on Brachiano--the joke of a fool using the words of a king. If they saw, instead of this joke, an allegorical correspondence between Brachiano and James, the joke, possibly a grim one, would have been on Webster" (Franklin, pp. 45-46). As Franklin notes (p. 47), Brachiano is attacked with impunity.

[30] To Franklin (p. 47), this speech embodies "white diabolism," insinuating guilt while pleading for dismissal of charges.

[31] Venice, unhistorically, Brown suggests, because of the city's reputation for prostitution (p. 77).

[31a] Bruder, p. 43.

[32] Larry S. Champion, "Webster's *The White Devil* and the Jacobean Tragic Perspective," *TSLL*, 16 (1974), p. 438.

[33] Benjamin, p. 12.

[34] Thomas B. Stroup, "Flamineo and the 'Comfortable Words'," *Renaissance Papers* (1964), pp. 12-16.

[35] Flamineo "suffers from a sort of mistaken Calvinistic fatalism; underneath his scorn, he believes he was lost from the beginning" (Stroup, p. 16).

[36] Lodovico's vow to Flamineo is a textual crux. Brown has it "Precious girn, rogue / We'll never part," from the first Quarto's "Pretious grine rouge," while Lucas adopts Q3's "Precious Rogue." Brown has "girn" in the two senses of "snarl" and "snare," referring to Flamineo's suggested alternative to a mirror: a saucer of a witch's congealed blood. Flamineo's conceit is "precious" therefore to Lodovico, not to the rogue himself (Brown, pp. 89-90).

[37] Henke's view (p. 640) of the connection between sexuality and spirituality, when they are figuratively presented through eating, is illuminating. "The lover is the 'god-eater' who seeks to partake of the vitality beyond reason that is the basis of all life." If sexual union is debased through gastronomic imagery in the play, just as spiritual communion is (as here), Webster might be seen as skeptical of consolation either by the spirit or by the world.

Chapter V

[1] For an extensive treatment of her heritage, see Marjorie N. Malvern, *Venus in Sackcloth: The Magdalen's Origins and Metamorphosis* (Carbondale, Ill.: Southern Illinois Univ. Press, 1975).

²John 29:17. See the Geneva Bible facsimile (Madison: University of Wisconsin Press, 1969).

³See Malvern, esp. pp. 37-38.

⁴All quotes from the play are from the edition in David Bevington, ed., *Medieval Drama* (Boston: Houghton, Mifflin, 1975).

⁵Jacob Bennett, "The *Mary Magdalene* of Bishop's Lynn," *SP*, 75 (1978), 1-9, emphasizes that the play is not static, but sharply individualizes Mary and emphasizes her "inner conflict."

⁶All quotes from the Tudor Facsimile Texts edition (London, 1908).

⁷Darryl Gess, *Measure for Measure, the Law, and the Convent* (Princeton: Princeton Univ. Press, 1979), esp. chapter 2.

⁸All quotes from *The Dramatic Works of Thomas Dekker*, ed. Fredson Bowers, II (Cambridge: Cambridge Univ. Press, 1964).

Chapter VI

¹Murray, p. 38.

²Holland, p. 46.

³Bliss, p. 120.

⁴Gunby, p. 37.

⁵His quote from the *Aeneid* suggests that he will now seek aid from Hell (Gunby, p. 37).

⁶Boklund, p. 110.

⁷"As pander [Flamineo] is 'like an old/ Proverbe, *Hold the Candle before the devell*'," (Murray, p. 45, quoting *Honest Whore I*, II.i.35-36).

⁸West sees "the devil's secretary," a traditional locution for one who has made a pact with the devil, as specifically alluding here to the Scottish Dr. Fian, whose witchcraft deeply interested James I, and who was known as "secretary to the devil," Bothwell (West, p. 50).

⁹The preceding action appears to be set *outside* the House. At Vittoria's entry, an interior scene is indicated (especially with the bed). What staging produced this movement is not clear (see Brown, p. 103).

[10] Bradbrook finds here Brachiano fulfilling the "perspective" motif begun in I.ii; he suddenly sees the "monster" hidden in the picture--Vittoria herself, when seen at the right angle. She is a devil, rather than a saint, in a reliquary (Bradbrook, p. 127).

[11] As a result of an ulcer's corruption; an element of the play's disease imagery that echoes the "exulceration" of sins proclaimed by the verbose lawyer in III.ii (Berry, p. 87).

[12] Revealing of how deeply Webster's Italy was perceived as England's mirror, the third Quarto (1665) of *The White Devil* reads, for "a great bridge," "London Bridge" (Brown, p. 110).

[13] Another example of the sentimental sexual stereotyping of Vittoria, and the difficulty of apprehending her true "self." With the last words, Vittoria "is not like the strumpet whose goal has been attained, rather like a very feminine woman who has been convinced against her better judgement" (Benjamin, p. 5).

[14] Surely, despite "coupling," there is no "insinuation of homosexuality" (Gunby, p. 40) here. Brachiano and Vittoria are male and female.

[15] It is based extensively on Hierome Bignon, *A Brief, but an Effectual Treatise of the Election of Popes* (London, 1605), excerpted in Brown, pp. 194-97.

[16] Berggren, p. 291.

[17] Brown, p. 196.

[18] For example, see Champion, pp. 454-455.

[19] Benjamin, p. 13.

[20] Boklund, p. 88.

[21] Hurt, p. 43. Monticelso's rebuke is, however often seen as "sincere" and as signalling his own disassociation, as Pope, from the conspiracy.

[22] Brown suggests (p. 123) that these include the ambassadors who have just witnessed Brachiano's excommunication. Therefore, "their mere presence on the stage would enforce Webster's often-repeated comments on the power of great men and the sycophancy of court society."

[23] See Dallby, p. 168.

[24] Francisco is "a white man with a black heart disguised as a black man with a white spirit," Samuel Schuman, "Theatre of Fine Devices'--The Visual Imagery of Webster's Tragedies," Renaissance and Reformation, 4, n.s. (1980), p. 89.

[25] Thomson, in John Webster, pp. 38-39.

[26] As in his metaphor of cudgelling a tree to make it bear fruit (V.i.183-85), where morality is reduced to pure physicality (Goodwyn, p. 86).

[27] "Flamineo believes he has a right to manage his own affairs; Marcello believes he has the right to tell Flamineo what to do. Each is a devil to his own brother" (West, p. 87). Brown considers (p. liii) Marcello's flaws limited to "smugness and self-pity."

[28] Inevitably the Oedipal allusion has been psychologized (see Hodge, p. 117). It would seem self-evident that there could be rivalry between Flamineo and Marcello for Cornelia's approval. But that Flamineo has any possibility or desire of gaining it, and therefore could be in battle with his brother for it, seems dubious.

[29] Alluding to the story in Pettie, that their hatred so burned that their bodies, united on the pyre, still gave forth separate flames flaring in opposite directions (Brown, p. 135).

Chapter VII

[1] Arthur Kinney, ed., Rogues, Vagabonds, and Beggars (Barre, Mass.: Imprint Society 1973), p. 110. See also A. V. Judges's classic anthology, The Elizabethan Underworld (London: Routledge & Kegan Paul, 1930).

[2] Kinney, p. 111.

[3] Kinney, p. 103.

[4] Kinney, pp. 164-65.

[5] E. D. Pendry, ed. Thomas Dekker: . . . Selected Writings (Cambridge, Mass.: Harvard University Press, 1968), p. 177.

[6] Pendry, p. 173.

[7] Pendry, p. 178.

[8] Pendry, p. 198.

[9] Pendry, p. 244.

[10] Pendry, p. 242.

[11] Pendry, p. 244.

[12] Pendry, p. 252.

[13] Pendry, p. 252.

Chapter VIII

[1] Holland considers her a "powerful tragic figure," and evocative of her Roman namesake, embodying ideals of Family and Motherhood in a manner not accessible to the present. Her verse "often suggests the mythic and moral implications of the actions of the major characters" (Holland, pp. 48-49). Murray sees her and the other ostensibly virtuous characters mainly governed by pride, self-righteousness, or hypocrisy (Murray, p. 40).

[2] Dent, "White Devil," p. 185.

[3] This stabbing must be what has made Flamineo into an "existentialist" for so many, and a practitioner of "gratuitous acts" (see Layman, p. 343), despite the weight of his heritage as a fusion of traditional limited "types."

[4] Cornelia alone can unmask Flamineo's "self-protective role;" in confrontation with her he exhibits his "ambivalence toward the persona he has fashioned for himself" (McElroy, p. 309).

[5] See J. R. Brown's analysis of this moment in his edition, p. xlvi.

[6] The poisoned beaver is the antitype of the "charm'd night cap" in which he watches Isabella die (McLeod, pp. 62-63).

[7] Goodwyn, p. 31.

[8] Based on Erasmus's colloquy *Funus*, which contrasts the deaths of spiritually and worldly-oriented men.

[9] McLeod, pp. 65-68.

[10] Can "Vittoria Corombona" actually be translated as "victory crowned" (Kroll, p. 19)? It might as well, and as ironically, read "Good-Hearted Vittoria." McLeod sees the cry signifying that Brachiano is "lost eternally"--in terms of world and spirit (McLeod, p. 68).

[11] Dallby (pp. 34-35) suggests that Webster originally planned a tight five-act "Tragedy of Brachiano" ending at this point, but that too many loose ends were left, requiring his addition of three more scenes, which comprise in effect a sixth act. Brachiano's non-dominant presence in the earlier scenes of the play might condition this speculation.

[12] As Brown notes ironically (p. 1), <u>everyone</u> in this play lives at court.

[13] Brown (p. 167) shows that although the first Quarto's "l" in lilly-flowers is actually an "I," the former reading, rather than "gilly-flowers"--seemingly appropriate since it was a euphemism for light women and bastardy--is preferable, in view of the emblematic tradition of lillies.

[14] Freer, p. 146.

[15] At lines 140-41, "a politically conscious Jacobean audience would have thought of Raleigh in the tower--held in prison from day to day for 13 years" (West, p. 58).

[16] As Gunby points out (p. 53), its details have careful parallels in earlier incidents. For example, here Hortensio seeks to warn the future victims, just as, in IV.iii, Monticelso sought to warn the future murderer.

Chapter IX

[1] See particularly R. W. Dent, <u>John Webster's Borrowing</u> (Berkeley: Univ. of California Press, 1960).

[2] Quoted in Millar MacLure, <u>The Paul's Cross Sermons</u> (Toronto: Univ. of Toronto Press, 1960), p. 233.

[3] MacLure, p. 234.

[4] All quotes are from volume II of <u>The Works of Thomas Adams</u> (Edinburg: James Nichol, 1862).

[5] S. R. Gardiner, ed., <u>Parliamentary Debates of 1610</u> (London: Camden Society, 1862), p. 7.

Chapter X

[1] Gill, p. 45.

[2] Pearson, p. 75.

[3] Pearson, p. 77. See Bliss, pp. 117-118.

[4] This and other details lead Brown (pp. liv-lvi) to assert that there is a deeply hidden, yet underlying, moral consciousness in Vittoria. He sees the book as unequivocally a devotional one, but notes that carrying one was a conventional dramatic figure for melancholy (p. 169).

[5] "This glorious white devil is rescued from her weakness only by the strength of the black devil" (Murray, p. 92).

[6] Gunby, p. 56.

[7] The view that "the courage and spirit with which Vittoria and her brother die is exceptional, and constitutes something wholly admirable in a world of treachery and baseness (Boklund, p. 173) seems difficult to sustain in the presence of these ambiguities.

[8] See, for example, Layman, p. 346.

[9] This and a number of other sententious lines in V.6 derive from William Alexander's tragedies--especially *Croesus* and *Darius*.

[10] Sullivan, p. 78.

[11] See Dallby, p. 134.

[12] Gill, p. 45.

[13] The spelling "limb'd" associates the painterly sense with the "limbs" of the dead (Brown, p. 186).

[14] Brennan, pp. 14-15, considers Giovanni a "prig," and the Red Bull audience dissatisfied, by Webster's own testimony, because of the play's "failure to conclude with an effective catharsis." She continues "A knowledge of *English* history, even of Elizabethan history plays, would have been enough to indicate to them that the reigns of hopeful young princes were not usually either long or uncorrupted by the ideas and actions of their advisors." If valid, mustn't this view apply to Prince Hal, not to mention Edgar and Horatio? And can it?

[15] See Brown, p. lviii, for a view of the ultimate "insecurity" here.

Chapter XI

[1] Helen Gardner and Timothy Healy, eds., *John Donne: Selected Prose* (Oxford: Clarendon Press, 1967), p. 25.

[2] *Prose*, p. 140.

³*Prose*, p. 152.

⁴This, and all further paginated references to *Biathanatos*, are from the 1646 London edition as reprinted by the Arno Press, New York, 1977.